PASTORAL LEADERSHIP

PASTORAL
LEADERSHIP

Andrew Watterson Blackwood

ABINGDON-COKESBURY PRESS
New York • *Nashville*

PASTORAL LEADERSHIP

COPYRIGHT MCMXLIX
BY PIERCE & SMITH

SET UP, PRINTED, AND BOUND BY THE
PARTHENON PRESS, AT NASHVILLE,
TENNESSEE, UNITED STATES OF AMERICA

Dedicated
to the
LOCAL MINISTERS
who have
asked me for this book

Foreword

W HERE can I find a book about pastoral leadership, or church management?" The question comes from ministers in fields of all sorts and sizes. The large majority of these men believe in the primacy of preaching and pastoral work, especially if the latter includes counseling. Every one of them wishes to keep his soul well and strong, so as to set an example of radiant living in a world that has almost lost the way to God. Half in despair ministers keep asking how they can do all this and still devote enough time to leadership of the local church.

"Where can I get a guidebook for a course in pastoral leadership?" "I want each student to have a volume with an over-all treatment of the minister as executive and organizer." In various forms this request comes from seminary professors of practical theology. These men know the literature of the subject, and esteem much of it highly. Still they wish something more. So do the students, especially after they have browsed through the books on reserve for this difficult course.

Many of the titles of works available will appear at the end of various chapters that follow. Other volumes equally useful may receive no mention. In certain fields, such as Christian education, literature abounds. Hence the maker of a reading list must select and omit, perhaps arbitrarily. In other departments, such as work among men, who can find a first-class book? Partly for such reasons, the discussion of some subjects may seem scanty, and of others profuse. Why linger over subjects, however important, when experts have already written much? On the other hand, why not discuss more fully what other books omit or pass over lightly?

Fortunately, any writer in this field can find help in works about business management. Sometimes we ministers smile at "bright spirits who utter the word 'planning' and expect the world to become angelic overnight." Anyone who goes through the current literature about business management, however, will find a wealth of ideas for students of pastoral leadership. To such writers I owe more than my footnotes make clear. From some of them, for instance, I have borrowed and adapted the distinction between the pastor as executive and as organizer.[1] According to these books a man who shines in executive work may not excel as an organizer, and vice versa.

As an executive the pastor makes the most out of the forces at hand. He does teamwork with others, both one by one and in groups. For example, as the main leader in public worship he relies largely on musicians and ushers. As an organizer he may help to bring about changes in the women's work, with which he has nothing to do, apparently, except to enjoy cups of afternoon tea. In actual life, according to these books, executive work and organization often overlap. So they do in the pages that follow. The same holds true of certain subdivisions, such as promotion of missions and work among women. Fortunately, overlapping proves less serious than overlooking. Hence this book deals broadly with the problems and the difficulties of local ministers today.

Every theory has come out of pastoral experience. Much of the light streams from my heroes no longer in the flesh. In dealing with such a practical subject a writer dare not ignore its history.[2] Fortunately, the mariner steers by the stars, not by the waves. In parish leadership, as in seamanship, the basic principles do not change. As for meeting conditions that shift as swiftly as sunshine and storm out on the sea, I must look to mariners now at work, and I never turn in vain. For these friends I daily give thanks. I look on them as the noblest men I know, and as the key men in the work of the Kingdom today.

To the following I owe more than I can tell: members of our family, notably my wife; colleagues on the faculty, especially Donald Macleod; students, past and present; library workers; lay officers; church secretaries; denominational leaders; and newspapermen. Pastors now on the field have aided me most of all. Some of them have shown me how to "live on twenty-four hours a day"; how to "live without worry, work without hurry, and look forward without fear." These men believe in God. By faith they have found the way

[1] See Thomas N. Whitehead, *Leadership in a Free Society* (Cambridge: Harvard University Press, 1937), p. 82.
[2] See a pioneer work in this field, Charles F. Kemp, *Physicians of the Soul* (New York: The Macmillan Co., 1947).

out of traffic jams and parish mazes. They too stand among my heroes.

Much as I value pastoral experience, I could not have written this book if I had remained out on the field. No one can appraise the team play of others while he takes an active part in the game. This I have learned anew from "the iron man of baseball." At first base for the New York Yankees Lou Gehrig took part consecutively in 2,130 games. Never once could he watch those teammates in action for nine innings. He did not even notice the team play between his two neighbors on the diamond, the second baseman and the shortstop. Afterward, when Gehrig could no longer play, he made a remark that would have delighted Paul as a lover of manly sports: "You'd be surprised how different a slant you get on a ball game when you see it from the bench. I mean, after you've been playing for years. For the first time I was looking at a complete game. For years I [had been] so busy taking care of my own position that I did not have time to take in the game as a whole." [3]

So let me introduce the book with a note of confidence, and that on a key distinctly Christian. If any man wishes to excel as a church leader, he should live much with Paul, in the spirit of prayer. Under the guidance of the Holy Spirit any pastor today can share the secrets of the Apostle as a master builder. "Paul knew but two sovereign themes—one was Jesus Christ; the other was the Church." [4] Let this master builder speak from heart to heart: "No other foundation can any one lay than that which is laid, which is Jesus Christ." (I Cor. 3:11, R.S.V.)

ANDREW WATTERSON BLACKWOOD

---

[3] Frank Graham, *Lou Gehrig, Quiet Hero* (New York: G. P. Putnam's Sons, 1948), p. 224.
[4] Charles E. Jefferson, *The Building of the Church* (New York: The Macmillan Co., 1913), p. 23.

Contents

PART ONE

THE PASTOR AS EXECUTIVE

CHAPTER I

The Goals of a Pastorate

HALF our local churches scarcely know why they exist, declares Bishop Fred P. Corson of The Methodist Church. In an address to pastors he insisted that many congregations could double their effectiveness if they would define their objectives, and strive to reach these goals. Speaking about conditions more broadly, Emil Brunner writes from Switzerland: "In recent centuries the Church has lost increasingly the consciousness of what the Church is and what the Church is for." [1] Wherever such a state of affairs exists locally one or more pastors of yesterday or today must bear part of the blame.

What then should an incoming minister plan in the way of strategy? Before he enters the field let him determine why the local church exists. He can do this thinking in advance, for these goals remain more or less constant. After he enters the field and sizes up its character, he can formulate a program for the coming year. He need not ever seriously alter the strategy, but he may have to shift the tactics often to meet changing needs. In like manner a scientific farmer or a merchant plans what he wishes to accomplish. On the basis of the strategy he works out tactics from year to year.

The people in the church also ought to see the goals. On entering a new field a certain pastor spoke the first Sunday morning about "The Ideal Church for Today." By that he meant the local congregation. In the evening he preached about "The Ideal Minister for Today." Then he asked the people to pray for him as he strove to live according to those ideals. Otherwise he might have seemed presumptuous. Needless to say, he stressed the church more than the minister. For that reason he put first the message about the ideal congregation. So important did he consider the truths in this opening

[1] See A. D. Lindsay and Others, *The Predicament of the Church* (London: The Lutterworth Press, 1944), p. 87.

sermon that he kept them before the people, in varying forms, as long as he remained in the field.

In the autumn many a pastor arranges for a planning conference. Or rather, he works with the officers in making such arrangements. At a quiet spot remote from the sanctuary the officers and other leaders spend an afternoon and evening thinking and praying about strategy and tactics. They need not employ these terms, but somehow they consider the need for objectives and plans for reaching them that Bishop Corson had in mind. When the planning conference adjourns, everyone ought to know why the home church exists, and what it hopes to accomplish this next year. How else can the congregation expect to do its part in winning the warfare against sin?

EIGHT MAJOR GOALS

The goals that appear below include the major objectives of any church today. Some of them, such as evangelism and Christian nurture, or home and foreign missions, ought to bulk larger than others that appear neither at the beginning nor at the end of the list. The order, too, might be shifted. Christian nurture might stand first, as second to nothing else in the work of the Kingdom. In fact, none of the items ought to seem insignificant. Since these objectives have become well known to the reader, they call for little comment. Unfortunately, they have not become well known to many of those to whom he ministers. At least the goals have not yet become what William James would term "living and vital options."

1. *New Testament evangelism.* This ideal calls on the church to present the claims of Christ to every man or woman, older boy or girl, for whose salvation the Lord holds the congregation responsible. This ideal appears almost everywhere in the New Testament. Ways and means ought to vary according to the community and the traditions of the church. But no congregation ought to remain content without trying to reach and win the unchurched and the unsaved in the community. Without sitting in judgment on the souls of their neighbors and friends, the workers can aim at bringing everyone into active touch with Christ and some local church. More of all this later.

2. *Christian nurture.* This ideal too will meet us again as we journey

along. In the days of His flesh our Lord set a little child in the midst. To this hour, perhaps even more than in other days, He bids the church train every boy and girl for Him and the Kingdom. These first two goals belong together, both in thinking and in practice. All too often a church becomes known either for zeal in evangelism, or else for enthusiasm about Christian nurture. Why separate what the Lord God has joined together? If anyone asks which of the two he should put first, let him begin with the one that the home church tends to minimize. So in athletics the coach of a football team plans to strengthen the weak point in the line or backfield.

3. *Household religion.* This goal needs to stand out more prominently than of late in most churches. Under God, everything here below depends on the welfare of the Christian home and church. If we had to distinguish between the two, by way of importance, we should give the primacy to the home. Especially today, when conditions everywhere imperil the family, no church should fail to stress the prominence of the home in the Kingdom of God.

4. *Church friendliness.* At first glance this objective may seem secondary, if not secular. But a careful reading of the New Testament and of church history will show that the spirit of Christianity calls for friendliness in church and community. Search the Scriptures and see whether these things are so. Then look at the home church and ask if it does not need to cultivate the family spirit that always obtains where people love the Lord. Especially amid a shifting population, every church needs to stress this objective more today than yesterday.

5. *Community betterment.* This goal too may surprise some laymen. In the past we may have let them think of such movements as secular, and therefore alien to the work of the Kingdom. Strangely enough, some of these friends, while so believing, have sought to promote the welfare of more than one community in Japan or India. The Scriptures also bid the people of God show concern about the place where they live and rear their children. For an extreme example, turn to the words of the seer about a place that some Hebrew exiles regarded as Godforsaken: "Seek the peace of the city whither I have caused you to be carried away captives, and pray unto the Lord for it: for in the peace thereof shall ye have peace" (Jer. 29:7). In the

home community today let not Christians tolerate the sort of social filth against which the Apostle protested at Corinth. Paul never ignored the community surrounding a church. Neither did our Lord.

6. *National missions*, commonly known as home missions. This work really belongs under the heading of evangelism. The home church strives to do its full share in making the nation Christian, as a whole and in every part. After Pentecost the Apostles began their soul-winning at Jerusalem, and from there branched out to other parts of the land. In our day, when large portions of the earth look to the United States for leadership, would that our country had already become Christian! Here again, the Church at large needs to formulate its strategy, and each congregation ought to set this goal high among its objectives. "New occasions teach new duties." According to Dr. Mark A. Dawber, executive secretary of the Home Missions Council of North America, "Protestantism must either adjust itself to a drastically changing world or else permit agencies lacking religious motives to relegate the church to the sidelines." [2]

7. *Universal brotherhood.* Like some of the other objectives, this one involves a spirit and an attitude rather than a program and a schedule. Here also, the Christian Church ought to labor indirectly, but it should do so with all its might. Both at home and abroad it ought to stand for the rights of the individual man, for the noblest of race relations,[3] and for the coming of world peace. According to statesmen in the Kingdom, we can reach these objectives most surely by such time-honored means as evangelism at home and missions abroad. We cannot hope to witness the brotherhood of man unless we begin with the Fatherhood of God, as we find this truth in Jesus Christ our Lord and supremely in His Cross.

8. *World missions.* Like evangelism at home, missions abroad belongs to the essence of New Testament Christianity. In fact, the two may differ but little save in respect to geography and language. Early in his missionary labors the Apostle Paul won converts in his own

---

[2] *The New York Times,* January 12, 1949.
[3] See Alan Paton, *Cry, the Beloved Country* (New York: Charles Scribner's Sons, 1948).

part of the Mediterranean world. Later he moved over into what we now call a "foreign land." There he employed the same methods, and won the same kind of recruits. In like manner Christian work among Mexicans residing in Texas may differ little from that among their kinsfolk across the Rio Grande. So let us agree that among all these eight objectives none looms larger than this of winning the world for Christ. How else can we ever expect to look out over "one world" wherein dwells righteousness and peace?

From this time onward we shall think about these goals as they concern the leader of the home church. In terms of music we may think of eight notes, out of which an artist can bring forth the harmonies of the Gospel for our day. What Arthur J. Gossip says about the work of the pulpit applies to all that the minister does in the field. To him these eight objectives surely afford "a theme worth hearing," and the congregation should become the instrument from which he can bring forth harmonies like those of heaven: "Preaching resembles music in this respect, that for a real success three things are required—a theme worth hearing, a sufficient instrument, and a master whose deft touch can draw from both what he finds in them." [4]

EIGHT MEANS TO THE GOALS

How does the pastor go about reaching these objectives? First of all, he relies on teamwork with the men and women of the congregation. This phase of his work bulks large throughout the first half of the present volume. Less directly, or at least less visibly, he relies on organizations of the church. This conception dominates the latter half of the book. He also plans to reach those objectives by work that he cannot share with laymen and their societies. These aspects of his calling do not appear prominently in the chapters that follow. For such matters we must look to treatises on homiletics, public worship and pastoral theology.

One conception undergirds the entire book. The leader induces the lay men and women to do as much of the work as their resources make possible. He enlists them both individually and collectively as laborers for the Kingdom. How? Largely by using the eight ways we shall

[4] A. J. Gossip, *In Christ's Stead* (New York: George H. Doran Co., 1925), p. 64.

now discuss. No man who wishes to lead an active church ought to neglect any one of these God-appointed means.

Here again, the list might appear in a different order. At present we shall begin with something general and lead up to the necessity for specific planning. Someone else might reverse the process. Later in the book we may seem to be piling up all sorts of work for the pastor. But let us remember that he can deal with any ministerial task in one or more of the eight ways that appear below. Since pastoral leadership consists largely in performing these God-given basic duties, we ought to regard it not as something apart from them but as work that the minister can do by excelling in these ways. All the while we should look on the minister as mainly a preacher and a pastor rather than a program-builder and a parish-promoter. His work should have much more to do with wings than with weights. So let us think about the minister's eight ways of leading people to the eight goals that we have set up for the congregation.

1. *Exalting the Church.* In time to come, when wise men record the history of our day, they will stress the rediscovery of the Church. In this respect, as in others, we have been returning to the ideals of the New Testament and of the Reformation. In the Gospels, it is true, the Kingdom bulks large, and the Church does not, at least on the surface. But in the remainder of the New Testament—especially in the Acts, in the Epistles of Paul, and in the Apocalypse—Christ and the Church stand out supreme. Let it become so in the life and work of every pastor. By exalting the Church as the agent of God he can guide the people toward all those goals.

2. *Leading in worship.* Many of us Protestants have rediscovered the importance of public worship. We may also look on it as an effective agency in pastoral leadership. In every form of corporate worship the pastor seeks first the glory of the Most High. He also seeks to promote the well-being of the friends whom he guides to the mountaintop. Whenever he brings them into the presence of Christ, he trusts the King to transform these waiting hearts. If he guides them well in common worship, he can also prepare them for tasks in the valley below. Only when people get right with God can they do their full share in making the world Christian.

3. *Preaching the Gospel.* Really we ought to think of preaching as an essential part of public worship, if not the most important part.[5] For convenience we can set the work of the pulpit off by itself. If any minister will examine his sermons for the past year, or his plans for the days to come, he will find that in almost every message he works toward one of those eight goals. Without some such target he might as well amuse the people by shooting arrows into the air. On the other hand, if every preacher would single out one of those goals at a time, and then prepare to reach it through the spoken word, the pulpit work of tomorrow would become far more interesting and helpful.[6]

For example, take a goal that we sadly neglect—household religion. At the First Methodist Church in Atlanta, year after year, the minister preaches a number of consecutive evening sermons on this subject. Recently he began in February a series about "God at Your Fireside." After the closing sermon in the series the director of religious education teaches a large group of young adults who wish to know what Christ has to say about courtship and marriage. Elsewhere the pastor might do this kind of pulpit work later in the season, perhaps after Easter, but that would bring the group meetings into early summer. The season and the method do not matter so much as the clearness of the objective in the eyes of both pastor and people, and the wisdom of the plan to reach the objective by messages from the pulpit.

4. *Teaching the people.* Once again our arbitrary divisions must overlap. Those eight evening messages about "God at Your Fireside" must have included more than a little about the teachings of Jesus. In fact, our day calls for a popular teaching ministry from the pulpit. The man who employs the pulpit for this purpose ought to have a teaching mind. If so, he cannot refrain from teaching whenever he comes in touch with human beings who need to learn the will of God more perfectly. Especially does our day call for such a pastoral ministry. During World War II our chaplains found among the sons

---

[5] See my *Preparation of Sermons* (New York and Nashville: Abingdon-Cokesbury Press, 1948), chap. xxiii, "The Sermon as an Act of Worship."
[6] *Ibid.*, chap. ii.

of Protestant homes and churches an appalling degree of religious illiteracy. According to Bernard Iddings Bell many a chaplain resolved: "If ever I get back into a parish again I shall teach and teach and teach. Everything which goes on which does not teach I shall regard as superfluous. I shall not call except to teach, nor preach except to teach, nor pay attention to guilds except to teach, nor go to a vestry meeting except to teach." [7]

5. *Doing pastoral work.* Whenever a ministering shepherd goes into a home he should have in view something he wishes to accomplish. While there he ought to deal with anything else that calls for attention and care. Before he leaves, somehow or other he should promote one of those major objectives. If he plans wisely, he stresses only one at a time, the one that the friends in the home need most. Which one to deal with in any particular case must depend on factors that no person except the minister can know. If many a church leader cherished such an idea of pastoral work, he would devote to it far more time, and make ready for it with far more care. Also he would derive far more satisfaction, and the people would receive far more benefit.

For example, a minister went into a congregation that had been split horizontally under his immediate predecessor and vertically under the one preceding. The minister found four groups as diverse as those in the church at Corinth. He determined to meet the situation by visiting, visiting, visiting. Neither in the pulpit nor elsewhere did he allude to past "unpleasantnesses." Little by little he promoted a spirit of friendliness. Thus he followed the counsels of Charles E. Jefferson.[8] Gradually the people began to let the dead past bury its dead, and to love each other in the Lord. Then the minister could lead them toward other Kingdom objectives. All the while he prayed for the church: "Peace be within thy walls, and prosperity within thy palaces" (Ps. 122:7).

6. *Counseling in private.* This form of pastoral work has received much attention of late, and rightly so. Never has any era called for more loving care of sick and burdened souls. Without going into

---

[7] *The Christian Century,* October 11, 1944.
[8] *The Building of the Church* (New York: The Macmillan Co., 1913), chap. ii, "Building the Brotherhood."

many other merits, let us single out one that has to do with pastoral leadership. Whenever a minister guides a layman out of distress into the sunlight of God's peace, this friend should feel ready and eager to show gratitude by work in the church. Here again we ought to think about the result rather than the motive. While the pastor listens intently to the outpourings of a troubled heart, neither of the two persons ought to be thinking about anything other than that heart and its need of God. Afterward, however, the "new man in Christ Jesus" ought to become a power in the work of the Kingdom. To this fact every pastor can bear witness: All through the years men with the shepherd heart have found in various forms of counseling a sure way to discover future workers and leaders in the church.

7. *Praying in the study.* In a sense the pastor's usefulness depends most of all on quiet times with the Lord. Here also the connection with practical affairs may seem remote and tenuous. Often we refer to the activities of parish leadership in terms of machinery and manipulation. This puts a mistaken emphasis on the pastor as an engineer. The more time and thought he spends in the study, the less he need devote to tinkering with machinery. Many a leader has discovered this "more excellent way." During the long morning hours, five days between Sundays, such a man lives in the study, close to the heart of God. Before he presents any matter to officers or people, he must receive the sanction of the Most High. And yet outsiders wonder why this man's church work flourishes, and why his people refrain from fighting!

For an example turn to Moses or Paul. In Bible days no one surpassed either of them as a leader of men. The former sometimes failed when he neglected to seek the counsel of God. The latter excelled because he sought and found wisdom higher than his own. Neither man's example would lead any minister to spend most of his study hours in struggling with church problems. Rather do those ancient leaders bid a minister live close to God and the Book, in the spirit of prayer. When he emerges from the study, he should feel ready to feed the sheep and guide them toward the promised land. Just as in law "cases are won in chambers," not in open court, so a minister does much of his best church work by way of the mercy seat.

8. *Planning with care.* In the spirit of devotion the minister plans for the church work as carefully as for the pulpit.[9] In all such planning everyone ought to work his own way. After a minister has become acquainted with the field and its working forces, he can figure out ways of leading the people toward the desired objectives. Such a project calls for intellectual ability and expenditure of time. But no man without unusual talent ought to enter the ministry today. No one who enters ought to begrudge the time it takes to plan ways and means of seeking first the Kingdom of God through the local church.

All of this requires dedication of self from day to day. Usually we think of a young man's giving himself to God as preacher and pastor. Amen! Let him do the same as church leader. If every seminary student did so at the beginning of his course, and daily thereafter as long as he served in the ministry, pastoral leadership would move on a higher level. The difficulties would not vanish into thin air, but they would yield before the man who relied on God for wisdom and power. In such a spirit of humility and boldness a young minister used to pray: "Take me, Lord, as an earthen vessel. Cleanse me by Thy Spirit, if need be through fire. Fill me and flood me with 'the light of the knowledge of the glory of God in the face of Jesus Christ' (II Cor. 4:6c). Then use me in leading this people to do Thy will today and throughout the years, in the Name of the Master Leader. AMEN."

Suggested Readings

Anderson, William K., ed., *Making the Gospel Effective.* Nashville: Commission on Ministerial Training of The Methodist Church, 1945.

Beaven, Albert W., *Putting the Church on a Full Time Basis.* Garden City, New York: Doubleday, Doran & Co., 1928.

———, *The Local Church.* New York: The Abingdon Press, 1937.

Bower, William C., ed., *The Church at Work in the Modern World.* Chicago: University of Chicago Press, 1935.

Dobbins, Gaines S., *Building Better Churches.* Nashville: The Broadman Press, 1947.

Fenn, Don F., *Parish Administration.* New York: Morehouse-Gorham Co., 1938.

[9] See my *Planning a Year's Pulpit Work* (New York and Nashville: Abingdon-Cokesbury Press, 1942).

Gray, Joseph M. M., *The Postwar Strategy of Religion*. New York and Nashville: Abingdon-Cokesbury Press, 1944.

Leach, William H., *Toward a More Efficient Church*. New York: Fleming H. Revell, 1948.

Lemmon, Clarence E., *The Art of Church Management*. St. Louis: Christian Board of Education, 1933.

Shelton, Orman L., *The Church Functioning Effectively*. St. Louis: Christian Board of Education, 1946.

Spangenberg, Leonard M., *Minding Your Church's Business*. Kansas City, Missouri: Beacon Hill Press, 1942.

Spann, J. Richard, ed., *The Ministry*. New York and Nashville: Abingdon-Cokesbury Press, 1949.

CHAPTER II

The Plight of the Leader

M ANY a pastor today suffers from tension between ideals and at-
tainments. Ideally he looks on church leadership as using the resources at hand in getting the congregation to seek first the Kingdom
of God. Actually he beholds a chasm between aspirations and achievements. Sooner or later he may have to lower the ideals or increase the
achievements. At times in despair he feels like crying out with the
Apostle, though in a different connection: "I cannot understand my
own actions; I do not act as I desire to act; on the contrary, I do what
I detest. . . . Miserable wretch that I am! Who will rescue me . . . ?"
(Rom. 7:15, 24, Moffatt).

SOME REPRESENTATIVE IDEALS

This typical pastor loves Christ and the Church. At the age of
sixteen he gave himself to the ministry of the Gospel. In college and
seminary he received the best training of the day. For ten years before the age of twenty-six he developed powers of intellect and charm
of personality. Then he married a young woman of equal gifts and
graces. Together they went out to the first pastorate, two starry-eyed
idealists. They had read a first-class book about *The Romance of the
Ministry*.[1] Better still, they could enter into the spirit of words from
the Book: "With joy shall ye draw water out of the wells of salvation" (Isa. 12:3).

On the first Sunday morning the young man preached about "The
Ideal Church for Today" (Acts 10:33b). He attempted more than
he could do well. But this "young man's large way of preaching" delighted his hearers, and left the speaker aglow. He had hitched his
wagon to a star. After a brief introduction suitable to the hour he said,
in substance, that the state of the times called for:

[1] Raymond Calkins (Boston: The Pilgrim Press, 1944).

26

I. A spiritual church.[2] In such a congregation—
   A. People love the Bible.
   B. They love to pray.
   C. They love to worship, especially at Communion.
II. A friendly church. As in a Christian home—
   A. The members love each other.
   B. They love their neighbors.
   C. They love the person in distress.
III. A crusading church. In a church with a passion—
   A. The people strive to win everybody for Christ.
   B. They strive to transform the community.
   C. They strive to redeem the nation.
   D. They strive to transform the world.
IV. A generous church. In a church that means business—
   A. The people give according to their means.
   B. They estimate their giving by the tithe.
   C. They give much more as they grow in grace.

Fortunately the young man could point to living examples of such congregations. Turning to a denomination not his own he told about the Chicago North Austin Lutheran Church, with 3,000 confirmed members. There the pastor, F. W. Otterbein, led the large majority of the households to erect and maintain the family altar. At one time an observer estimated that 90 per cent of the homes had family worship. Without knowing much in detail about that congregation, one feels that it can qualify as spiritual. In our day people who worship God in their homes tend to do everything else the Lord and the pastor lead them to do.

Later in the message he gave another example, showing how a church of that denomination has helped to transform the community. At Frankenmuth, Michigan, 95 per cent of 1,300 inhabitants belong to the neighborhood church. In its history of over a century the community has never had a crime of violence. During the past twenty-five years no one has been put in jail. During the depression no one in the community went on relief. The town has always been first in the state to report all its taxes paid in full. The commu-

---

[2] See Edgar S. Brightman, *The Spiritual Life* (New York and Nashville: Abingdon-Cokesbury Press, 1942).

nity has always assumed more than its share of responsibility for philanthropic causes.[3] The Lord Jesus must have had His way in that church and in those Christian homes.

Three years after his introductory message the young minister sat down to take stock, mentally. In so far as he could judge by external signs, the home church could not qualify on any one of those four major tests. It seemed not worthy of note as spiritual, friendly, crusading, or generous. At first glance the people appeared to have increased their giving, but on closer view they proved to be contributing less, proportionately, than twenty years ago. In many a field today the people give through the church a smaller proportion of their income than in any former decade.

We might go further into detail. Take church attendance. This example will illustrate the trend in many a parish.[4] Perhaps unwisely, a pastor in New Jersey ran the following item in the monthly church letter, which went out over the community and far beyond: "In 1900 our church had 396 members. The average attendance was from 400 to 500 at the morning service, from 200 to 300 at the evening service, and from 100 to 150 at the midweek service. In 19— our church has 672 members. The average attendance is from 175 to 200 (at morning worship), and from 15 to 30 at the midweek service. These facts tell their own story."

What story do they tell? Much else, no doubt, but just now this: a growing tension between that man's ideals and his achievements. Rightly or wrongly, a pastor blames himself for such statistics. His tension increases when he takes an inventory of working methods. For this point of view we turn away from that Jersey parish, which holds only one service on the Lord's Day.

On the evening of his first Sunday in his new pastorate another young man preached about "The Ideal Minister for Today" (Ezra 7:10). Without any semblance of self-assurance he set the standards high. Toward the close he asked the people to pray for him as their pastor and friend. Here is a summary of his sermon:

[3] See the *Chicago Tribune*, December 25, 1946.
[4] For conditions on a larger scale see Emil Brunner and others, *The Predicament of the Church* (London, The Lutterworth Press, 1944).

The state of our times calls for a minister who dwells in the house of the interpreter. According to Bunyan, the interpreter had eyes lifted up to heaven, and the best of books in his hands. The law of truth was upon his lips; the world was behind his back. He stood as if he pleaded with men, and a crown of gold did hang over his head.[5] So let us think about—

 I. The interpreter over at the parsonage, as a student.

 II. The interpreter out in the parish, as a shepherd.

 III. The interpreter up in the pulpit, as a seer.

Three years later, when the young man takes stock, he discovers that the study has become an office, with telephone jingling and people knocking at the door. Month after month he finds more and more difficulty in getting sixty consecutive minutes for thought in the spirit of prayer. Half or more of each morning he must devote to matters of business detail. In like manner pastoral work suffers because he must keep adjusting and repairing church machinery. In the pulpit on the Lord's Day, feeling jaded and nervous, he preaches and prays as well as he can, with all that inner tension. What an atmosphere when a man speaks on "Christ's Remedy for Nerves"!

Does the picture seem overdrawn? If so, bring it down to the right dimensions. Really it affords a composite view of many parish ministers today, though not all. Consequently more than a few feel restless. The man in the small church thinks that if he had a secretary he could put first things first. The one with a secretary longs for a staff. The one with a staff finds that administrative burdens have increased. So we might go on to consider the most pressing problem in the lives of pastors with Christian ideals. As a rule, the loftier the ideals, the more the tension. Sometimes, indeed, it threatens to cause an explosion.

What an example for a minister to set before men and women who already have nerves frayed by distractions! As Woodrow Wilson used to say, a minister's calling consists in being something. Every pastor ought often to read Bushnell's sermon about "Unconscious Influence." The sage of Hartford makes clear that a minister accomplishes far more for God by what he is than by what he says and does. The pastor should also read Bushnell's other famous message

[5] *Pilgrim's Progress*, chap. V, par. 4.

"Every Man's Life a Plan of God." [6] The Lord never intended one of His ministering servants to become so busy here and there as to lose the vision of the Kingdom.

No one can tell how much the low estate of many a church comes from the pastor's squandering time and strength through inner friction. The lack of spirituality on the part of the people may have contributed to his feeling of distraction. But the minister should accept the major share of the responsibility. What then shall he do? Let him make two resolutions:

First, "This congregation ought to have a new pastor. By the grace of God I am going to become that new leader." One minister even made such a declaration from the pulpit. Other men wisely reserve such things for their Lord.

Second, "As the pastor of this church I need a new vision." About this, too, he prays. The light may come from John Bunyan. The Evangelist is speaking to a pilgrim, perhaps a young minister, who feels bewildered, and knows not which way to turn.

> "Do you see yonder wicket-gate?"
> The man said, "No."
> . . . "Do you see yonder shining light?"
> He said, "I think I do."
> Then said Evangelist, "Keep that light in thine eye, and go up directly thereto. So shalt thou see the gate, at which when thou knockest it shall be told thee what thou shalt do." [7]

That wicket gate may lead to the home of an older man with a shepherd heart. From this ministerial counselor the overburdened young pastor can learn much he ought to know about church leadership. Every young minister ought to have such a mature person as a father confessor. In the Protestant Episcopal Church a young rector can turn to the bishop. Among Methodists the young pastor can also look to the district superintendent. So in other branches of the Church a local leader need not bear his burden alone. But in more

---

[6] See my *Protestant Pulpit* (New York and Nashville: Abingdon-Cokesbury Press, 1947), sermon 8.
[7] *Pilgrim's Progress*, chap. I, at the end.

than a few denominations, some of them large, the church machinery
provides no oversight for the inexperienced minister.

Fortunately any young pastoral leader can adopt a master builder
of churches, and look to him in time of need. In like manner a young
physician may counsel with an older one about any case that threatens
to become critical. The mature pastor will gladly advise the young
friend about matters of details. The mentor will do far more good,
however, if he goes down to bedrock. He may begin by pointing
out laws of business management, as developed by the late Frederick
Winslow Taylor, and by other experts in "business administration."
In the average congregation a young minister deals with young men
and women who know about the "Taylor system," though perhaps
under a different name. In the rural church some of the young farmers
have gone through the state college. There they have learned the
principles of scientific agriculture. They expect the pastor also to excel in his line of work.

The young leader of such laymen needs to know these basic principles. He can find them in the Book, and that in a simple form. In
Ex. 18:13-27 is the record of how Moses learned from his father-in-
law what the young pastor ought to learn from his confessor. These
words from Exodus might well hang on the study wall as a motto. If
the young man reads them day after day, in the spirit of humility and
prayer, he may begin to mend his ways. The words from Jethro suggest the following observations:

1. Many a pastor today has no broad plan for the field.
2. He does not seek advice from men who excel in his line.
3. He tries to do everything himself, as though he alone knew how.
4. He consumes time and energy on details. No statesman!
5. He lives on his nerves, and gets on other people's nerves.
6. He does not delegate responsibility to his teammates.
7. He does not discover and enlist new leaders.
8. He does not let strong men work in their own ways.
9. He does not inspire loyalty to the Kingdom.
10. He does not gain a reputation for knowing how to lead.

These statements may seem unkind and unfair. Jethro said much the same, but positively and constructively. He encouraged Moses to use the manpower at hand, and so to carry out the will of God. According to the record, Moses entered upon a career that made him the foremost leader in the Old Testament. The principles he learned from Jethro still apply to the work of the local minister. In terms of today, and positively, they suggest the following plan:

1. *Size up the situation.* Each church differs from every other. So does a field change from year to year. Partly for this reason a pastor may succeed in one church and not in another. His methods suit one field but not the next. In the same church, plans that prove effective for a while may lose their force. Hence the pastor may have to change his methods or else move. Many a young minister moves too often, and an occasional older one not often enough. Whether or not a pastor flits from field to field, he needs to size up the local situation at least once a year.

Because of varying local needs, no guidebook or teacher can tell a young man how to proceed. He should seek and follow the guidance of the Holy Spirit. The Spirit works according to a knowledge of local needs. For example, He enabled young Joseph to size up the situation at a crisis hour in Egypt. At a time when the world of that day faced famine, with resulting years of depression, the Spirit led Joseph to see the "road away from revolution."

2. *Plan the work*, at least for the coming year. Before an incoming minister starts to formulate a program, he ought to confer with the lay officers and the leaders of the various groups. After he has surveyed the field, and learned what these friends think best, he should have in hand an over-all program, not too detailed. As for ways and means, he can leave most of them to others, who stand ready for service under his leadership. When he turns to them for aid, he should never refer to a proposal as "on trial." So insist the experts in business management. Also, he should refer to the program, truthfully, as coming chiefly from the laymen. For an object of such executive leadership, this time from a layman, turn to the records about Nehe-

miah as a builder. Note in Nehemiah 2–6 how he let strategy determine tactics.

3. *Secure co-operation* from the officers and other lay workers. Unlike Old Testament leaders a pastor today can rely on women for the sort of helpfulness many of them already show in the Red Cross and elsewhere ouside the church. If he gains the friendship and esteem of men and women, he can get them to do many things he has neither time nor ability to accomplish. On the other hand, if he tries to push through any project that does not appeal to the majority of these workers as necessary or feasible he may forfeit their esteem. Such short-sightedness may pile up trouble for him and for the next pastor or two.

4. *Enlist new leaders.* From time to time one or another church organization must have a new head. Often the friends in the group know not where to turn for a leader. If they come to the pastor for counsel, he may guide them to the best man or woman for the post. Nothing the "chief" does all year may contribute more to the work of the church than this inconspicuous ministry as an expert on personnel. In such a quiet fashion the president of a large college or university builds up a teaching staff. He relies on the friends in charge of each department, and he never goes over their heads. When the time comes for him to act, he knows how to find and enlist a new leader. By such means Woodrow Wilson brought to Princeton University half a hundred young preceptors, many of whom became the most brilliant professors in the history of the institution.

5. *Promote teamwork.* As Jethro told Moses, leadership consists largely in delegating both opportunity and responsibility. When Bernard M. Baruch accepted the chairmanship of a national commission on atomic energy, he announced the names of his associates. Then he said, with a smile, "You know I never do anything myself." He never does anything he can get someone else to do! As Dwight L. Moody used to insist, "It is better to get ten men to work than to do the work of ten men." What an honor strong men and women count the privilege of serving with such a chief! They see in him an object lesson of how to work, and they follow his example. Team-

work becomes largely a matter of contagious enthusiasm on the part of the leader.

This kind of chief never goes over the head of a committee chairman or anyone else in charge of church work. The leader never refers to such a person as a subordinate, or an underling. Even if a certain part of the work lags, the chief does not take it over. He waits until the work picks up, or until the friend in charge gives up the post. This sort of ending seldom occurs among the co-workers of a pastor who excels in selecting lay leaders, and in filling them with zeal like his own. On the other hand, he knows how to support and encourage any worker who falters, even temporarily. The pastor should excel in the fine art of appreciation, and of giving thanks, both privately and publicly. In short, leadership resolves itself into Christian relations.

6. *Inspire loyalty* on the part of the team. For example, the coach of a high-school basketball squad welded a group of inexperienced lads into a championship team. In that city the Rotary Club recently entertained as guests of honor the coach and the members of the squad. In his words of thanks the coach said that the boys deserved all the credit. Then the captain and other lads arose to protest that the team owed everything to the coach. They had entered the season without a star player, without prestige, and without hope of winning a game. But they had learned how to play as a unit. How many winning churches there would be if every pastor knew how to inspire such loyalty on the part of the entire team!

The high-school coach could not have qualified as a genius, or even as a man of talent. But he knew basketball, and he knew boys. Better still, he believed in them, and he led them to believe in him. The same ought to hold true of the man who serves as coach of workers in a church. When he takes charge in a new field, he ought to size up the members of the squad, both collectively and individually. During long, quiet hours of meditation he should lay plans for a winning team. Then he ought to inspire the friends with a desire to excel as workers for Christ and His Kingdom.

Such ability as a leader of men and women calls for practical wisdom rather than brilliant powers. For example, think about the presidency of the United States. As a witness hear a British statesman of yesterday, James Bryce. He has written the ablest treatise about the American form of government. At one time he served as ambassador from Great Britain, and he loved our country second only to England. In writing the words that follow he may have had in mind two presidents whom he knew and liked, Grover Cleveland and William McKinley. Bryce saw that neither of them showed marks of genius, and that each of them in his own fashion excelled as an executive.

A president need not be a man of brilliant intellectual gifts. . . . His main duties are to be prompt and firm in securing the due execution of the laws, and [in] maintaining the public peace; careful and upright in the choice of the executive officials of the country. Eloquence,—whose value is apt to be overrated in all free countries,—imagination, profundity of thought, all are in so far a gain to him that they make him a "bigger man," and help him to gain a greater influence over the nation, an influence which, if he be a true patriot, he may use for its good.

But they are not necessary for the due discharge in ordinary times of the duties of his post. A man may lack them and yet make an excellent President. Four-fifths of his work is the same in kind as that which devolves on the chairman of a commercial company or the manager of a railway,— the work of choosing good subordinates, seeing that they attend to their business, and taking a sound, practical view of such administrative questions as require his decision. Firmness, common sense, and most of all, honesty, an honesty above all suspicion, are the qualities which the country needs in its Chief Magistrate.[8]

Suggested Readings

Anderson, William K., ed., *Pastor and Church*. New York and Nashville: Abingdon-Cokesbury Press, 1943.

Bach, Marcus L., *Report to Protestants*. Indianapolis: The Bobbs-Merrill Co., 1948.

Boisen, Anton T., *Problems in Religion and Life*. New York and Nashville: Abingdon-Cokesbury Press, 1946. See the bibliography.

Craig, Clarence T., ed., *The Challenge of Our Culture* (Inter-Seminary

---

[8] *The American Commonwealth*, vol. I. Copyright 1893 by Macmillan & Co., 1910 and 1914 by The Macmillan Co., 1921 by Rt. Hon. Viscount Bryce. Used by permission of The Macmillan Co. p. 80.

Series, vol. I). New York: Harper & Bros., 1946. Chap. V, "Personal Tensions in Modern Life."

Gladden, Washington, *The Christian Pastor and the Working Church.* New York: Charles Scribner's Sons, n. d.

Leiffer, Murray H., *In That Case.* Chicago: Willett, Clark & Co., 1938. Chap. X, "The Minister's Role as a Professional Man."

————, *The Layman Looks at the Minister.* New York and Nashville: Abingdon-Cokesbury Press, 1947.

Man's Disorder and God's Design (Amsterdam Assembly Series). New York: Harper & Bros., 1948.

Spann, J. Richard, ed., *Christian Faith and Secularism.* New York and Nashville: Abingdon-Cokesbury Press, 1948.

Young, Kimball, *Personality and the Problems of Adjustment.* New York: F. S. Crofts & Co., 1940.

CHAPTER III

The Problems of the Church

MANY a church has become problem-conscious. When the officers meet they discuss local problems. In Protestant novels about the church and the minister, the clergy seem like a sickly lot. On the other hand, Roman Catholic writers keep away from problems about their churches and priests. Such novelists would not dare to wash dinner dishes in the presence of invited guests, or display soiled linen to the public gaze. In Catholic fiction priests and the sisters of charity appear as messengers of "sweetness and light." The parish church seems like a heaven on earth.

Much in Protestant novels corresponds with facts. Both in the church and in the pastor we have treasure in earthen vessels. A congregation without difficulties would soon become weak and flabby. But why fix our gaze on problems? The term never appears in the New Testament, and the idea seldom emerges there. The stress falls on opportunity, in the spirit of "apostolic optimism." Once the Apostle wrote: "A wide door for effective work has opened to me, and there are many adversaries" (I Cor. 16:19, R.S.V.). He seems to have put the opportunity first because he wished it to bulk larger than the problem.

THE PROBLEMS IN APOSTOLIC TIMES

In the apostolic church, as in our day, many problems had to do with "church leadership." By dealing with those difficulties, one after another, the leaders turned problems into opportunities. The apostolic attitude toward such a matter appears in the sixth chapter of the Acts. The record shows how those leaders faced their problem squarely and dealt with it at once. In a case of petty pinpricks they would have ignored minor unpleasantnesses. If the matter had concerned only one person or two, the leaders might have dealt with it privately. The problem at hand involved the peace of the Jerusalem church, and probably its continuance as a united body. Hence all the leaders faced that problem in the spirit of prayer. Then they solved it in a way pleasing to God. By faith and works they transformed it into an opportunity for larger service.

In the "First Church of Jerusalem" that problem grew out of the revival at Pentecost. Sometimes we say with a sigh: "If only we had a revival like the one at Pentecost, our problems would fade away like mists before the rising sun." Perhaps so! But other difficulties would spring up to fill the vacant places. Whenever a church witnesses an ingathering of new members, the leaders must face new problems. As at Jerusalem, many of them have to do with the leaders themselves. Today, also, the Holy Spirit waits to guide in such a transformation. What an opportunity!

Now let us turn to the record: "In these days when the disciples were increasing in number, the Hellenists murmured against the Hebrews because their widows were neglected in the daily distribution" (Acts 6:1, R.S.V.). In terms of our day the problem concerns newcomers, over against persons of longer standing. These new members come from one racial background and the old stand-bys from another. The issue relates to women, whose cause enlists the support of the men. Like many another problem that threatens to engulf a local enterprise, this matter has to do with business. The issue relates to money. In either home or church a squabble about money may lead to divorce. When people who mildly love each other begin to dispute about money, charges and countercharges spread like a forest fire.

Those apostolic leaders dealt with their problem behind closed doors. In the presence of God they brought out the facts and laid them before Him in prayer. After a time of deliberation they learned the will of God, and then they felt ready to act. They called a meeting of the congregation and there the leaders declared: "It seemed good to the Holy Spirit and to us." At last they could move forward with boldness. They brought the facts out into the open and then made a specific proposal. The people accepted the proposal, and their difficulty began to disappear. Through waiting upon God in prayer the officers had discovered a way of transforming their problem into an opportunity for larger Christian service.

This account tends to oversimplify the picture. Such a solution does not always follow at once, and never comes of itself. Still the record says that after the solution of that problem the work of the Lord increased. The people had been spending their God-given powers in bickering with each other. Under apostolic leadership they began to use that energy in building up the church, and then they loved their ministers all the more. Had not those leaders dealt with the parish problem in the spirit of Christian statesmanship?

In the record note the form of the solution. It called for a change in "the boards of the church." The congregation elected seven new officers, all with Hellenistic names. Up to that time the officers seem to have come from the ranks of the Hebrew Christians. In like manner today the leaders may wonder why certain young people feel disaffected, even hostile. Let the leaders deal with the problem constructively. Why not give the young people adequate representation on the official board? In every way get them to feel and to say: "This is our church because it belongs to Christ, and so do we." The same principle would apply to newcomers in a congregation where the old stand-bys cling to all the offices.

The newly elected officers at Jerusalem appear to have become deacons. In the Greek record both a noun and a verb come from a root that we transliterate into the term deacon. One of these pivotal words appears in the statement of the problem: "Their widows were neglected in the daily *ministration*." The other key word stands out in the solution: "It is not right that we should give up preaching to *serve* tables." Whatever their name and their rank, those new officers assumed the oversight of the business matters that had threatened to disrupt the First Church of Jerusalem. Because of that change in form of leadership the apostles had time and strength for the work God had called them to do. "We will give ourselves continually to prayer, and to the ministry of the word."

THE PROBLEMS IN MORE RECENT TIMES

This text about freedom from serving tables once led Thomas Chalmers to preach a sermon that afterward became famous. At the age of thirty-five he had gone to Glasgow from a rural church at Kilmany. In that smaller field he had learned how to keep first things first. But in the new city charge he soon found himself swamped. During the second year in the field he preached a sermon about "The Christian Ministry Secularized." He had intended to deliver another message of the same kind, but he desisted when he found he had accomplished his purpose. In the words that follow he refers to things right in themselves, but not directly concerned with the calling of a pastor:

Were I to obey the call of these winged messengers, and to ply my weary round among all the committees which they announce to me, and to take my every turn of the bidden attendance, and to give my mind to every subject of every deliberation we are expected to share in, and to bow my neck to the burden of all the directorships and president- and vice-presidentships which are habitually laid upon us,—then, my brethren, might I retire from the ministry of the word and prayer altogether, and give not a single half hour in the twelve month to the work of Sabbath preparation, and bid a stern refusal to every imploring call of the sick and desolate and the dying, and bid a final adieu to the whole business of family ministrations. . . . I might in this way, I assert, sink all that originally belonged to the office of minister of the gospel, and yet earn the character among you of being a most laborious, hard-working, painstaking, and in a great variety of ways most serviceable minister.[1]

Through that sermon Chalmers brought about a change in the leadership of the church. As long as he ministered at Glasgow, in two different fields, he rendered far more service out in the community, and he carried on that work far better than before. But the pastor and his clerical associate did not permit their own ministry to become secularized. Like the apostles, they gave themselves to "prayer and to the ministry of the word." Never again could he tell the people:

The whole flavor of the spiritual relation between a pastor and his flock is dissipated and done away. There is none of the unction of Christianity at all in the intercourse we hold with them; and everything that relates to the soul and to the interests of eternity and to the religious cure of

[1] *Sermons of the Late Thomas Chalmers Illustrative of Different Stages in His Ministry* (New York: Harper & Bros., 1849), pp. 367-68.

themselves and their families is elbowed away by filling up their schedules, and advising them about their moneys, and shuffling along with them in the forms and the papers of a most intricate correspondence.[2]

In other words, let Christ's minister be nothing but a minister!

Here in the United States, also, such problems have a way of disappearing before the right sort of leadership. In New York City a certain Episcopal parish had become known as almost hopeless. Friendly observers of the work expected it to die. But to it came a young clergyman who insisted on looking at the field in terms of opportunity. Whenever he and the lay officers faced a problem, he led them to deal with it in the spirit of "apostolic optimism." Again and again, largely through his leadership, they transformed problems into opportunities for wider service. Consequently the work prospered. Such experiences have encouraged many of us to believe that under the right sort of minister any church can solve each problem as it arises, and then use it as a stepping-stone to higher things.

Throughout this chapter we have seen that the change comes largely through leadership. Many of the outworkings appear elsewhere in the book. Here we call attention to some of the underlying principles. They appear in another saying from Thomas Chalmers. He believed in church leadership, but only as a means to Christian ends. In the excerpt below he stresses the human side of the matter:

There are two distinct elements which constitute the practical efficacy of a religious establishment. The first is the existence of an adequate machinery; the second is working that machinery well. If the machinery has been ill worked, or not worked at all, it by no means follows that it is itself to be despised. Such a state of things affords no reason at all for our pulling it to pieces. We must apply our remedy to the element which is defective; we must improve the working of the machinery; we must endeavor to man it better; it will then bear with prodigious force on our population.[3]

PROBLEMS INVOLVING THE PASTOR

Sometimes the problem concerns the pastor or his wife. For convenience we shall think only about him. If anyone hurts his feelings

[2] *Ibid.*, p. 373.
[3] Adam Philip, *Thomas Chalmers, Apostle of Union* (London: James Clarke & Co., 1929), p. 124.

he ought to ignore the matter. Better still, he should go out of his way to show the other person kindness. Probably the offender meant to inflict no hurt. Even if he acted with open eyes, still he may become a friend and supporter of the minister who accepts a slight in the spirit of the Master. To all of this any mature pastor can say "Amen."

When the fault lies with the minister, even in part, he ought to make amends, and that at once. Since these cases usually have to do with what he says, he ought often to read the words of the Apostle: "The tongue is a little member and boasts of great things. How great a forest is set ablaze by a little fire" (Jas. 3:5, R.S.V.). However, if a man's tongue gets him into trouble, it can get him out again. He can go at once to the other person and talk things over. If the pastor has spoken unwisely, he should express regret. If he has said nothing he ought to retract or soften down, he can talk about something else, as friend to friend. Or the minister can explain the matter to a third party and ask him to serve as peacemaker. First of all, however, the minister should pray for guidance.

Even with the best of intentions a pastor may err. Before he learns how to order his days he may forget an engagement, and promise to be at the same time in two places miles apart. He may show favoritism in appointing committees or in according praise. Apart from divine grace every leader tends to commend his own appointees and ignore wheel horses whom he has inherited. These workers may accept neglect, but their wives demand fair play. So in time the pastor may become known as "the man with the big head and the big stick."

An extreme instance from life will show how not to deal with a personal problem. A minister received anonymously a letter that charged him with follies of which he never had dreamed. Like King Hezekiah the pastor should have laid the missive before the Lord, and asked Him what to do. Then he would have burned the letter, knowing that he could never forget what it had taught him. Unwisely, this man tried to identify the handwriting. When he thought he had done so, he went to the woman he suspected, and demanded that she retract what she had written. Too late he discovered his error in diagnosis. Up to that hour she had looked up to him as a Christian gentleman. But when she discovered her mistake, she withdrew from the church. If she had insisted on her rights, she might have demanded his resignation, as a dunce unworthy to serve in the ministry.

Today when the world seems to be drifting toward the abyss, a church leader may ask: "Why devote attention to little things?" Somehow an egotist thinks a matter inconsequential unless it injures himself personally. He forgets that the little things of life start troubles worse than any forest fire. According to Anne R. J. Turgot, "The greatest evils in life have their rise in things too small to be attended to." The Christian way of dealing with many a problem is to prevent it from arising. In the words of Phillips Brooks, "You will never have in your parish a problem which you could not have prevented, or come out of one without injury to your character and your Master's cause." [4] Here follow a few suggestions about preventive measures:

1. *Be a happy pastor.* People have troubles enough of their own, and they need not know about yours. If anyone has done a deadly wrong and comes to talk about the error of his ways, do not pass the matter off with a jest. Remember what W. M. Clow terms "the dark line in God's face." In dealing with people who try to live aright, show the meaning of Christianity in terms of "love, joy, and peace." For a living example of a happy pastor and preacher, study the career of Brooks at Trinity Church in Boston.[5]

2. *Cultivate a sense of humor,* but never exercise it on anyone save yourself. Learn to laugh away the recollection of a slight, a sting, or a snub, that might keep you awake half a night. With Brooks learn to relieve a situation by seeing the ludicrous where you might look for the tragic. But if you have a sense of humor beware lest it become dislocated. Then it might work more havoc than the jawbone of an ass.

3. *Be pastor of the whole congregation.* Treat all the people alike. Pay special heed to anyone in trouble, even if it seems to you inconsequential, or imaginary.

4. *Fall in love with the people,* collectively. Show that you love them, and enjoy being their pastor. Within Christian limits they will

---

[4] *Lectures on Preaching* (New York: Thomas Y. Crowell, 1877), p. 103.
[5] See A. V. G. Allen, *Life and Letters of Phillips Brooks* (New York: E. P. Dutton & Co., 1901), 3 vol. ed.

do anything for a man they love, partly because he first loved them. Be a man of God, who is love.

5. *Believe in the people* and their possibilities. Unless a minister takes care, he may never publicly speak well about anyone who lives today and resides in the town. On the other hand, the Apostle Paul, foremost church leader, started each of his epistles, save one, with words of commendation. In every church except the Galatians he could find something to praise.

6. *Expect much from the people,* both one by one and as a congregation. Not only expect great things from God; do the same with His children. Strange as it may seem, you may have less difficulty in persuading them to do something large and hard than in getting them to attempt something cheap and easy. Avoid "the Lilliputian heresy."

7. *Pray for them.* Whenever you feel tempted to start scolding any group, pray for those friends. Prayer has a way of opening prison doors, and of making ready for new achievements.

8. *Live in hope.* Such an attitude goes far to avert troubles that might otherwise spring up in the parish. Even if disaster looms on the horizon, the man who keeps on hoping in God can find a way of transforming a problem into an opportunity. What a working philosophy of church leadership!

9. *Use all your brains.* The chief test of intellectual power lies in the ability to use the resources at hand in solving each problem as it arises.

10. *Trust in the Lord Jesus.* Learn to say with the master church leader, "I can do all things in him who strengthens me" (Phil. 4:13, R.S.V.).

Suggested Readings

Harner, Nevin C., *The Educational Work of the Church.* New York and Nashville: Abingdon-Cokesbury Press, 1939. Chap. III, "Bringing Order out of Chaos."

Leach, William H., *Toward a More Efficient Church.* New York: Fleming H. Revell Co., 1948. Chap. II, "Unity in Administration."

Chapter IV

The First Year on the Field

AS in a honeymoon, the first year in a pastorate goes far to determine its effectiveness, or its failure. The most frequent causes of failure, or of dissatisfaction, find their roots here. By the end of the first eleven months the pastor and his wife have succeeded or failed in securing the confidence and esteem of those they wish to lead. Afterward one or both can bring about a change of opinion on the part of disaffected persons, but this kind of transformation calls for uphill work, in the spirit of prayer. Meanwhile, according to a denominational leader, half of the two hundred congregations in his area have become dissatisfied with their pastors, and the pastors with the people. And yet this official has no power to initiate any transfer.

In four cases out of five, wisdom and tact during the first year would have averted such deep-seated feelings. If an incoming minister gains the reputation of being a strong preacher and a kind pastor, he has made a good start. If he knows the people, one by one, and wins their friendship, the church leader has cleared the path for future relations on a Christian level. "A stranger will they not follow, but will flee from him: for they know not the voice of strangers." (John 10:5.) Hence a wise man begins with "human relations," not with church machinery. He wins friends right and left, preferably in their homes. He knows people by name, and cares for them as a shepherd loves his sheep.

ENTERING THE NEW FIELD

At the beginning of a pastorate, unfortunately, a minister and his wife may not appear at their best. In addition to financial worries, they may feel all worn out, with nerves on edge. They miss loved ones far away, and find everything near at hand unfamiliar, if not forbidding. All the while they ought to look radiant. Like Abram of old, a pastor should enter a new field with a spirit of adventure. By faith he should fare forth into the unknown, free from fear (Heb. 11:8). On the other hand, anyone who has moved with a family knows how much difficulty the pastor and his wife meet in looking and acting like Christians during these first few weeks.

At first a wise minister asks for no changes. He seeks no alterations, other than those that have entered into the arrangements for the call. In an occasional church, conditions may have become so critical that they require surgery, immediate and radical. In such a case a minister without experience and ability as an ecclesiastical surgeon ought not to undertake the work. As for a fairly normal situation, he should not think of resorting to surgery before he has taken time for diagnosis. The patient will not succumb if the physician waits to study the clinical findings.

For an example of "watchful waiting," without action, take Phillips Brooks. At the age of thirty-three he took up work at Trinity Church in Boston. During the ten years previous, in two parishes of Philadelphia, he had gained distinction, locally. There he had tried to help run the nation and the world. After a study of the Boston field he determined on another course. As a native son he knew the city well, and he might have instituted a policy of reform, both in the community and at Trinity Church. On the contrary, for the first few months he did practically nothing, openly, except the work of pulpit and parish. That he strove to do with all his might.

During those first months he kept sizing up the situation, in both city and parish. As the son of a businessman young Brooks could have excelled as an administrator. But he determined to leave that sort of work largely in the hands of others. Then he could devote himself to pulpit and pastoral work. All of these facts appear in various biographies, especially in the most comprehensive, by A. V. G. Allen, and there at best in the three-volume edition.[1]

While the young man is appraising the church, the people are doing the same with him and his wife. They wish to know whether they have secured two sweet and gracious Christians, or two young upstarts. Some of the people may sense the need of enriching the hour of worship. Another group may feel ready for changes in the local

[1] *Op. cit.*, vol. I, pp. 314-16.

machinery, or the church edifice. A different group would oppose any alterations or innovations. They prefer the olden, golden glory of days gone by. Naturally the minister does not know which group to favor. If wise, he determines to become the pastor of the whole congregation. He wishes not to disturb the status quo until the people as a whole feel ready to move forward with gladness.

At the age of twenty-eight Henry Sloane Coffin became the pastor of Madison Avenue Presbyterian Church in New York City. There he found rented pews, a system in which he did not believe. If he had insisted, he might have secured a change to free pews almost at once. But he waited a few years until the officers to a man favored that sort of Christian democracy. Such a minister values the peace and harmony of the congregation far more than any improvement in methods. To his amazement he finds that even with rented pews the heavens do not become as brass.

Early in September at another large church the incoming minister first met with the governing board. He knew that some of the most prominent members had not yet returned from their summer vacations. Still he proposed a discontinuance of the Sunday evening service. When the matter came to a vote, that same meeting, he cast the deciding ballot in favor of the "innovation." Another leader would have kept the matter from coming to a head, especially since the absentees practically all believed in the continuance of those services. Such executive caution does not depend on the merits in the case, so much as on the desire to promote harmony in the church. In the case before us haste in making the change did not contribute to the felicity of Zion. However, the pastor weathered the storm.

This experience raises a question about the best season of the year to enter a field. Many prefer springtime or early summer. If a man begins the first of June, he has eight or ten weeks to become acquainted, and do his sizing up. In August he can hie away for a brief vacation, perhaps covering only a single Lord's Day. This free time he ought to take at a distance so as to see the work large and see it whole. How else can he expect to lay plans for the coming year? [2]

[2] See my *Planning a Year's Pulpit Work* (New York and Nashville: Abingdon-Cokesbury Press, 1942).

No one can formulate a program for the work while he keeps busy with routine tasks. If we had more strategy on the part of pastors we should have fewer debacles among lay workers.

In a large congregation the minister does better to start the first of May, or soon after Easter. Then he has three months or more to win friends and get his bearings. In any case the August holiday affords a natural break. In most parishes the fall season has become "the springtime of the church year." In September everyone ought to feel ready for a new beginning. Since the leader has come to know the officers and the people, with their traditions and ideals, he can begin with them where they are, and guide them to better things. Again, how simple it all sounds!

It may be that a minister will be led to a field in early autumn. If so, he can view the months before Christmas as a warming-up period —to warm up every heart, including his own. During a lull at the holidays, or else a few weeks later, with the approval of the official board, he can take a ten-day leave of absence. At a distance from home and church he can map out a campaign for the months ahead. Why must a pastor's vacation always come in August, and always include consecutive weeks? Whatever the time of year, he can spend an hour or more every day getting ready for the months ahead.

The worst time to enter a new field may come a month or so before Easter. If a man has been serving effectively in another church, the friends there think he ought to remain with them until they have passed the climax of the year's work. If he undertakes new tasks during the busiest season, before he knows the lay leaders, he may not adapt himself to the onward sweep. After the first few weeks he will sense the anticlimax.

In actual life, however, Providence may lift a man from a place where he feels much at home and set him down in another church where everyone mourns the loss of a leader who has gone home to God. In such a case, perhaps just before Easter, a young minister can take up the mantle of the departed hero, and pray for a double portion of his spirit (II Kings 2:9). The new pastor may also apply to himself words that originally referred to something else: "It is not for you to know times or seasons which the Father has fixed by his own authority" (Acts 1:7, R.S.V.). Alas, however, we often insist on having our own way instead of relying on God's Providence.

THE PLANS FOR THE FIRST YEAR

How then shall a newly ordained pastor begin? Unless a young man takes care, he may carry over into the pastorate habits he has formed at the divinity school. He has responded to bells not of his ringing, and to schedules not of his making. He has used intellectual muscles chiefly at night, and he has formed the habit of putting off until tomorrow what he should have done yesterday. No one could devise a worse system for a future pastor. Who can wonder that we ministers have gained the reputation of being unbusinesslike? Hence the time has come for the young pastor to begin forming habits he will never need to change. As a witness hear Phillips Brooks:

No one dreads mechanical woodenness in the ministry more than I do. And yet a strong wooden structure running through your work, a set of well-framed and well-jointed habits about times and ways of work, writing, studying, intercourse with people, the administration of charity and education, and the proportions between the different departments of clerical labor is again and again the bridge over which the minister walks when the ground of higher motive fails him for a time. . . .

One of the most remarkable things about the preacher's methods of work is the way in which they form themselves in the earliest years of his ministry, and then rule him with almost despotic power to the end. I am a slave today, and so I suppose is every minister, to ways of work that were made within two or three years after beginning to preach. . . . He is the happiest and most effective old man whose life has been full of growth and free from revolution.[3]

By way of starting aright think of certain self-made rules. At no point can we stop to consider exceptions.

1. *Plan for a permanent work.* Do not look on the first charge, or any other, as a stepping-stone to higher things elsewhere. Only a dunce would try to fix in advance the length of his pastorate, and then tell people how long he expected to remain. Usually a young minister stays in his first charge only a few years. Even so, he ought

[3] *Op. cit.,* pp. 92, 104.

to prepare for an abiding work, and not feel eager to fly away before the Lord bids him go elsewhere.

2. *Tarry at home throughout the week*, except on the pastor's day of rest—or it may be two half days. For the sake of the people, and your own contribution to the Kingdom, reserve such a rest day, or else Saturday afternoon and Monday morning. Remember that the remainder of your time between vacations belongs to the home church. An occasional speaking appointment elsewhere, perhaps once a week, may do no harm. But the man who leaves his own bailiwick repeatedly may become shallow, or else break down. In all such matters exceptions must occur. In case of frequent or prolonged absences, seek the approval of the official board.

3. *Systematize the work of the study.* A young man owes himself long quiet hours there five mornings every week. Later in the ministry, after he has formed the habit, he will continue to toil. Strange as it may seem, ministers with large ability and heavy responsibilities usually study harder and longer than men who envy those other leaders their places in the sun. Without habits of mental toil a pastor may be burned out when forty years old. Then old age will come as an anticlimax.

If the officers wish the pastor to study at the church, he should do so. If not, during the first year or two, before children begin to make themselves heard, he may prefer to work at home. In that case an upstairs room serves better than one down near the front door, or close to the wife in her duties. As for equipment, the pastor needs a flat-topped desk, a typewriter, and books, all sorts of books about Christianity. Works of other kinds he may read elsewhere. In the study he should deal only with books in his special field.

The hours of the day ought to be fixed and kept sacred. At the age of twenty-six John Henry Jowett went to his first charge, at Newcastle-on-Tyne.[4] There he determined to be at his desk when the members of the congregation trooped by on their way to the factory. To those long hours of quiet study he owed much of his prowess in later years. In South Carolina a young pastor could study

[4] See Arthur Porritt, *John Henry Jowett* (New York: Doubleday, Doran & Co., 1924).

from nine in the morning until two. When he moved north, the lunch hour came earlier. There he shifted to the period between eight and twelve-thirty.

The working schedule ought to include something about the apportionment of hours. Indeed, certain writers have attempted to formulate schedules that an ordinary person could scarcely remember from day to day.[5] Every young minister ought to determine these things for himself, and keep them simple. He may set apart the first hour each day for work on the Bible, in the spirit of prayer. After this opening period he can use the remaining time according to his plans for the year and the season. In an emergency he should drop everything and hurry to the assistance of any person in distress. Otherwise, not being a genius, he needs all these morning hours. Early in his first pastorate, and at times thereafter, he may put in the bulletin a personal note: "The pastor appreciates the kindness of the people in helping to safeguard his morning hours of study. Except in an emergency, please do not call him by telephone, or ask to see him, during the morning hours."

4. *Spend five afternoons a week among the people.* If a man knows how to use God's time, he can visit more than a few persons in two or three hours. At Baltimore, Maltbie D. Babcock became the most popular minister in the history of the city. In his calling he seldom tarried long at a home. If he were a pastor now, he would probably ask people to confer with him at the church. Somehow he would schedule the time so as to keep in touch, one by one, with wounded spirits that need a radiant presence and a healing touch.

During some afternoons funerals interfere with the schedule. A wise man determines to accept them as they come, and to use them as means of doing pastoral work. So with other interruptions—he should learn from the Master to look on them as open doors for usefulness. If not busy otherwise after dark, he may plan to visit then. In that event he ought not to call during the afternoon. Few ministers can profitably give themselves to parish visitation, or to counseling, more than two or three hours a day.

[5] See Cleland B. McAfee, *Ministerial Practices* (New York: Harper & Bros., 1928), pp. 23-26.

5. Do not study after dark. If you do, you may break down. As a man grows older he may have few evenings free, except on Saturday, an evening that belongs to the Lord, in the way of rest and relaxation. During World War II General Marshall planned his days so that he could retire at nine o'clock and be at his desk by seven-thirty the next morning.[6] He would agree with psychologists and physicians that intellectual labor after dark imposes on the system a needless strain. When Sir Walter Scott had reached the age of thirty-three, he gave up all writing after dark.[7] The late A. T. Robertson of Louisville attributed his usefulness as an elderly man partly to the fact that early in the ministry he had formed the habit of not studying after sundown. What a way to conserve one's strength!

6. Set apart a time for business details. Do not let such things come first, lest they usurp a large share of the hours best for creative work. Form the habit, day after day, of doing the big thing early in the morning. In a pastor's life the big thing means preparation for leading in worship, for preaching the gospel, and for shepherding the flock. Later in the day attend to business that has accumulated. Also make plans for the next day.

Form the habit of dealing with practical affairs in businesslike fashion. According to rumor the majority of clergymen do not reply to letters immediately, and sometimes not at all. Sir Walter Scott, amid all his activities, and without clerical help, answered every business letter the day it came to hand. A pastor may set as a limit twenty-four hours, with a week for mailing a social note. This includes thanks for courtesies received. Of course no person feels obliged to answer a form letter.

Learn to write a clear, short letter, or else a note. If the matter seems important, file with the original communication a carbon copy of the reply. Such materials go into the minister's files alphabetically. If you accept an invitation, or make an appointment, confirm the agreement in writing. Make clear the date, the hour, and the place. Then retain a carbon copy until you have fulfilled the engagement.

[6] Katherine T. Marshall, *Together, Annals of an Army Wife* (New York: Tupper & Love, 1946), p. 67.

[7] John Buchan, *Sir Walter Scott* (New York: Coward-McCann Co., 1933), p. 88.

The act of writing out the data will help to impress them on the memory. The carbon copy may also explain an apparent failure to carry out an engagement.

7. *Do not put on paper anything you would blush to see in print.* If you feel obliged to utter anything unpleasant, go to the person and say it, if possible with a smile. When you have anything good to communicate, write it out and send it through the mail. In this connection listen to John Ruskin: "I never wrote a private letter to any human being which I would not let a bill-sticker post six feet high on Hyde Park Wall, and stand myself in Picadilly and say, 'I wrote it!' "

8. *Do not anywhere try to impose plans imported from outside,* or borrowed from a book, including the present volume. Especially in a rural field, do not pattern after a metropolitan minister with a multiple staff.

9. *Be at your best every day,* both spiritually and physically. No one can do all the work of a parish unless he plans for more than a forty-hour week. Neither can a minister stoop to indulgences that may seem harmless in other men.[8] If in doubt, a minister prefers to stand on the safe side. Not only must the pastor remain in right relations with God and with himself. He must also gain and hold the esteem of the people in the community. They expect him to "endure hardness as a good soldier of Jesus Christ."

10. In short, *plan to serve with all your redeemed powers.* If at times the discipline seems exacting, what else does it mean to be a Christian, especially a church leader? "If any man will come after me, let him deny himself, and take up his cross, and follow me." (Matt. 16:24.)

Sometimes the cross seems heavier than a young pastor and his wife can bear. Contrary to all their plans and dreams, they meet with disaster. But if they accept it in a Christian spirit, they find that Emerson's law of compensation still holds. Some of us have never known this law to fail: when a young man's ministry starts with serious illness, or other disaster not affecting morals, the Lord blesses the pastorate from that time onward. The people begin to pray for

[8] See Nolan B. Harmon, *Ministerial Ethics and Etiquette* (Nashville: Cokesbury Press, 1928), chap. II, "The Man."

their minister, and he learns to love the people. So does his wife. In such an atmosphere of love and prayer every other grace flourishes. But they must both accept their cross, and bear it bravely, with strength from above.

For a living example look at Charles H. Spurgeon. At the age of nineteen he went to a run-down church in South London. During the first year or two he met with criticism and abuse from many people not in his church. Keenly as he felt those attacks, which he did not deserve, he never entered into a kicking match with a mule. Within less than a year after he went to London he had to cope with a plague of cholera. Returning one day from a funeral, weary in body and sick at heart, he saw in a shoemaker's window a text that brought him courage and strength. Largely because of diligence and endurance throughout that plague, he found his way into the hearts of people all over London, and far beyond. Note the text: "Because thou hast made the Lord, which is my refuge, even the most High, thy habitation, there shall no evil befall thee, neither shall any plague come nigh thy dwelling." (Ps. 91:9-10.) [9]

Suggested Readings

Brown, Charles R., *The Making of a Minister*. New York: The Century Co., 1927.

Church Management, issued monthly, Cleveland, Ohio.

Clausen, Bernard C., *The Technique of a Minister*. New York: Fleming H. Revell Co., 1925.

Harmon, Nolan B., *Ministerial Ethics and Etiquette*. Nashville: The Cokesbury Press, 1928.

Hewitt, Arthur W., *Highland Shepherds*. Chicago: Willett, Clark & Co., 1939.

Leach, William H., *Toward a More Efficient Church*. New York: Fleming H. Revell Co., 1948. Chap. III, "A Program for the Local Church."

Leiffer, Murray H., *The Effective City Church*. New York and Nashville: Abingdon-Cokesbury Press, 1949.

[9] See *The Autobiography* (Chicago: Fleming H. Revell Co., 1898), vol. I, p. 371.

McAfee, Cleland B., *Ministerial Practices*. New York: Harper & Bros., 1929.

Palmer, Albert W., *The Minister's Job*. Rev. ed. New York: Harper & Bros., 1949.

The Pulpit Digest, issued monthly, Great Neck, N. Y.

Van Vleck, Joseph, *Our Changing Churches*. New York: The Association Press, 1937.

CHAPTER V

The Attitude Toward Equipment

W HAT a man's body means to his soul, a building means to a church. In either case a minister has to labor with something less than ideal. When he goes to the first parish, he may look for heaven on earth. Soon he will find that Christian people have "this treasure in earthen vessels." As in apostolic days, believers today must worship God amid limitations. In New Testament times only one congregation seems to have had a church building of its own. These facts suggest a working philosophy.

1. The minister should *learn to love the building* where he must spend most of his working hours. Such an attitude appears in Ps. 122, where the man of God exults in the home church. He shows loyalty to God by love for the church and its visible home. He delights in it when present and desires it when absent. In the first part of the psalm the poet sings about presence at the church; in the central part, about praises of the church; and in the last part, about prayers for the church. All of this, in as far as it relates to the premises, affords an index of a minister's fitness for leadership.

The same conception appears in favorite hymns.

> I love Thy Church, O God!
> Her walls before Thee stand.

> Glorious things of thee are spoken,
> Zion, city of our God

Often we spiritualize these songs, as perhaps we ought. We should also take them literally. Do we not dedicate the church building? That means setting it apart for God's use in the community, where it gives to the work of the Kingdom a sense of visibility and permanence. If our bodies can become temples of the Holy Spirit, how much more the places where God makes His glory known! So the minister ought to set the people an example of reverence for the house of the Lord. Then he can lead them to sing with "the spirit and the understanding" an old Latin hymn:

> To this temple, where we call Thee,
> Come, O Lord of hosts, today;
> With Thy wonted loving-kindness
> Hear the people as they pray;
> And Thy fullest benediction
> Shed within its walls alway.

2. The incoming pastor should *accept what he finds* in the way of equipment. With the right spirit God's people can worship Him in any kind of structure. Without such a spirit they will not worship Him anywhere. Also, not every "improvement" in a church building will commend itself to coming generations. Before Thomas Hardy became a master of fiction he served as an architect. Later he wrote about his youthful folly in tearing down Georgian Colonial edifices to erect mid-Victorian monstrosities.

Some of us have had to put up with equally unfortunate "improvements." Before the turn of the century church leaders erected Sunday-school buildings according to the Akron Plan. They also gloried in a sloping floor leading to a corner pulpit. They transferred the pipe organ and the choir from the rear balcony to a newly-made niche behind the pulpit. Much the same zeal, not according to knowledge, led to memorial windows with pictorial scenes. Today experts tell us that stained-glass windows ought to embody truth in symbols, and not show persons in action.[1] In our time, also, many a pastor and building committee do not know enough about art and architecture to improve on the work of the fathers. Incidentally, the study of architecture and stained-glass windows affords the pastor and his wife a hobby full of fascination and profit.

What attitude should the pastor adopt toward the central pulpit or the central altar? Let him accept what he finds, and make the most of it. The uplift and power of worship depend on spirit and content

[2] See Charles J. Connick, *Adventures in Light and Color* (New York: Random House, 1937).

far more than on the architect's plan for the interior of the sanctuary. Some of us have had churches with both arrangements. We have found it possible to lead in worship acceptably with a central pulpit or a divided chancel. If the local program calls for a new sanctuary, the architect will probably advise a chancel arrangement with a side pulpit. The trend of late has been moving steadily in that direction. Meanwhile, in most nonliturgical churches, at least nine out of ten pastors must conduct the service and preach the sermon from the central pulpit. Why then force an issue? Learn to say with the Apostle, "I have learned, in whatsoever state I am, therewith to be content" (Phil. 4:11*b*).

3. The leader ought to *make the most out of what he has.*

For example, the grounds may need attention. Early in General Marshall's career as a commanding officer he served at military stations where the premises showed need of loving care. His wife has written that

ere long the changes seemed to come of themselves, with none of the irritations of a new broom sweeping clean. . . . If the post was shabby, with poorly kept grounds, he began fixing up his own garden and lawn. Within a few weeks all the gardens and lawns down the line began to take on a different complexion. There was never a word spoken, never an order given.[2]

At a church the improvement may not come so quickly. Especially at first the minister has less authority than the commander of an army post. But if the new church leader knows how to win friends and influence people, he can encourage the officers to make the premises attractive. Also, he can set an example at the parsonage. At the church any such program may call for shrubbery and trees, with grass neatly mowed, and other marks of loving care. The building itself may need repairs and paint, so that no place in town will look more inviting. Such an ideal filled the heart of an old-time warrior, King David: "The palace is not for man, but for the Lord God" (I Chr. 29:1*c*).

This kind of leadership calls no attention to itself. In most branches of the Church the minister does not belong to the congregation. In

[2] Marshall, *op. cit.,* p. 12.

things temporal he exercises as much or as little authority as he wins by personality—and no more. Even if he had a right to issue orders, he would work less directly. In a well-regulated church, as in a household, one person ought to feel responsible for the cleanliness and attractiveness of the whole, and of every part. This kind of upkeep calls for money. More than that, the work requires personal supervision of the sort a woman gives a house, a garden, or a lawn that she loves. For these reasons the pastor should deal with such matters through the chairman of the appropriate committee.

4. *Conditions may call for structural changes.* If so, face the matter frankly. Wait until you feel sure about the need for alterations. Then speak to the chairman of the board or committee in charge of such concerns. Sooner or later you may get this group to see the light. Until they do, let the matter rest. Never think of going over their heads and asking the congregation to act. If the officers recognize the need, encourage them to start making plans. To outline and discuss the various steps in a building program would call for a separate volume. Fortunately such a book exists.[3]

Here we can think only about leadership by the pastor. In view of countless other duties he must leave such matters largely to laymen. When the plans come before the congregation, lay officers should take the initiative. Throughout all the work they should lead. After it stands complete they ought to receive the credit, or the blame. For example, conditions may call for a new organ. Here again wise men move with caution. Before Albert Schweitzer went to Africa, he spent much time and energy in Europe keeping parish churches from removing old organs and replacing them with new instruments, far inferior.[4] Nevertheless, even in the judgment of such an expert, the old organ may have gone to pieces, like the poet's "one-hoss shay."

In another church the size and shape of the sanctuary permit the erection of a partition, partly of glass, to shut off a portion of space near the main entrance. Such a foyer, narthex, or lobby, contributes much to the orderliness of worship, and to the spirit of friendliness.

[3] See William H. Leach, *Protestant Church Building* (New York and Nashville: Abingdon-Cokesbury Press, 1948).
[4] See George Seaver, *Albert Schweitzer* (New York: Harper & Bros., 1947), chap. III, "Organs and Organ-Building."

At a church in Easton, Pennsylvania, an improvement called for a change of the rear balcony into an enclosed space where mothers could sit with wee children. Today while the little ones keep out of sight mothers can see the minister and the choir. Sounds from the pulpit and choir up front come to these mothers through the amplifying system, but the noise of the children never disturbs the worshipers below.

Any such changes may or may not commend themselves to the people. Probably some of them will feel pleased, and others will find fault. In the latter case why should they criticize the pastor? They did not secure him as an expert in structural engineering, but as an interpreter of God's holy will, and as a shepherd of the flock. If they lose confidence in his judgment as a church leader, they may begin to feel restless under his preaching. Why should he run such a risk? Many a young pastor has had to move to another field because he has begun to make rash demands for costly innovations. If he had waited for time and tact to do their perfect work, he might have led the people to make the changes with never a ripple on the waters.

5. In time the situation may *call for a new church edifice.* In that case the people ought to enjoy the services of a pastor with maturity and experience. As we have seen, after Phillips Brooks had been in Boston long enough to get his bearings, and to win confidence as a leader, he guided in the removal to another location, and in the erection of a new sanctuary. In as far as we can judge, if Trinity Church had not moved to that other site and built a new edifice, he and his people would not have wielded such an influence throughout Boston and the world. Other well-known parish ministers of yesterday first prepared the way and then led to the erection of new church buildings. For examples, turn to the records about Charles H. Spurgeon, Henry Ward Beecher, and George W. Truett. In each case the pastor first established himself in the esteem of the people. Then he led them to taste the joys of building a church they saw needful.

In looking forward to a new building, encourage care in the choice of a site. What Bishop Warren A. Candler said about missionary property in Cuba applies equally well to churches in the States: "We must have Protestant church buildings that will command attention

and respect. . . . I refuse to buy one inch of ground in obscure back streets. . . . Why set our men to work in shanties and back streets?" [5]
All of this assumes that a church requires a central location, easily accessible. In a city such an edifice ought to stand out prominently, and not be overshadowed by business houses on every side. In a certain center two churches of the same denomination stand close together. Through the years one has prospered and one has not. The difference in popular appeal has been due in part to matters of location and prominence. Only the church out in the open has made its mark on the city and the surrounding country. In all such concerns we Protestants can learn much from Roman Catholics.

The plans for a new building ought to include provision for offices. The number should vary according to the size of the staff. Where space is limited an office during the week can serve as a meeting place at night or on the Lord's Day. Ideally, however, each office ought to serve only one person or group. Here we shall think only about the parts that concern the pastor and the secretary. When not in use the quarters of either ought to be kept under lock and key. Otherwise members of classes or groups might handle his books or disturb her files.

In the arrangements now before us the pastor has a study at the church. The secretary answers the telephone and guards him from interruptions.[6] She watches over his morning hours as precious in her eyes. The pastor's study needs to be quiet, comfortable, and somewhat inaccessible. No one should be able to enter without first getting permission from the secretary. Her office ought to be prominent and easy of access from the street.

Somewhere near the church office and the study, if space permits, he may have a conference room. There he can meet with persons who wish to consult him, and he can reserve the study for its original purpose. In a large congregation the officers also need a board room, where they can meet in comfort, and have access to records. Ordinarily the same room can serve as the pastor's office by day and

---

[5] Alfred M. Pierce, *Giant Against the Sky* (New York and Nashville: Abingdon-Cokesbury Press, 1948), p. 103.
[6] For an opposite view see Calkins, *op. cit.*, pp. 57-60.

as a board room at other times. All these matters have begun to bulk larger than formerly in the thinking of building committees and church architects.

7. Before they start to build, encourage the officers to *sit down and count the cost*. Urge them to avoid piling up debts that will prove a burden, and interfere with gifts for benevolences. The pastor should know, as many laymen do not, that congregations contribute much more readily to a building program than to debt reduction. Also, an enlarged building requires an increased budget. Few committees think about the need for additional janitor service, heat and light, with upkeep and repairs after the first few years. For such reasons many a new stone edifice gleaming in the sunlight seems like a white elephant eating up provender difficult to provide. Once again, the pastor may have to bear the blame for what looks like extravagance.

As a rule people build a new church during days of so-called prosperity. With hands full of pledges stretching out over the next five years the officers run up bills that call for cash payments in ninety days. Sooner or later a depression may come and many pledges remain unpaid. Then the faithful who did not see the need for all that outlay must meet interest on the church debt. Some of them may quit giving liberally to benevolences. Consequently the spiritual life of the church declines. At length the pastor may resign, and his successor must stagger along under a load of debt.

More than one minister with ability to build has spent his life in fields where he has led in liquidating debts that never should have been contracted. If such a man had his way he would encourage the people not to build until most of the money lay in the bank. He would not dedicate a building until the people had paid all the church debt. Why dedicate to God what belongs to the bank? Fortunately the spirit of Protestantism does not require costly edifices in most communities. However, the downtown church in a city constitutes an exception.

8. Whether the building be new or old, ask the governing board to *determine how it shall be used*. Encourage the officers to let people out in the community use the building for any purpose in keeping with its character. "Let the church be the church." Also let it become a

meetinghouse. In most states church property enjoys freedom from taxation. Why should the premises not minister to the needs of the people near by? If it ever seems needful to charge outsiders for use of the sanctuary at a marriage, let the amount cover only the cost. On the other hand, the officers may direct that all the music before the wedding ceremony be in keeping with the holiness of God's house.

In a one-room building it may seem necessary to use the sanctuary for purposes not in keeping with such ideals. As a rule exceptions need not apply. Let the officers go on record as reserving the sanctuary for worship. That would keep any group from charging admission at the door, applauding a performance, taking photographs during public worship, and throwing rice or a bride's bouquet while in the house of God. "My house shall be called a house of prayer for all people." Such regulations obtain at the Gothic Chapel of Princeton University, but no one thinks of ascribing them to the chaplain in charge. In all these matters the officers of a church ought to take the responsibility, and if need be, accept the blame.

As an example of such regulations consider the statement below. It first came out in the weekly bulletin or calendar. The regulations now appear in the social rooms of the First Baptist Church at Huntington, New York. On the wall a neat copy, typed and framed, attracts the attention of everyone who visits that part of the church premises. In other congregations the content and wording ought to differ, but the idea calls for emulation. Why not forestall abuses, rather than correct them?

I. The language and general conduct of all present in the church building shall at all times be in keeping with the spirit of reverence due the House of God. No smoking shall be permitted in any part of the church or Sunday-school building.

II. There shall be no activities—outside of the regular church and auxiliary organizations—scheduled for any part of the church building until permission has been granted by the House Committee. All such appointments, when approved, to be entered on the "Activities Calendar" to be posted in the church parlors. No part of the church is to be used for other purposes during the time of any regular or special church service. Only for very special occasions shall the church building be used on Saturday evenings.

III. There shall be proper adult supervision at all exclusively boys' and girls' activities in the church building. All such activities shall cease at ten o'clock P.M.

IV. Request is made in the interests of economy that all present in the building feel responsibility for extinguishing unnecessary lights.

Suggested Readings

Anderson, Martin, *Planning and Financing the New Church*. Minneapolis: The Augsburg Publishing House, 1944.

Conover, Elbert M., *The Church Builder*. New York: Bureau of Architecture, 1949.

Drummond, Andrew L., *Church Architecture of Protestantism*. New York: Charles Scribner's Sons, 1935.

Leach, William H., *Protestant Church Building*. New York and Nashville: Abingdon-Cokesbury Press, 1948.

Ritter, Richard H., *The Arts of the Church*. Boston: The Pilgrim Press, 1947.

Scotford, John R., *The Church Beautiful*. Boston: The Pilgrim Press, 1945.

Stafford, Thomas A., *Christian Symbolism in the Evangelical Churches*. New York and Nashville: Abingdon-Cokesbury Press, 1942.

Webber, F. R., *Church Symbolism*. Cleveland: J. H. Jansen, 1938.

CHAPTER VI

The Different Kinds of Boards

I N an ideal setup the government of the church rests with a single body. Usually it goes under the name of an official board; sometimes it is called a church council, or pastor's cabinet. For convenience we shall adopt the first of these titles. In many churches the minister acts as chairman. However, if denominational law or local custom bids him step aside, he should do so with alacrity, especially when he can aid in choosing the layman to preside. Needless to say, a minister's effectiveness as church leader depends largely on his ability to do teamwork with the official board and its committees.

The large majority of pastors serve in bodies affiliated with denominations. In any such case a man ought to know and abide by the rules in his branch of the Church at large. When he goes into a field, he ought also to conform with the best local traditions and ideals about ways and means of doing the Lord's work. For the present, however, we shall think about a setup more or less ideal. Afterward we can deal with some of the many exceptions. In like manner students of medicine think first about the ideal.

Let us begin with a congregation of five hundred resident members, and an official board of thirty-five, the majority of them men. These friends hold office for one year, and are eligible for re-election. In other cases the body consists of a number divisible by three, perhaps thirty-six, who hold office for three years, one third of them retiring or being re-elected each year. As for the manner of election, that varies widely in different denominations and local churches. One plan calls for a nominating committee, which reports to the annual meeting soon after the close of the fiscal year. Ideally the board includes a representative of the young people's work, and of the women's societies. The system lends itself to all sorts of variations within the denominational framework.

This way of working calls for centralized authority, with as much diversity of function as local needs require. The stress falls on the teamwork of the everlasting whole. Within such a board the plan may call for four departments, or commissions, with a larger number in a church of unusual size. Within each department the details should be delegated to committees. As a rule the larger the church and the official board, the more numerous the committees. In most churches four departments can include all the activities of the parish. They appear below in tabular form:[1]

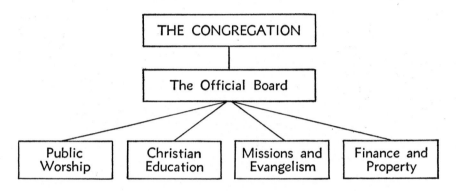

The department of public worship may operate through committees in charge of such concerns as music, pulpit supply, and use of the church. In a small body all of these may be handled by a single committee. Usually one mature layman serves best in deciding about the use of the premises. The department of Christian education sometimes goes under the name of a board. In any case it strives to coordinate and promote all the educational activities of the parish. The committees may have to do with the Sunday school, the other young people's groups, the daily vacation Bible school, and the special activities for boys and girls. Ideally the list should include work among women, but usually they prefer to think of their labors as missionary rather than educational. Let the good women have their way. They will do so anyhow!

The department of missions and evangelism calls for committees on such affairs as promotion of missions, visitation evangelism, conserva-

[1] Diagram adapted from Nevin C. Harner, *The Educational Work of the Church* (New York: Abingdon Press, 1939), p. 65.

tion of new members, and community betterment. The department of church finance and property may require these subdivisions: maintenance, stewardship, every-member canvass (or some such heading), publications, publicity, and auditing of accounts. If the program calls for a new church edifice, or educational unit, that will necessitate one or more special committees.[2] Experience has shown the wisdom of limiting the number of committees, provided they can take care of the work in hand, with due regard for the morrow.

With various modifications such a plan may operate in almost any branch of the Protestant Church. In some denominations the unitary system has the right of way; in others it has been winning favor. Here and there congregations have been turning to plans for such unified supervision and control. They have made the shift, not because of tradition and custom, but because the unicameral way of working appeals to laymen as in harmony with the best practices in the business world today. Many pastors also like the plan because it tends to simplify the machinery of the church, and to promote harmony among the officers.

Under favorable conditions such a system gives the work of the church a sense of unity. The plan leads representatives of various societies and groups to become acquainted with each other and with the different activities of the church. Otherwise in a large congregation one group may scarcely know what others have in hand. This line of thought applies especially to women and to young people. When their representatives belong to the official board, these groups feel that they have received a place on the main floor of the enterprise. However, they have yet to win their case in the higher courts!

This kind of system opens the way to pleasing and wholesome diversity. As the work expands, or as local conditions change, ways of working may shift. No longer need the setup in a large city church resemble that in a wayside chapel. In either field the system should enable workers to meet the needs of the field, both today and tomorrow. Here again we look at the facts ideally. If the estimate seems too glowing, ask why churches here and there keep shifting to

[2] See Leach, *op. cit.*, part I, "Planning and Financing."

the official board plan, whereas congregations that have given the method a fair trial rarely turn back to other ways of working. All of this, to be sure, does not come of itself. It calls for skillful leadership on the part of the minister, and for loyal teamwork on the part of lay leaders. Otherwise a small group of willful men may hold the reins from year to year. Then the causes they like may receive much attention, and other interests may lag through lack of concern. The larger the board, and the more diverse the parts, the more does it need symmetry and balance. Partly for this reason a minister who leads well enough in a church with two or three governing bodies may flounder when he first becomes the guide, philosopher, and friend of an official board. In some churches he must feel content not to preside, or even belong. Still he ought to serve as the moving spirit, "the very pulse of the machine."

TWO GOVERNING BOARDS

Another way of working calls for two governing boards. One of them, at least in theory, may hold the final authority. This body deals with what have become known as the "spiritualities." In a congregation of three hundred resident members this board may consist of eight or ten persons. In a larger church the system may call for one such officer to represent approximately fifty members, or perhaps a hundred. In some congregations these friends serve for life. In fact more than a few cling to the office after they have ceased to do more than simply "stand and wait." As a rule, under the rotary system, they hold office for three years. Year after year one third of them go off the board or else are re-elected.

In many churches this bicameral system works well. Those charged with the spiritualities accept their duties as from the Lord, and do their parts diligently. In after years one of the successive pastors may go into other work, and then he will look back on the meetings of this group with a feeling close to nostalgia. One such minister reports: "I had always thought of such a board as a Scotch-Irish debating society. Instead of that I found a group of Christian gentlemen who sat down together and talked about the spiritual interests of the Kingdom. When they differed in outlook, they did so as members of a brotherhood where everybody loved and trusted all the rest. In one such body for seven years I never heard of a divided vote."

A case from life will show how this plan lends dignity and power to such an officer who serves year after year. In Buffalo a congregation with twenty-five hundred resident members had fifty of these spiritual leaders. In addition to various other duties each of them served as lay pastor of about fifty members in a geographical group. Once a quarter, during the week before the celebration of the Sacrament, he called on every household, or communicant member, to deliver Communion tokens. These he felt bound to take in person, and not to send by mail, or through any hands other than his own.

Today, twenty years after he removed from that city, one of those officers tells about that service as the most gratifying and fruitful experience in all his life. Through the score of years intervening he has cherished the recollection of those contacts with fifty brethren on the board, and fifty other parishioners in their homes. In the congregation where he now labors he wonders why the brethren do not adopt some way of encouraging spiritual leaders to become assistants to the pastor, each with a flock of his own.

In view of these facts, why do some of us question the wisdom of having more than a single board? Partly because of the officials to whom we now turn. These men have in charge the business interests of the church. Women too may serve on either board, and in some cases they do, but let us keep the picture as simple as we can. As a rule the financial board consists of men younger than those on the spiritual body. What unfortunate nomenclature, as though both groups did not need spirituality! As a rule the financial board, also, does its work faithfully and well, and yet friction may arise within the official leadership of a church with two efficient boards more or less independent.

Sometimes the friction involves the pastor, at least indirectly. Over one board he may preside, and with these men he may have no special difficulty, either collectively or one by one. He knows them and loves them in the Lord; so he wins their affection and esteem. He can lead them in the oversight and promotion of Christian education, evangelism, missions, or any other cause dear to the heart of Christ.

Many who have enjoyed long years in such relations cherish only happy recollections, but not every minister can say as much about his dealings with the financial board. Here again many of us have no bitter memories, but still we question the wisdom of letting the second board remain practically independent of the other, and of the minister.

To the financial board the pastor may not belong and at the meetings his presence may not seem welcome. He may find the majority of this group zealous about the budget for current expenses and lukewarm or cold about expenditures for missions overseas. If friction develops between the two governing boards, he may feel like siding with the spiritual leaders. After one or the other body has gained ascendancy over the church as a whole, he may find difficulty in shepherding the entire flock. If all of this sounds fanciful, think of an actual case, of a sort not rare.

In a church where the spiritualities were in the hands of elderly men, most of them semi-invalids, the business board practically assumed control of the church. They liked the minister as a man but looked on him officially as head of the passive board. At a juncture when the active group felt the need of extensive repairs and improvements they laid all their plans for a building campaign and summoned a meeting of the congregation. In none of these deliberations and actions did they consult the pastor beforehand, or notify him afterward. Even if they acted according to the letter of their church laws, surely they did not follow the Golden Rule. If their program had appealed to the congregation, the minister would have had to lead in raising all the extra money.

A THIRD GOVERNING BOARD

A congregation with more than one board may have three. The third one, also, may constitute a problem, though not serious. These friends may have in charge the distribution of money for relief of the needy. Except in "hard times" the congregation may include few persons in dire distress. So the pastor may find difficulty in keeping these men employed. Sometimes he wonders about the wisdom of continuing the board without a sufficient reason for its existence.

As time goes on he may find satisfaction in being able to call on a group of minute men eager to relieve him of any task within their powers. Under his tutelage these friends can unconsciously prepare for service on a more responsible board. Or if the body goes under the name of "junior board," they can deliberately make ready for larger tasks in the Kingdom.

In a field with two or three governing boards the new pastor should accept the system he finds. With this way of doing the Lord's work he can lead to solid achievements. In time he may foster among the lay officers a desire for a unified board. Meanwhile he can suggest that the two or three bodies function informally as a single governing board. If they act discreetly and fairly, these men invite to serve with them representatives from other groups in the church, especially among the women and the young people.

A wise pastor summons a special meeting of such a body only when the occasion warrants. In any movement or emergency that vitally affects the welfare and progress of the church they all love, he can lead these representatives collectively in working out ways and means for doing the will of God. We might go on to consider his ability to get along with other official leaders of church societies. Soon we shall turn to such matters, more in detail. Meanwhile let us set up a working rule, which almost never permits an exception: Look on the peace and harmony of the church as more important by far than any improvement in methods of constituting boards.

> We are not divided,
> All one body we,
> One in hope and doctrine,
> One in charity.

CHAPTER VII

The Relation to the Official Board

D EALINGS with any official group or groups afford a test of a minister's piety and brain power. Almost a hundred years ago a master preacher declared: "It takes more high manhood, more wisdom, firmness, character, and right-seeing ability, to administer well in the cause, than it does to preach well." [1] How much more would Horace Bushnell feel this way if he served as leader of the governing boards in a going concern today! So let us render homage to every local minister who excels in this part of the Lord's work.

Experts in business management insist that the matter resolves itself largely into one of human relations. Even in such a specialized field as engineering, or railroading, understanding of human nature counts for more than technical knowledge and skill. For this reason a far-seeing divinity school has worked out a plan by which every prospective graduate has to go through an internship, either in a factory or in an office. Listen to a part of what he should learn from serving under a foreman in a shop or an executive at a desk:

Management is the development of people and not the direction of things. It affords the opportunity to bring out the best in free people, working in an organization so that they will enjoy their work. . . . The successful administrator gets people to work with him, not primarily because he has power over them, and can order them about, but because he is the kind of leader for whom they want to do their best.[2]

Experts in the business world stress leadership, not drivership. They look on technical competence as essential, but as almost worthless in itself. A church leader must know more than how to drive mules; he must like men, and believe in them as friends and equals. Instead of

---

[1] *Building Eras in Religion* (New York: Charles Scribner's Sons, 1910), p. 215.
[2] See Paul Pigors and C. E. Meyers, *Personnel Administration* (New York: McGraw-Hill Co., 1947), pp. 4-6.

trying to become a parish pope he should humble himself, and be willing to take advice. No man called of God to lead a flock dares think of his own plans as inspired and infallible. On the other hand, he should look on himself as indirectly responsible for the effectiveness of all the work in the church. In order to see how these principles work, let us think about them in a difficult realm, that of money. The finances of a church present much the same problems whether they are handled by a separate body or by a committee within a unified board.

RELATIONS WITH THE FINANCIAL OFFICERS

From his first day on the field a pastor should encourage both officers and people to magnify the importance of the church finances. If the friends in charge of the Lord's money handle it with skill, and keep the property shipshape, he should go out of his way soon to express appreciation and delight. If he receives an invitation to attend one of their meetings, he can thank them as a group. Otherwise he may put in the church bulletin or newsletter a note of appreciation. On the contrary, a new pastor once publicly referred to the church treasurer of the current funds as the congregational "Judas"! What ministerial asininity!

Somehow an incoming pastor can gain the good will of these officers. He can show that he admires teamwork such as the group displays. Otherwise he might stand aloof and wait for those "cold-blooded businessmen" to make the first advance. They in turn might look on him as a starry-eyed idealist. If he puts their mutual relations on a friendly level, distinctly Christian, he may receive an invitation to attend a meeting. He should accept with alacrity and, when he comes, express pleasure in getting to know these friends more intimately. For a while he may keep such relations on a level of Christian friendship, rather than church management.

A wise pastor trusts the officers in charge of the Lord's business. After a few months, even if not invited to a regular meeting, he may plan to be present fifteen or twenty minutes ahead of time. Then he can greet each friend on arrival, and chat about something of mutual concern, not relating to business in the hands of these laymen. If the chairman insists on his remaining after they convene, the pastor can lead in a short opening prayer. He can thank the friends for all they keep doing, and then ask to be excused. If anyone wishes him to answer a question, the minister opens up his heart. He should talk briefly, and then hie away to another engagement, which must not seem fictitious.

An incoming pastor, unfamiliar with the setup, should not try to impose his will on these officers. In a rare case a new man may have to start by "cleaning house." If so, the situation calls for a pastor with experience and prestige as a leader in church business. Otherwise laymen may look on the "stranger" as more or less of an expert in spiritual matters, but as an amateur in business affairs. Unfortunately they may have suffered much at the hands of former pastors with good intentions but little executive ability. If they find the new man "reasonable," they will begin to confide in him as their friend, and in time they may ask his advice about matters of business.

Throughout the first year or two must the leader sit by and watch these men lay plans for twelve months to come? When they draft the budget for current expenses, must he remain a spectator, with no right to speak? God forbid! How can he persuade people to oversubscribe a budget in which he only half believes? In ways honorable and Christian he can win the friendship and esteem of the chairman, the treasurer, or some other man of force in the business group. As man to man, friend to friend, the minister and this lay officer can talk about any matter of church business.

Without any semblance of dictation or wire-pulling the pastor with vision and tact can promote any enterprise that concerns these officers. Working indirectly and inconspicuously, he can lead the group as a whole into a larger vision of why the church exists. Even if he does not get far the first year or two, he can guide in the election of business officers who love the Lord and seek the coming of His dominion over land and sea. On the other hand, if he does not lead such officers away from provincialism, how can he expect the congregation to seek first the Kingdom of God?

Certain practices relating to money often call for correction. These changes the pastor can bring about gradually, and without fanfare.

In most cases the conditions have grown up because of carelessness. With an exception here or there, men who serve gratuitously as lay officers wish to do the Lord's work properly. They enjoy it all the more after they begin to do it with distinction. Once again, the situation affords a test of the pastor's ability and resourcefulness. Can he bring about reforms without precipitating a little revolution or rebellion?

1. *Counting the Lord's money.* One person may count all the money that comes through the weekly offerings. This friend may enjoy a reputation as spotless as snow, but why expose anyone to possible misunderstanding? From the time the money goes on the collection plates until the count has gone on the church records, let two or more persons be present. In one congregation the members of the board tarry after church and enjoy each other while tabulating the returns. At least two persons should be able to vouch for every penny they receive, and for the accuracy of the resulting records.

2. *Not paying bills on time.* The church treasurer may have become dilatory about the payment of bills, and the congregation may have become a byword in the community. How can the pastor win recruits for Christ among merchants who cannot collect debts from the church? The men in charge should instruct the treasurer to pay all bills immediately, or at least by the first of each month. If necessary, he can borrow money and pay interest at the bank, rather than imperil the name of the church. As for larger obligations, the officers ought to make honorable business arrangements.

3. *Delaying payments to church agencies.* In a congregation with one treasurer the friend in charge may distribute benevolent funds at rare intervals, perhaps only once a year. Ideally he ought to send them out, prorata, the first of each month. If that would involve dealing in small sums, he may tarry until the end of the quarter. If he waits for a whole year, he helps to put the larger church agencies "in the red." Throughout most of the church year why should they pay interest on money that the Lord's people have given months ago?

3. *Misusing benevolent funds.* Worse yet, the treasurer may use benevolent money in paying current expenses, and never dream of doing wrong. Why not give-and-take between the two accounts, as

husband and wife do with their budgets? Unfortunately, benevolent funds always do the giving, and current expenses do the taking. Despite all rationalizing, look on such a practice as wrong. Lead to watertight divisions between the two funds, with a single treasurer, or else to the election of two treasurers, with accounts at separate banks. The latter plan seems more nearly ideal.

4. *Carelessness in collecting pledges.* As a rule the treasurer borrows from the benevolent account because the amounts coming in for current expenses do not enable him to meet bills as they fall due. The men in charge may have grown careless about collecting pledges for church support. They need to adopt such measures as we shall consider when we deal with raising the annual budget.

5. *Failure to audit accounts.* The laws of the denomination may call for a careful accounting of financial records and books once a year. Many a treasurer seems ignorant of such regulations, and of the reason for their enactment. He may resent a suggestion that the pastor or somebody else questions the accuracy of the accounts. In such a case the pastor may bide his time. When a new treasurer stands ready to take charge—or two treasurers—the pastor can lead to an auditing of all the books, up to date. Then he can insist on such a procedure at the end of every fiscal year. How otherwise could the men in charge make a proper report at an annual meeting, or quarterly conference? As for the treasurer, if he thinks twice, and calmly, he will wish a careful auditing for the sake of his own reputation.

6. *Absent treatment of the sanctuary.* At more than a few churches some of the men in charge of temporalities seldom attend public worship or show concern about such services. In an extreme case these men come every Lord's Day and tarry until they have taken up the offering. Then they repair to another part of the edifice to smoke cigarettes and tell shady stories while they count the Lord's money. To remedy the situation have the officers adopt a more worshipful way of presenting these gifts before the Lord. After a prayer of consecration they may leave the offering plates at the altar on a table set apart for that purpose. There the gifts should remain until after the benediction.

These solutions may sound simpler than the facts warrant. Only by tact, indirectness, and patience can a new pastor lead to the correction of abuses. Even if he succeeds, apparently, he ought to know that the causes usually lie deeper. The right sort of lay leaders do not indulge in such practices. Both people and officers need instruction about the meaning and dignity of all worship and work in the church. When God's people do away with the old pagan distinction between sacred and secular, they will choose for financial officers men who love the Lord as much as those who serve as spiritual leaders.

WOMEN AS FINANCIAL OFFICERS

Meanwhile we must deal with conditions as they obtain in more than a few quarters. The easy way to remedy existing defects in the financial organization might be to have women serve with men. To such a procedure, at least in theory, few of us object. We have long felt that women have far too little part in the deliberations of higher church bodies. Locally we wonder why men should constitute a minority of the membership and yet hold nearly all the offices. For example, look at the fourth page of the bulletin in a church that does not know how to use the space profitably. Note the number of men's names on the upper half of the page—the more important part—and the paucity of women's names. And yet in the pulpit we often prate about Christian democracy, with equality between the sexes! "There is neither male nor female; for you are all one in Christ Jesus." (Gal. 3:28*b*, R.S.V.) All one! Yea, verily, but which one?

Practically, however, many of us hesitate about letting women displace men in the handling of finances. Some of the reasons appear in a case from life. A congregation with a thousand members had fifteen financial officers. In as far as the young pastor could judge, they did all their work faithfully and expertly. When a "class" had served for three years, no one but the treasurer could succeed himself. After the lapse of a year any of those men could come back by way of re-election. Most of them, however, declined in favor of new men. Consequently a large proportion of the leading laymen in that church became intimately acquainted with its inner workings. Partly for this reason the membership and the church attendance on the part of men equaled that among women.

No pastor as head coach would willingly break up such a winning combination, but more than a few women began to agitate for representation. They insisted that men did not know how to provide equipment and maintenance for the kitchen and the social rooms. On the other hand, the officers concerned wanted only men at their Tuesday night meetings. After they had transacted the business in hand they would hie away to a soft-drink parlor and enjoy a "stag party," with no wife or sister to cramp their style. Not knowing how else to avert what looked like disaster, some of them conferred with the minister. He thanked them for coming, and asked them to leave the matter in his hands. They were to do and say nothing about it until after they had heard from him or from the women.

The pastor saw that he must act at once, for if the matter came out into the open the women would win their way. Since he knew that the executive committee of the women's association was scheduled to meet in a few days, he asked the president for the privilege of speaking a few minutes at the opening. Then he prepared as carefully and prayerfully as for any address from the pulpit.

In the meeting, after a brief prayer, he thanked these friends for all that they and other women had done and were doing through the church. He thanked them, also, for loyalty to him as pastor. He assured them, truthfully, that he relied on the women of the church more than on any other group. Then he spoke a few more words, quietly:

"As your minister and friend I have come to beg a favor. I cannot give you my reasons, now or ever, but I assure you that they have to do with the welfare of the church we all love. My plea is this: Do not ask for the election of women on the board in charge of our business interests. As your friend and co-worker, I feel confident that I can secure from these men everything you leading women deem necessary in the way of equipment and maintenance. In the name of the Lord whom we men and women love and serve, let us all go forward from victory unto victory."

Then the pastor smiled, bowed, and left the room. He never knew what took place behind closed doors after his departure. He had no reason to inquire, for he never heard anything more about that restlessness among the women.

In another field this pastor would have followed a course almost the reverse. Nobody but a fool would try to standardize such human relations and procedures in two different parishes. This other case from life concerned a rural church with two hundred members. Six of them, five men and a woman, dealt with matters relating to business, and with money for current expenses. If any person had begun to agitate for the removal of that woman, the pastor would have striven tactfully to stop the agitation, and to keep her on the board.

Those five men felt delighted with her presence at every meeting. They looked on her as "a perfect woman, nobly planned, to warn, to comfort, and command." The "commanding" took the form of insisting that they convene every month at her home, where at times she fed them and their wives with the bounty of God's good earth. For many reasons the work of finance went forward better than at any time in the history of that venerable church. Only a bungler would have dreamed of breaking up that winning combination. As long as the motor of an automobile runs smoothly, a wise man refrains from tinkering with the machinery, and from trying to take it apart. So in church leadership often we find it "better to bear those ills we have than fly to others that we know not of."

FRICTION BETWEEN TWO BOARDS

More than one pastor has to deal with friction, or perhaps aloofness, between two boards. Ideally he may wish they would merge into a single body. Meanwhile perhaps he can lead to the election of a man to serve on both boards. Without seeming to carry water on both shoulders, a liaison officer of the right sort can help each group to understand how the other one feels. He can also make clear and attractive the program of the denomination with reference to the local church. Above all he can promote the spirit of harmony and cooperation.

The pastor himself can do even more to bring about a reconciliation, but he must not expect to close an old breach overnight. Better still, he can help to avert ill feelings and strife. For instance, look at a case. In an ancient and honorable church the spiritual leaders were elderly men who stood up for the faith of the fathers. The financial officers welcomed more light from their own day. As practicing physicians a number of them felt concerned about cases of lip cancer among friends who took Communion. By unanimous vote these younger men asked the older group for permission to purchase and install an individual Communion set.

The young minister, new on the field, could see the makings of a conflagration such as once before had done lasting harm. He knew something about the bitterness that attends verbal battles between stand-patters and progressives. In this case he presided over the men who believed in the *status quo*, and he sympathized with those who wanted to move forward. Wisely he determined to hold his peace and see what happened. He knew that the older group agreed with John Henry Jowett: "Never move with small majorities. Never take an important step in church life if a large minority is opposed to your proposals." [4] Those elderly brethren had also formed the habit—except in an emergency—of never settling an important issue at the meeting when it first arose. Ordinarily they did not believe that the Lord's business required haste.

When these brethren received the request about the Communion set, they voted to send a letter of thanks to the other group for this and all their concern about the Lord's work, and to ask time for dealing with the matter deliberately. Note that word "deliberately"! During the informal discussion two thirds of the elderly brothers showed that they did not believe in the proposal. At the next meeting, and at the third, their opinions remained much the same. At the fourth monthly meeting one of the men, not himself in favor of the innovation, made a new suggestion: "Brethren, the people have honored us by electing us to represent them on this board. Let us find out what they want us to do about this Communion set."

During the ensuing month each of those men talked about the matter with his friends out in the congregation. When the group convened again, and came to this part of the docket, man after man re-

[4] *The Preacher, His Life and Work* (New York: George H. Doran Co., 1912), p. 224; see also chap. VI, "The Preacher as a Man of Affairs."

ported that the large majority of his friends wanted the individual Communion set. After all these reports one of the men, not originally in favor, moved that the board authorize the proposal. That motion carried, unanimously and heartily. Then one of the brethren, not originally in favor, asked the privilege of donating the Communion set as a memorial to a loved one. When it arrived and went into use, the pastor could see no ripple on the surface of the waters. Then and afterward he never heard anything but commendation for what those officers had done. And yet he felt certain that if they had pushed the matter through at the first meeting, and had decided it either way, they might have touched off a powder magazine. From that experience in watching a group of elderly men wait on the Lord for unanimity he learned the practical wisdom of certain Quakers who tarry until they all can move together in brotherly love.

THE DIGNITY OF LAY LEADERSHIP

In all contacts with officers and people the minister should dignify the work of lay leaders. He should encourage them to magnify church office, looking on it as the noblest of earth's distinctions. If the customs of the church call for a service of ordination and installation, he can help to make the ceremony an event, not merely an incident. In any church he can recommend a special service of recognition by the people assembled to worship God. He may bring a message about the Christian Church, or about the Holy Spirit as the power of God in the lives of men (Acts 1:8). Then he can lead in a stately ceremony that will lead these men to dedicate themselves and their all to the service of Christ and the church.

At other times, also, he can honor officers who give largely of time and strength. If the seating arrangements permit, he can have such a board sit with him during the service and later stand with him when he baptizes candidates for church membership, or publicly welcomes those who have recently joined. In the bulletin and in other announcements he can keep the officers before the eyes of the people, favorably. Whenever he refers to a new proposal, he can speak of it, truthfully, as issuing from the officers, not from the pastor. In sermons and in pastoral contacts he can gradually educate both people and officers to think of such work as almost on a par with that of the minister. This appears to have been the ideal in the New Testament, for the apostles never alluded to laymen as an inferior order of church leaders.

Occasionally a young minister asks how to deal with a senior lay officer who bosses everybody, including the pastor. Some of us have had no such experience, but lack of experience never deters anyone from giving advice. Thank God that the brother takes his duties seriously! When you become his friend, you may find beneath his gruff manner a heart of gold. If you suspect that he has a blind spot, remember that you may have one of your own. Whenever you can do so with a clear conscience, follow the counsel he offers freely. In any case thank him for all his concern. Go out of your way, with your wife, to show the other members of his family kindness. At first you may feel that they need commiseration.

All the while, even if you do not admire the man, respect his office. Never let anyone tell you about his faults and foibles. Above all, do not strive to unseat him. Such a scheme may backfire. Deal with him as a football coach does with a star who tries to outshine the rest of the team. Develop other players so that they too will render effective service. In some such fashion Lincoln dealt with star members of his cabinet, where he found man after man willing to take the reins out of the president's hands. The chief would not let anyone find fault with a one of those associates. Soon he established himself as leader of them all. What else does church leadership mean than ability to engage in teamwork with masterful men?

A glance back over this chapter will show the pastor in action as an executive. These same priciples, as they apply to the business world, appear in a current volume by an expert. As for elements more distinctly Christian, they will emerge later.

> Executive work has become primarily a matter of successfully operating and steering one's ship. . . . All executive work is navigation—knowing where you want to go, what shoals you must avoid, what the forces are with which you must deal, and how to handle yourself, your ship, and your crew, effectively and without waste, in the process of getting there.

Whatever the nature of the organization, it must establish its goals, make its plans, create its organization, set up levels of authority and co-ordination, supervise workers, provide leadership and inspiration, . . . educate its employees concerning the objective of the enterprise, secure their wholehearted co-operation, be assured that the public is getting the sort of service it desires, and that its complaints are adequately met, and adjust the plans and programs of the enterprise to the social forces which ultimately determine its survival.

The successful commander is he who has the best balance of physique, mentality, personality, technical equipment, knowledge of human behavior, social adaptability, ability to understand and get along with people, and a sense of purpose and direction.[5]

[5] Marshall E. Dimock, *The Executive in Action* (New York: Harper & Bros., 1945), pp. 1, 6, 11.

CHAPTER VIII

The Dealings with the Staff

EVERY church of any size needs a staff of full-time workers, each on a salary. With a few hundred members the officers may feel able to employ only a pastor and a sexton. In a larger body the budget may also warrant a full-time secretary. When the number of members increases, the staff may include a director of Christian education, a minister of music, or an assistant pastor. Rarely has experience shown the wisdom of combining two of these functions, except when the assistant pastor directs things educational. Starting with a pastor and a sexton, we may think of an additional full-time worker for every five hundred members, or major fraction thereof.

A congregation of five hundred resident members, or more, needs a pastor, a sexton, and a secretary. So we might go up the scale, numerically. The Roman Catholic Church, with relatively few parishes, tends toward a multiple ministry. Protestantism, especially in the United States, often operates with smaller units, sometimes too small for effective service. When a congregation includes one or two thousand members, with as many additional adherents, the work may become understaffed. Then critics may wonder why the pastor falls short in his multitudinous duties.

Any kind of expanding staff brings additional difficulties. When money abounds, churches cannot secure and keep competent full-time workers. In days of depression many a congregation feels unable to support a staff, and trained workers go about seeking positions. Hence the average church struggles along without enough paid workers. Especially in the country it may feel content to secure and keep a minister with a seminary training and a sexton with a mind to work. In all these matters the average church needs far more strategy.

THE CHURCH SEXTON

The average pastor has to learn his business as an executive. If he had an assistant or a secretary, the minister would not know how to keep either of them profitably employed.[1] Even at first he should know how to get along with the sexton. With the hiring and firing of such a scapegoat the pastor should have nothing to do. Rather should he treat the sexton as a friend. The dear man may have become the errand boy of all the organizations, and the subject of endless bickerings. With long hours, small pay, and meager thanks, he receives orders from almost everybody, and criticism from irresponsible persons.

Occasionally, however, a friendly observer of churches runs across exceptions. In five different places recently I have watched sextons who have lifted their work out of the doldrums. In a fashion all his own, each of them is making a distinct contribution to the Kingdom. These men have come to middle years or even more. One has retired from heavy work as a machinist. Each of them loves both church and people. Without demanding his rights such a man expects and receives courtesy and consideration from every member of the church, except a few of the Lord's feeble-minded.

One of those caretakers labors at a church in our capital city. There his brother serves as an important member of the governing board. The sexton rightly thinks of his work as on a par with that of his brother. Both show loyalty to the Kingdom by devotion to the church and its people. What follows on the part of the sexton? Foresight, order, system, cleanliness, thrift, and all the other qualities that our Lord commends in His parables.[2] The people, in turn, look on him as their friend. They call him Mr. _____. In another congregation, where such a worker did not relish the name of sexton, the people referred to him as the custodian. Such a congregation secures and retains a worthy helper much as a good woman keeps someone at work in the home. A certain housemother always has paid help, even in boom times, and that without ability to pay top wages. The mistress knows the meaning of kindness and justice. The two women look on each other as Christian friends.

The pastor too should learn how to show kindness. If he has ever worked with his hands, he knows about the trials and problems of

---

[1] Ideally every seminary student would take an internship of two years before graduation, and every church would employ a full-time secretary.
[2] See *The Jesus of History*, by T. R. Glover (New York: George H. Doran Co., 1917) pp. 129-30.

the sexton. The minister should understand what every workingman craves: fair play, a living wage, recognition for work well done, and security for the future. All of this a pastor can encourage the officers to accord the custodian. He ought to receive instructions from only one person, and that not the minister. In a well-regulated household the maid gets instructions from no one but the mistress. From the head of the household she receives appreciation, with an occasional gift, all in the spirit of Christian love.

In short, be a gentleman. Treat the caretaker as a human being. Do not hesitate to tell him kindly that the house committee has granted the use of the church for a wedding next Tuesday evening at eight o'clock, with a rehearsal at nine the evening before. See that he gets extra pay for added work, especially for outsiders. Be content with making positive suggestions, and not many of these. As for issuing orders, finding fault, and picking flaws, leave all that to the committee in charge. Some of us have never known a sexton who would not respond to friendship from the pastor as a Christian gentleman.

If a new caretaker begins well, a note in the bulletin may cheer him on the way toward permanent usefulness. So will an occasional note, sent through the mail, thanking him for a special kindness. The board or committee in charge should see that he has a living wage, a free day every week, or perhaps two half days, and a reasonable number of working hours, especially on the weekly "day of rest and gladness." At Christmas and at other times he and his family will appreciate tokens of thanks. In other words, treat him as a man, not a mule. Look on his work as a position, not as a job. He in turn will save much that a misfit would waste.

THE CHURCH SECRETARY

By the time the young minister has learned to deal with a sexton, the staff may also include a secretary. Here the human relations differ in detail, but not basically. At the start both she and the pastor ought to understand her duties and privileges. Otherwise she may have to serve him and his wife as a sort of hired girl. With the business arrangements he should have nothing to do, directly. But he can suggest to the committee that she ought to have regular office hours, with a free day every week, or two half days, especially if the work keeps her occupied on Sunday. Unless she serves as full-time secretary to the pastor, both of them should know at the start whether she ought to write out sermons from week to week. Seldom does the regular work afford her the time to deal with his personal correspondence, and his wife's telephone calls.

In most cases a mature woman serves better than a younger one without experience, who is also likely to marry. Whatever the age, the minister treats her as a Christian gentlewoman. During office hours both of them keep to the work in hand. When he dictates letters he sits on the opposite side of the desk. After the first few weeks their relations should become as natural and friendly as in any other office where Christ has His way. The pastor and his wife can entertain her at their home, and the wife can send an occasional gift, especially at Christmas. Each of them should follow the Golden Rule.[3]

Before a man goes to a church with such a full-time worker he should learn how to deal with a letter. In this case, as in no other, a pastor needs to dictate. He may ponder these suggestions that have come from long-suffering secretaries. They report that few pastors excel in this part of the work, and that some of them treat a secretary like a moron. Others expect from her the wisdom of Solomon, or else they muddle along and make her work a mess. Why not plan this part of the Lord's business?

1. *Set apart a time* for the day's correspondence, with anything else that calls for dictation. Try to handle all such matters at the same hour each day.

2. *Act as in a business conference.* Keep to the matter in hand. Many a pastor who complains about lack of time wastes minutes that belong to the Lord and His people.

3. *Have everything ready, and in the right order.* When you first read a communication that calls for a reply, jot down on the margin any items that need attention.

4. *Sit down and remain seated.* Keep from seeming nervous. Es-

[3] Either of them can secure without cost a pamphlet, *The Perfect Secretary, A Handbook of Office Behavior*, from the Eaton Paper Corp., Pittsfield, Mass.

pecially during the first weeks, a minister who fidgets may set the secretary's teeth on edge.

5. *Dictate clearly, but not loudly.* Speak at an even rate, with few words at a time. Try about 130 a minute. If she prefers, talk a little faster.

6. *Encourage the secretary to ask questions* about anything not clear. Receive suggestions courteously. Remember that in her field she knows more than you do.

7. *Leave the original correspondence,* so that she can verify name and address.

8. *Let her deal with matters of routine,* and in her own name. As for intimate letters, write them yourself, preferably with a pen.

9. *Read word for word every paper,* communication, or document you expect to sign.

10. *Remember that loyalty works both ways.* If you treat the secretary as a Christian friend and helper, she will work with you as the most influential man in the community.

OTHER MEMBERS OF THE STAFF

If the staff includes another person or two, the opportunities for misunderstanding and friction increase. In a church with a thousand members the pastor may wish for a lay assistant rather than a minister, and a woman rather than a man. In days when the demand exceeds the supply the officers may have to take what they can get. Ideally the work may call for a layman as minister of music, or a woman as director of Christian education. In either case, the work of the associate ought to supplement that of the pastor. The other person should not wish to do half the pulpit work, or outshine the pastor in his own field. In any case the situation calls for a clear understanding of the privileges and duties involved. Vagueness may lead to friction. If anything of that sort develops, the pastor should rely on frankness. Man to man, in dealing with a male associate, the two can talk things over in the spirit of prayer.

A pastor deals with associates in one of two ways. Ideally he should keep hands off, except to commend work well done. At Free St. George's Church in Edinburgh Alexander Whyte had a succession of young ministerial colleagues, each of whom later rose to distinction in the Church. After Whyte had gone home to God, each of those younger men gave thanks for the privilege of having worked with such a leader. They all appreciated his letting them do the work in their own way, without suggestions or criticisms. But not many young helpers seem ready for such uncharted freedom.

Another pastor nearer home follows a course almost the reverse, and with almost equal success. He secures from the divinity school young graduates without pastoral experience. Then he outlines the work of each ministerial assistant, and calls for regular reports, detailed and in writing. This pastor looks on himself as a coach. In effect he gives each ministerial associate a postgraduate course in practical theology. What else does many a seminary graduate need? If he tries to pray in public without making ready, or if he blunders into a hospital room without securing permission, someone with authority ought to take him in hand, teaching what he should have learned at the divinity school.[4]

Much of this training may go under the name of internship. Someday all our denominations will require every prospective minister to serve as an apprentice for at least a year, preferably two years, before he receives ordination. The value of such a discipline varies according to the ability of the local pastor as a coach. Does he know how to supervise teamwork, or does he attempt to do everything himself? Does he develop the young man's powers or try to keep him in a strait jacket?

Whenever an ordained minister serves as assistant pastor, friction may arise. Then each party may blame the other. Even if the two get along amicably, the younger one may begin to look for a field of his own. Soon the work of finding an assistant must start over again. For many reasons a pastor may prefer to work with a mature associate, whether or not ordained. In a large church such a teammate can assume responsibility for the business administration. A Y.M.C.A. secretary, for example, may retire at the age of sixty. Then he can serve a church for the next ten years or even longer.

[4] See my *Pastoral Work* (Philadelphia: The Westminster Press, 1945), chap. XXVI, "The Work of a Paid Assistant."

If the staff includes two or three ministers fully ordained, one of them can serve mainly as preacher, another mainly in pastoral work and personal counseling, a third mainly as director of young people's activities. These distinctions need not stand out in the public eye. In a published list of the church staff, the name of the minister in charge ought to appear first. Then should follow the names of the other ministers in the order of seniority, or any other order the minister in charge deems best. If a number of lawyers can work together for years in the same firm, and a group of physicians in a clinic, so can ministers of the Gospel. In every such case the team must have a captain to whom the others defer.

As a rule the director of young people's work needs to be fairly young in years. After this friend draws near to middle age he or she may transfer to another part of the staff work, such as calling on the sick and holding personal conferences. Among ordained men no longer young, more than a few would welcome an opportunity to work on the staff of a large congregation. As in a college faculty, a church staff may call for one person with years of experience and for others with the zest of youth.

We might go into detail about other members of the staff, and about staff meetings. But why attempt to lay down rules? Effectiveness here depends largely on the ability of the chief both as strategist and tactician. Can he formulate plans for the work of the staff? Can he work with these friends in carrying out the program? If so, he can become the leader in a church with a multiple ministry. If not, he may serve as a member of a staff, rather than as its head. The day has come when Protestants ought to expect from any parish minister more than ability to speak effectively and be a kind pastor. He ought also to excel as a member of a church staff, whether as the chief coach or as one of the associates.

In either case a young minister would profit from a course of reading about business personnel and related subjects. If a man does not know how to embark on such a course, he may plan for a summer vacation near the state university. At the reference department of the library he will find experts ready to guide in such reading. Before long he will discover that leadership of a staff calls for two qualities that do not always appear together: businesslike efficiency and Christian considerateness. In the following excerpt the latter stands out as more important. A correspondent of the London *Daily News* has been discussing one of the infrequent disturbances in the Salvation Army:

If a regiment rises against its colonel, the colonel is to blame. "There are no bad soldiers, only bad officers." . . . I worked under one of the biggest and most successful executives in the world. . . . One of the departmental chiefs who had brought his division of the undertaking to a high degree of success never went further. . . . Finally he disappeared. Someone asked the man at the head the reason. "So-and-so," said he, "had the most discontented staff of any in my employ. They were unhappy and he had to make frequent changes. Such a man is no good to me even if he does double his output in a couple of years." [5]

Suggested Readings

Bernard, Chester I., *The Functions of the Executive*. Cambridge: Harvard University Press, 1938.

Dimock, Marshall E., *The Executive in Action*. New York: Harper & Bros., 1945. Contains annotated list of related works.

Landis, James M., *The Administrative Process*. New Haven: Yale University Press, 1938.

Leffingwell, William H., and Robinson, E. H., *Textbook of Office Management*. 2nd ed. rev. New York: McGraw-Hill Book Co., 1943.

Meriam, Lewis, *Public Personnel Problems from the Standpoint of the Operating Officer*. Washington: Brookings Institution, 1938.

Mooney, James C., and Reily, Alan C., *The Principles of Organization*. New York: Harper & Bros., 1939.

Pigors, Paul, and Myers, C.A., *Personnel Education*. New York: McGraw-Hill Book Co., 1947.

Scott, Walter D., et al., *Personnel Administration*. New York: McGraw-Hill Book Co., 1941.

Schell, Erwin H., *The Technique of Executive Control*. New York: McGraw-Hill Book Co., 1946.

Smith, Howard, *Developing Your Executive Ability*. New York: McGraw-Hill Book Co., 1946.

[5] P. W. Wilson, *General Evangeline Booth of the Salvation Army* (New York: Charles Scribner's Sons, 1948), p. 203.

Tead, Ordway, *The Art of Leadership*. New York: McGraw-Hill Book Co., 1935.

Tead, O., and Metcalf, H. C., *Personnel Administration*. New York: McGraw-Hill Book Co., 1941.

Whitehead, Thos. N., *Leadership in a Free Society*. Cambridge: Harvard University Press, 1937.

CHAPTER IX

The Friend of the Musicians

I N every church the organist and the other musicians need the support of the pastor. Perhaps they have gained the reputation of being sensitive; and they might not deny the charge. They feel almost as touchy and easily hurt, or pleased, as the minister and his wife. Sometimes musicians have difficulty among themselves. More often they do not give satisfaction to many of the people. Whatever the difficulty, church musicians look to the pastor for sympathy and help. He in turn may regard them as a problem. At ministerial conferences, where a seminary professor deals with pastoral cases, many of those submitted have to do with musicians.

THE PROBLEMS ABOUT MUSIC

For example, take a situation that has become common. The young people and some of the older ones feel that the organist has outlasted her usefulness. The music committee and most of the older folk insist on retaining her year after year. As time goes on, the issue becomes acute. Which side shall the minister and his wife favor? How can they remain neutral? Theoretically he ought to serve as pastor of the entire congregation. But how, with reference to the music?

Another problem has also become common. In fact, these two may exist together, like typhoid fever and pneumonia. Young people returning from college and university have learned to enjoy the music of Bach, Beethoven, and Brahms. With them side other devotees of culture, no longer young, save at heart. Many of the older folk, and some not advanced in years, prefer the gospel songs of Fanny Crosby and Frances R. Havergal. Even in the same family such a cleavage may appear. Once again, which side shall the pastor and his wife favor? How can he "turn the heart of the fathers to the children, and the heart of the children to their fathers"? (Mal. 4:6a.)

One thing he knows. The musicians need sympathy and help. Not even a chorus of angels from the realms of glory could satisfy both factions. Sometimes the musicians do not try to please more than one of the warring groups. The minister and his wife may agree with those who want classic music. But as pastor of the entire church he ought to deal with people as they are, musically. In time he may lead them to love and sing "O sacred head, now wounded," or "The spacious firmament on high." At present he may content himself with choosing hymns easier for non-musical folk. Without seeming to dictate he may suggest to the choir leader the inclusion of special selections notable for rhythm and melody rather than harmony.

The issue may come to a head when the congregation needs a new hymnal, or the church school a new songbook. The wise pastor shows confidence in the musicians by conferring with them before he determines what to advise the music committee. In the end the committee may decide on the standard hymnal of the denomination, or on a smaller work for the church school. In almost every case the denominational books seem best for the local church. The pastor need not base his preference on the merits of the hymns and the music so much as on the wisdom of keeping in line with other churches of the denomination. If this looks like playing politics, remember that almost every denomination now has a first-class hymnal, with adequate songbooks for other purposes. Why look further?

The problem may seem less acute if the church holds two services on the Lord's Day. For some reason lovers of classic music usually think of it in terms of the morning service, or perhaps vespers. Most of them do not object to something else at the evening hour, especially if they do not attend. Since the music at the two services ought to differ anyway, so as to meet varying needs, why not give the preference to statelier songs in the morning, and to more informal music at the evening hour? If the church holds vespers, however, the stately music ought to come then, and the more informal songs at the earlier service.[1]

THE SELECTION OF HYMNS

In any case the minister should know how to select hymns. Otherwise he may never gain the respect of those who understand music.

[1] See my *Fine Art of Public Worship* (Nashville: Cokesbury Press, 1939), chaps. V and VI.

For a special service, as at Easter, or just before Christmas, he may choose all the hymns with reference to the sermon, or rather the theme of the hour. Even then the three hymns should follow a sequence, forward-looking and climactic. At a regular hour of worship why let all the hymns sound the same note, and reflect the same tone color? As for the wisdom of having three main hymns, after the opening burst of song, almost one third of the songs in any first-class book ought to come after the sermon. If you wish to have a singing church, let the people sing! Over at Dumfries in Scotland, the pastor of St. Michael's Presbyterian Church has five hymns at every service, and he holds four services on the Lord's Day. Thank God for a faith that teaches us to sing! What a Protestant heritage!

In choosing hymns the man who knows his business may follow such principles as those below. They appear in the preface of the songbook at the chapels of Yale and Princeton universities. The songs themselves would not suit the needs elsewhere, but this paragraph contains practical wisdom about the choice of hymns for any congregation:

The more objective type of hymn, expressing adoration, praise, [or] thanksgiving, appropriate for the beginning of worship, forms one group. The more intimate type of hymns, appropriate for the central part of the service, is a second group. Hymns appropriate for the climax of the service are grouped together according to the emphasis on consecration [dedication], service, or social appeal. The seasonal hymns for the Church Year and for special occasions follow in a group by themselves.[2]

If the better type of music dominates the morning service, no one should object to something else at night. The hymns and special music need not all belong to the gospel-song family. If those who attend in the evening so desire, they may have a song service during the first fifteen minutes. In some churches the young folk and some of the older ones tarry after the hour to enjoy a sort of old-time singing school. Then the members of the group can ask for what they want. If the minister keeps his eyes and ears open, he may learn much

[2] E. M. McKee and R. R. Wicks, eds., *University Hymns* (New Haven: Yale Univ. Press, 1931), p. vi.

about dealing with people as they are. So can the friends in the choir, if they deign to attend what has become known as a "singspiration."

Meanwhile people in many churches do not join heartily in the musical portions of the service. Few of them sing hymns at home or at their work, as their fathers and mothers used to do. Why not? Perhaps partly because the musical policy of the pastor and the choir does not take into account the present degree of musical appreciation among the people. Gradually the choir can lead almost any congregation to love and sing the noblest hymns from every land and every time, such as "Now thank we all our God."

THE HOME MISSIONARY OF MUSIC

In order to become a home missionary of music the pastor needs to know about its prominence in the Bible and in the history of the Protestant Church. On Reformation Sunday he may tell the people how much that movement had to do with music. Luther, Calvin, and other reformers gave music back to the people, and opened the way for congregational singing. Two hundred years later the Wesleyan Revival gave a large place to the ministry of song. What else does it mean to have a Christian church today?

A true philosophy of music gives a worthy place to the organ. The pastor and his wife should think of the pipe organ as the most wonderful thing that has come from the hands of men. In a church not able to afford such an instrument, the musicians find that any sort of organ in tune serves better than a piano, which cannot sustain a tone. More than a few small churches have installed electric organs, and have found them satisfactory, within their limits.

The pastor should regard special numbers by the choir as more important than selections from the organ. Also he may think of a mixed chorus as better than a quartet, and a quartet as better than a soloist, or two singers. "Better" does not here refer to the quality of the music, but to uplift in the public worship of God. The larger the number of friends in the choir, if properly garbed and reverent in demeanor, the less do people notice the personality of any singer. However, if conditions temporarily do not permit the training of a choir, a precentor may lead the congregation as a single chorus. Who could ask for more uplifting songs?

The minister should give the first place, musically, to singing by the people. More than a few worshipers appreciate the beauty of organ music; a larger number prefer selections from the chorus, usually when supported by the organ; almost everyone loves the right sort of congregational singing. In the course of a year or two, if the pastor works hand in hand with the organist and the choir, these guides in worship can foster the use of first-class music, and lead to delight in first-class hymns.

All of this has much to do with parish leadership. If the people are to sing well, they need to learn how, and that early in life. In a church of any size the officers may secure a full-time minister of music. Instead of paying the members of a quartet to come in from without and entertain lovers of beauty, the church ought to develop its own musical resources, especially among the boys and girls. Hence the minister of music ought to organize singing groups of various ages. He may have as many as six choirs, at different age levels. For the first year or two the music by the ablest of these groups may not compare with that of the former paid quartet. After a while, however, the volunteer singers will find themselves. Then they will render music worthy of the God they adore.

Year after year some of the older members will keep dropping out of the adult choir. As these friends take their places in the congregation they will tend to raise the musical level. Hence the congregational singing ought to keep improving. But even if it does not, think of the opportunity to enlist and train boys and girls, beginning with the "cherub choir," with wee treble voices not in tune. "Out of the mouth of babes and sucklings hast thou ordained strength" (Ps. 8:2a). This plan of enlisting and training groups of various ages may constitute the chief contribution of America to the music of the Christian Church.

Such a program goes far to meet a common criticism. Ill-informed folk often look at the church budget and sneer at the amount set aside for music, over against that for the church school. They forget that almost half of the money for current expenses has to do with

Christian education. If the church program calls for a full-time minister of music, they could list his work under Christian education. Except in the Scriptures, where can the church find such a storehouse of sacred learning as in a standard hymnal? If the minister of music leads the people, young and old, to love and sing the noblest songs of the Church, both from yesterday and today, why not call his work Christian education?

The pastor should encourage the officers to invest money freely in the musical leadership and training of the people, the younger the better. The officials ought to keep the organ in tune, and even the chimes. The music committee should secure an organist able to bring out of both organ and chimes the most heavenly harmonies. The plan locally may call for the same person to act as organist and director, or else for two musicians: a part-time organist and a full-time singer, with the latter as minister of music. This friend in charge should never seek to entertain. Only in the public worship of God can the average church excel, musically. As for entertainment, let the people find it elsewhere. Musically, as in every other respect, let the church be a church, not a place where performers call attention to themselves and away from God. Why compete with the world in a field where it often excels?

As home missionaries of music, the pastor and his wife need not play the pipe organ and sing like stars in grand opera. If they do not regard themselves as experts, they may not interfere with the music. However, both of them ought to know enough about it to appreciate excellence in others, and also lead in carrying out a constructive program. Fortunately, any person with intelligence can cultivate a love for first-class music. When William Lyon Phelps of Yale arrived at manhood, he awoke to his lack of such culture. Then he set himself to become a lover of music. In later years he could talk entertainingly about an art of which he had never become a master. "The way to appreciate beauty," he wrote, "is to keep looking at it, to appreciate music is to keep listening to it, to appreciate poetry is to keep reading it." [3]

[3] *Autobiography with Letters* (New York: Oxford Univ. Press, 1939), p. 209.

We have been taking for granted that the pastor looks on the musicians as friends and helpers in the public worship of God. The point of view may become clearer in the light of a few negations.

1. The minister and his wife should *have nothing to do with employing musicians.* The proper committee ought to deal with all that, and then accept either the praise or the blame. The chairman ought to confer with the pastor about matters of policy, but the people should not blame the minister for the choice of any musician or the quality of any special number. The dear man has burdens enough without assuming those of the music committee. Let them bear the responsibility for what has become known, unwisely, as "the war department of the church."

2. Unless the friend in charge invites him to be present for a special purpose, occasionally, the pastor *need not attend choir rehearsals.* If he wishes to secure expert leadership for the responses in reading from the Psalter, he may ask the privilege of taking a few minutes to explain the matter, especially the rhythm. With the choir he may go through a selection or two, in order to explain their responses. He can get them to follow the tempo he sets for the psalm, according to its tone color. Ordinarily, the pastor should leave the rehearsals in the hands of the friend officially in charge of the music.

3. Both publicly and privately the pastor and the musicians should *refrain from finding fault with songs that people like.* If he or the minister of music spoke slightingly about "I and me hymns," or "the glory song," such sarcasm might hurt the feelings of good people who live up to all the musical light they have received. Many such friends respond to constructive musical leadership, which relies on the expulsive power of a new affection.

4. *Encourage the leader of the music.* No one in the parish, unless it be the superintendent of the church school, needs so much pastoral encouragement as the director of the music. As a rule no one else goes through the year with so little commendation as the organist. If the pastor receives more than his share of adulation he may pass some of it along to her. Years ago a young minister began his work in a home

mission station. After about three months he drove out twenty-five miles to visit the organist, a farmer's wife. On the piano he saw every scrap of writing he had handed her during those thirteen weeks. After that, in fields of different sorts, he tried never to let a month go by without giving the organist a visible token of gratitude for her part in public worship. In various ways, thereafter, he tried to do much the same with the other musicians. In short, treat them as friends. They will respond by loyalty to you and to the church.

Suggested Readings

Ashton, Joseph N., *Music in Worship*. Boston: The Pilgrim Press, 1943.

Julian, John J., ed., *Dictionary of Hymnology*. New York: Charles Scribner's Sons, 1915.

Kettring, Donald D., *Steps Toward a Singing Church*. Philadelphia: The Westminster Press, 1948.

Marks, Harvey B., *The Rise and Growth of English Hymnody*. New York: Fleming H. Revell Co., 1938.

Smith, H. Augustine, *Lyric Religion*. New York: The Century Co., 1931.

Chapter X

6 2 4 5

The Believer in the Ushers

THE student choir of a certain divinity school visits more than a hundred churches every year. These young men hear and see much that gives them pleasure, but they do not always admire the ushering. They feel that somebody ought to enlist and train men who will make this part of the work a means of grace. Such an undertaking need not consume much of the pastor's time and energy. If he has learned what Jethro told Moses, the parish leader finds that ushers respond to such a way of working, indirectly. It consists largely in the fine art of appreciation.

DUTIES OF THE USHER

The importance and the difficulty of ushering vary according to the field. In a large congregation, without a commodious sanctuary, these friends have much to do. Even in a church with pews not overflowing, the ushers need to look out for strangers. All of this may apply even more to the evening service, or to vespers, than to morning worship. At any hour the right sort of ushering helps in working toward two ideals that seem to conflict: reverence in the house of God, and friendliness among His people.

"They that feared the Lord spake often one to another; and the Lord hearkened, and heard it, and a book of remembrance was written before him for them that feared the Lord, and thought upon his name" (Mal. 3:16). In the heavenly book of remembrance the recording angel surely writes the names of church ushers, with other leaders in public worship. So do ushers find a place in the heart of the pastor who believes in doing everything "decently and in order." They magnify their office by coming to the sanctuary at least fifteen minutes before time for the service to begin. In exceptional cases ushers find it needful to be present half an hour in advance. They strive to make an attractive appearance. At a Christian Science service on Sunday morning the ushers may appear in formal attire. That calls for an oxford-gray cutaway coat, striped gray trousers, not too dark, but not conspicuously light, together with a boutonniere. In many a rural church such attire might smack of display. However, ushers find that even the poorest of God's people, in terms of money, enjoy belonging to a church with a building full of beauty, and officers in their best attire.

Courtesy bulks much larger than dress. The ideal usher makes everyone feel at home, but without seeming effusive and fussy. He notes that certain strangers like a hearty greeting, and that others prefer to enter a sanctuary unobtrusively. He may offer an arm to an elderly woman, and greet the next one with a friendly nod. He can seat a newcomer without embarrassment or delay. Often this means taking him to a pew where church members know how to make a stranger feel at home, without disturbing friends near by. The usher can even get people to sit well forward, so that there need be no chasm yawning between the speaker and his hearers.

The work of an usher in a crowded church calls for skill and resourcefulness. While the people are assembling, he studies the part of the sanctuary over which he presides. After the vocal worship has begun, late-comers may at times threaten to fill the aisles, but he knows where to find seats not far from the rear. In our day ushers serve more often where they encounter no difficulties due to congestion. Still they can arrange to distribute people so that the sanctuary will not seem vast and empty. All the while they wonder why people prefer the rear pews, whereas in other places they pay extra for the privilege of sitting up front.

Even with skill and tact an usher may hurt someone's feelings. How can one deal with a man who insists on sitting next to the aisle, in a pew that ought to hold five other people? Worse still, when an aged man faints, or suffers an attack of angina pectoris, the ushers must act. If in the midst of the service someone calls out "Fire," the ushers ought to avert a panic, with its resultant loss of life. In such a crisis they need the support of the pastor. During a disturbance not near the front of the sanctuary, and involving only one person, he may continue the service without interruption.

At a time of crisis the pastor should take command. Without leaving his station or showing excitement, he should do what the Spirit directs. At one time he may ask the people to remain silent. He knows that the organist will begin to play the sort of music that quiets troubled souls. Again the pastor may ask the people to sing a familiar hymn, and if need be, he can start the tune himself. In case of fire, or a fire alarm, even if false, he may bid the people leave the sanctuary quietly and in order, under the leadership of the ushers. Then he will understand why the fire department chief does not allow chairs in a church aisle.

Such a crisis may come to a pastor only once in forty years. But that one time may almost break his heart. Spurgeon went through such an experience soon after he began to serve as pastor in London. In a vast assembly at Surrey Hall someone started the cry of "Fire." In the stampede that followed, a number of people lost their lives, and many others suffered injuries. During the next few weeks the young pastor suffered a complete collapse. In after years he never regained all of his health and strength. Through that ordeal he learned much that he needed to know as a leader of men.[1] "No man has any more religion than he can command in an emergency."

In an occasional crisis, as in routine worship, the pastor thanks God for ushers on whom he can rely. Even when on a midsummer holiday he depends on these associates to greet the visiting minister who arrives fifteen minutes before the hour of worship. Not only should they make the guest feel at home. They can insure him the sort of satisfaction that comes from feeling that "all things are now ready." On the other hand, here and there, in churches far from small, the visitor feels that when the pastor leaves home everything suffers a slump.

In general, the peripatetic preacher gains a favorable impression of the ushering. Indeed, he feels that these friends deserve far more commendation than they receive. Almost never does he see in print or hear anything good about church ushers. In full view of these excellencies here are some suggestions:

1. An usher should *never show favoritism*. He should treat all per-

[1] *Op. cit.*, vol. II, p. 192.

sons as guests in the house of God. However, he should go out of his way in showing kindness to a stranger, and to anyone else in need.

2. Such a guide should *never point*. Let him conduct. When he escorts strangers to a pew, he should not scurry away. If the people are singing he may hand one of the newcomers a hymnal open at the proper page.

3. In escorting a person to a pew up front, a capable usher should *never lose anyone in transit*. He can form the habit of walking on the right-hand side, and not swiftly. By glancing over the left shoulder he can keep in touch with the persons in convoy. If they take refuge in a pew not far forward, he should accept the inevitable. How foolish he might look if he tried to keep on leading sheep that had ceased to follow!

4. An usher should *never embarrass the minister* by bringing up notices to be read from the pulpit. When an usher receives anything of the sort, he should hand it to the chief usher. If the latter deems the matter important, he may slip the notice into the pastor's hand at the time of the offering. Ordinarily, any such procedure seems unwise. It may encourage exhibitionism. If the ushers respond to one request of the sort, why not to others? Like begets like. Perhaps unconsciously, some active women or even an usher may enjoy the publicity that attends the reading of a special notice. Such a situation calls for teamwork and tact.

5. When the ushers take up the offering, they should *never rush forward* as to a fire. In coming up to get the plates, in receiving the gifts of the people, and in bringing the offerings to the altar, they ought to move as in the presence of the King. His worship never warrants the sort of haste that calls attention to itself and to His servants. In a sense, the best church usher seldom is seen. He calls no attention to how he serves the Lord.

6. After the people begin to assemble, these men should *refrain from conversation*, even in whispers. If the church premises include a lobby, or narthex, the ushers ought to remain there, except when at work within the sanctuary. Even when they stand in the foyer, their reverent demeanor should suggest to incoming friends the spirit of awe in the presence of God. After the late-comers have arrived,

each of the ushers but one may be seated with his wife and children.

7. In a building of another sort the ushers must remain in full view of both pastor and choir. If so, they should *never flit about after the service has begun.* How can the pastor, or the tenor soloist, set his affections on things above if he has to watch half a dozen big men shifting back and forth near the rear of the room, talking together in whispers, or turning their backs in order to read notices on the bulletin board? All of this, by no means uncommon, springs from lack of thought, and not from a desire to distract. Even the best of inexperienced ushers needs supervision and training.

8. Capable ushers *never make it hard to worship God in the rear pews.* They plan to seat any late-comer at an interval when he will not disturb those who have come on time. If feasible, the ushers try to reserve some of the rear pews for those who cannot come promptly. All of this points to an ideal not often attained where a host of people assembles in five or ten minutes.

9. The usher should *never absent himself from the sanctuary before the benediction.* He should look on himself as an aide to the pastor and stand by till all is finished. Both of these men ought to join heartily in all the worship to the end of the hour.

10. After the benediction, he should *never hasten away from church.* When the people make ready to depart, he should station himself where he stood when they began to enter. He should show a friendly spirit and be ready to lend a helping hand. For instance, women, even more than men, can enter the house of God and leave it again without feeling at home among friends. He should try to arrange for such newcomers to meet church women with tact and charm.

11. The usher should *think of his work as a man-sized job.* A friendly observer of churches wonders about the wisdom of committing such work to teen-age boys, or anybody else, without expert training and supervision.

Pastor, appreciate your ushers. A visitor among many churches feels that some pastors do not sense the importance of this work, or give it a large enough place in the plans for leadership. Where else will a little time and thought bring larger returns than in securing efficient ushering?

GUIDANCE FROM THE PASTOR

In all these concerns the minister should work indirectly. Ideally, he can have as expert and dependable a group of ushers as he once watched in an edifice of the Christian Scientists. Practically, he may find this work in the hands of mature men not willing to alter their ways. Sooner or later he can lead to the selection of the right man as head usher. Then gradually the new chief can gather about him a corps of first-class associates. The right sort of head usher needs little or no supervision and counsel. However, he will absorb an amazing amount of appreciation if it is sincere.

Through the official board the minister can also help to determine the age group of the ushers. Local conditions may call for the use of young men, or even boys of high-school age. In a certain congregation such lads had begun to hold aloof from what they dubbed "the old folks' church." The official board requested the chief usher and his assistant to enlist and coach twelve lads about eighteen·years old. On the first Lord's Day they marched down the aisle, two abreast. A little lad counted them, two by two. Then he asked in a loud whisper, "Mama, are those the minister's twelve apostles?"

Such lads may deal with the offering adequately. In other parts of ushering they need to work with older men. A first-class usher would excel as a traveling salesman, and no reputable wholesale house would entrust its incoming business to a group of boys, however full of zeal and promise. Even if the ushers comprise men thirty years of age, they need to serve under a man with experience and skill. In churches that present few difficulties inexperienced ushers may meet all the requirements, except in an emergency. Then certain older officers, standing ready as "minute men," should take charge and avert disaster.

Where young men do the ushering, the leading church officers, or some of them, can serve as a committee of welcome. Before and after each service two of them may stand at each entrance. There they can greet all who enter or leave, especially anyone who has not attended before, or has been absent for a while. If the committee of welcome changes its personnel from month to month, people will begin to feel that the officers care for the members of the church and for the stranger within the gates.

Under these circumstances the pastor may not think it necessary to stand at the main entrance after the service. However, he should defer to the traditions of the parish, and the desires of the official board. After the benediction at Riverside Church in New York City the three ministers station themselves at the foot of the steps leading up to the chancel. On either side of them stands one of the senior church officers. To this group the ushers and other church members can bring anyone who wishes to meet the ministers. On the other hand, where local custom bids the pastor stand at the main entrance after the service, the head usher should arrange to protect him from the draft. An up-to-date church provides him with an outer mantle or cape when the weather grows cold.

In a large congregation the pastor may request the official board to sanction the formation of an ushers' association. This group may consist of the men who now serve as ushers, with their predecessors as honorary members. Once every three months the association may meet to discuss the work on the Lord's Day, and enjoy an evening hour, socially. If the church budget permits, the work for the year may culminate in an ushers' dinner, or banquet, with the wives as guests. The men themselves can arrange the program for the evening.

At such a banquet the speaking may have to do mainly with ushering. The program need not last long, but it ought to include something constructive. Three or four members can report briefly about ushering they have seen up in Toronto or out in Denver. A man with a sense of humor, and ability to impersonate, may take off the sort of exhibitionism he has witnessed far from home. Then the ushers will want a few words from their friend, the pastor. In the name of the Lord he can thank them for all they have done throughout the past year. How could he better spend an evening late in June than by adding his presence and good cheer to this gathering of his teammates and friends, the ushers?

In the bulletin and elsewhere the pastor can express his appreciation publicly. For example, at a church in Baltimore the following letter from Maltbie D. Babcock as minister appeared in the "Monthly."

Some of the details would not fit everywhere. For instance, in Babcock's day that spacious sanctuary was filled to overflowing.

The ushers of Brown Memorial are thoughtful men, held in honor for their works' sake. . . . They earn a salary which is never paid, except when the members of the church, by words of sympathy and recognition, warm their hearts.

In several ways we can heighten their spirits and lengthen their lives. Come punctually to church. It helps the order of God's house. It will give you a short preparatory service. To be a little ahead of time costs but a little thought, and will prove an investment from which fine dividends are drawn all through life.

Tell the usher, as you enter church, of any vacant seats in your pew. . . . If you find your place taken, remember that the usher is but "dust and ashes," like yourself, and that this is a well-regulated family. Smile on him and say, "It is all right. I will take the stranger's chance today." So you will relieve his fears and find a saint's niche in his esteem. The service may be blessed to you from a new point of view.[2]

Suggested Readings

Beaven, Albert W., *Putting the Church on a Full-Time Basis.* New York: Doubleday, Doran & Co., 1928. Chap. IX, "The Usher as Host to the Congregation."

Garrett, Willis O., *Church Ushers' Manual.* New York: Fleming H. Revell Co., 1924.

---

[2] John T. Stone, *Footsteps in a Parish* (New York: Charles Scribner's Sons, 1908), pp. 19-20.

CHAPTER XI

The Counselor of Committees

THE executive work of the pastor consists partly in dealing with committees. His success or failure as a leader may depend on ability to appoint a committee, especially the chairman, and also confer with a committee chairman of a society in the church. A wise leader never thrusts his opinions on a committee or a chairman. But after the laymen come to know and trust him as their leader, the chairman of one committee after another will seek his help or advice. Such quiet conferences consume time. But he should know that some of these contacts afford the best openings for Kingdom work. Also, he may enjoy this kind of pastoral counseling.

Unfortunately, a minister of a certain type looks down on committee work. He cannot hope to excel in what he does not like, or deem essential. If such a Moses of today would turn to a modern Jethro for counsel, the latter would insist that dealing with a committee through the chairman affords a test of a man's ability as a leader. Hence every young minister ought to study the technique, and also consult with his pastoral adviser, a man like Jethro.

A case from life shows how an able executive regarded this part of the work. When Frances Willard was finding her way as head of the national W.C.T.U. she asked Hannah Whitall Smith to serve as chairman of an important committee. That Quaker woman answered as she smiled: "If thee wants anything done, Frank, just put on two other women with me. Only let one be a permanent invalid, and the other out of town." [1] As head of the whole movement Frances Willard practically adopted this policy. For each department she chose a superintendent, and then let this associate do the work in her own way. The president held each of these women responsible for her part of the work. Largely for this reason Frances Willard made the W.C.T.U. a power as a national body, and in its local branches.

[1] Ray Strachey, *The Life of Frances Willard* (London, 1912), p. 212.

109

Facetiously Miss Willard used to say: "If Noah had appointed a committee, the Ark would still be on the stocks." Practically, her way of doing teamwork shows much about the art of dealing with committee chairmen. The biographer insists that the effectiveness of her leadership, under God, depended on her ability to select associates: "She not only chose good workers, but she *made* them." Often she would select for an important post a friend who felt sure she would fail. But the new chairman did not fail, largely because she knew that the chief expected her to surmount every obstacle and reach the goal. All of this takes for granted in the chief a gift for discerning a potential leader. A man without such a gift from above may have no business in the ministry today.

In order to advise with committees, and increase their loyalty, a pastor must know how to deal with various types of persons, one by one. Whenever he can do so, the minister confers with the chairman alone, and then lets the chairman thresh things out with the rest of the committee. The chairman receives the credit if things go well, and the blame if they do not, because of his bungling. In one case the pastor may let the chairman formulate plans and carry them out. As a wise master builder the minister knows that the other man wishes approval from the chief before any new adventure. Human nature being human, the chairman wishes to stand well in the eyes of the chief. The layman does not relish taking orders from the boss.

This way of allowing liberty seems ideal, but it does not always work. In conferring with a chairman who lacks experience and confidence the pastor may need to suggest ways and means. The gist of them may have more to do with the chairman's gaining self-assurance than with the work in hand. Every executive ought to give first aid whenever an associate desires encouragement and help. A wise pastor would not watch a committee chairman flounder, and not reach out a hand to show that somebody cared. If the chairman proves to be big enough for the post, he soon begins to gain the right sort of self-confidence.

An English writer lists the following as the chief faults in the work of committees:

Irrelevant discussion
A self-centered chairman
One or more members desire to impress the chairman
Failure to state the problem
Failure to prepare for the questions discussed
Indifference of certain members
Failure to permit certain members to take enough part
Failure to present questions in a thought-provoking way
Failure to postpone chairman's statement of his position
Bias due to ulterior motives
Fixed ideas on the part of chairman or members
A tendency to jump at conclusions [2]

1. *Do not multiply the number of committees needlessly*. Busy men and women grow weary of serving with nothing worth while to do. They ask each other, "Why meet for the sake of meeting?"

2. *Do not rely on a few pastoral pets*. Throughout all the work choose representatives of various households and groups. Remember the human desire for recognition. Everybody wants to be wanted. In a college annual a student likes to see his name associated with the leadership of an important group. What if a few of the college president's pets held all the offices, so many that they could not do the work properly? Then others would feel left out in the cold.

3. If feasible *do not keep the same committee personnel* year after year. Try to secure rotation in office. Develop new leaders. Also get different people to know the inner workings of the machinery.

4. *Encourage the keeping of minutes and records*. When a new chairman takes charge he should appoint a secretary. In a small group, the chairman may do this work himself, but not ideally. Somehow the committee should have at hand in every meeting the relevant facts about previous meetings.

5. *Never fail to have a committee report after it has acted*. The action will come more surely if the chairman expects to report at a definite time in the near future, and to submit the report in writing.

6. *Never go over the head of a committee chairman*. Many a church

[2] Lyndall Urwick, *Committees in Organization* (New York: Institute of Public Administration, 1937).

leader wonders why he secures little co-operation from a certain person of ability who serves with distinction in community causes. If the minister glanced back he would see that he once took work out of this person's hands, or else made an important decision, and left the chairman with nothing to do but dreary drudgery. Herein lies the main weakness of many an executive. Unconsciously, he suffers from an inflated ego. As a boy he may have driven mules; he should have learned to lead sheep.

7. *Never let a timid chairman flounder.* Encourage him to consult with lay leaders in other fields. Suggest churches where lay leaders bubble over with enthusiasm, which becomes contagious.

8. *Do not let a new chairman remain idle at first.* Encourage him to convene the committee and lead the other members in canvassing the field. If the new committee goes over the ground in the spring, the members can think about the subject during the summer. In the autumn they should feel ready for a progressive movement. In work for God the fruits come most surely after careful planning over a stretch of time, and all in the spirit of prayer.

9. *Do not bungle or falter as chairman of a committee.* For a discussion of this matter turn to the next chapter. It relates to presiding over gatherings of various sorts. The principles, however, apply to the head of a committee. In carrying them out a man needs all sorts of practical wisdom and resourcefulness.

10. *Do not begrudge the time spent in counseling with a committee chairman.* Learn from the Lord Jesus to accept any interruption graciously. In order to do so, approach the whole matter in the spirit of prayer.

Positively, for an object lesson of the principles, turn to the late William Temple, before he became Archbishop of Canterbury. Writing intimately to his brother, this churchman tells about committee work under his supervision:

When I have learned the ropes I shall be able to settle which committees, etc., I should attend. Just now I shall go to all of them to see what they do and how they do it. Knox [the predecessor] attended them all and largely ran them. But that I won't do. Probably I shall be thought lazy, but there are plenty of other things to do.[3]

Suggested Readings

Baxter, Bernice, and Cassidy, R. F., *Group Experience.* New York: Harper & Bros., 1943.

Cooper, Alfred N., *How to Conduct Conferences.* New York: McGraw-Hill Book Co., 1946.

Dimock, Marshall E., *The Executive in Action.* New York: Harper & Bros., 1945. Chap. XV, "The Technique of Delegation."

Urwick, Lyndall, *Committees in Organization.* New York: Institute of Public Administration, 1937. 49 pp.

Walser, Frank, *The Art of Conference.* New York: Harper & Bros., 1933.

[3] F. A. Iremonger, *William Temple* (New York: Oxford Univ. Press, 1948), p. 329.

CHAPTER XII

The Chairman of a Gathering

S OONER or later a minister has to preside over a gathering of consequence. Sometime he may have to do so without time for special preparation. Fortunately, he can gain experience and poise by serving as chairman of groups in the home church. He may or may not preside over this body or that, according to church law and custom. Somehow in the course of a year or so he should learn most of the basic principles. In time he may become known as a master of assemblies. As long as he lives, however, he may keep learning more about such mastery.

The conscious preparation may begin early, the earlier the better. A pastor ought to know Roberts' *Rules of Order*. He may never have to employ some of these procedures, but knowledge of them ought to give him the right sort of self-assurance. Much more thoroughly should he master the book of government and discipline —under whatever title—in his branch of the Church. He should also encourage the lay officers to acquaint themselves with approved practices in the denomination. In a body where the local church makes its own rules, pastor and people should know how to conform. If the leaders of the home church make a careful study of correct procedures, they will render far more enthusiastic and efficient service. The laymen too should gradually learn how to preside.

THE NEED OF A DOCKET

The man who takes the chair at any gathering ought to have in hand a docket, with a list of the agenda. At a special meeting, with only one purpose, he may rely on memory. Even there, he ought to have in view the entire trail up to the time of adjournment. Then he will not waste the time of busy people, or make some of them wish they had remained away. In a regular meeting he should feel able to rely on the secretary, or permanent clerk, to prepare the docket.

In that case the two should confer privately before the meeting starts. Without seeming to decide any matter of business, the pastor should inform himself about what is to come before the group.

A minister soon learns to rely on the secretary or clerk of the governing board. To this friend the young pastor may owe more than to anyone else in the parish, except his wife. The gifts and the experience of the two men often supplement each other. In matters of routine the pastor seeks and follows the judgment of the other man. At a time of uncertainty or dread the younger one may find the older friend a tower of strength. But why look on the matter so solemnly? Both of them ought to enjoy these gatherings with their teammates and friends.

The docket of business meetings everywhere tends to follow much the same course. Probably a sample appears in the manual of the denomination. This docket one feels free to modify within limits, according to the business in hand. The pastor does well to follow the procedure to which the laymen have become accustomed. Occasionally, however, he may suggest the possibility or the wisdom of bringing up an important item of business fairly early in the hour. Otherwise he might come to it after the men had begun to look at their watches and wish for home.

Gradually a minister with tact can lead any such group to deal with matters more or less important. Then they can refer details to the appropriate committees—it may be with power to act. Otherwise the chairman may get a reputation for concern about trifles. If he expects members of the group to attend every meeting, he should prepare each time to set an inviting table. Within the limits prescribed, he should look out for a degree of variety. So let us assume that the brethren have assembled and that the hour has come for the meeting to start. Without following the docket item by item we may glance at certain parts.

A chairman ought always to convene the gathering exactly on time, and never before. Instead of leading in the opening words of prayer, he may call on one of the laymen. If so, let this friend know in advance. Somehow make clear that you prefer a brief prayer, and not a survey of world conditions. From time to time call on the men in the order of seniority. Keep a private record, so as not to show partiality. A pastor should have no pets. After the funeral of the most saintly member of the official board his widow asked the minister why he had never called on her husband to lead in prayer. The young man did not know that he had singled out all the other officers, some of them more than once. Never in a small group or open meeting had he shown any awareness of the dear saint, who best knew how to lead others to the mercy seat. The pastor's eyes filled with tears as he begged her pardon.

After the prayer comes the calling of the roll. With a small group the man in charge often omits this item, unwisely. It takes but half a minute, and has a wholesome psychological effect. The roll call shows that every member ought to attend each meeting, and be present on time. When out of town, or ill in bed, a member ought to send a note of regret. Even in a small group such niceties tend to foster a sense of loyalty and *esprit de corps*.

Next comes the reading and approval of the minutes from the last meeting. This act tends to make everyone feel the importance of keeping an accurate record of all that occurs. Ordinarily the secretary knows more about keeping minutes than the minister yet knows. If so, the latter ought to keep his ears open. Someday, perhaps without warning, he may have to serve as the "recording angel" of a ministerial group. Then he should know how. Also he may enter a church where the brethren have grown careless about the meetings of the governing body. Lovingly and tactfully, in conference with the secretary, the pastor can start a reform. This lay officer may begin by conferring with the corresponding officer in an adjoining parish, where brethren do things decently and in order.

After the reading and approval of the minutes may come reports from permanent committees. These may report every time in the same alphabetical order, or the docket may call for rotation. After each report the presiding officer should open the way for questions on the business of the committee. He himself ought to serve as the guiding spirit of the meeting, and not as "speaker of the house." All the while he has to keep the balance between rushing things through and throttling discussion, or dawdling along and wasting time. Ordinarily he should encourage full discussion of important matters and quick action about anything else. The impetuous man needs to put on internal brakes, and the easygoing one ought occasionally to accelerate the speed.

Then follow reports of special committees. Here the procedure varies widely in different churches of much the same size. One body tends to rely on permanent committees, more than a few. The other policy calls for a special committee to deal with anything temporary that does not logically fall under the jurisdiction of an existing committee. Some of us favor the latter procedure, if the way is clear. The meetings afford more variety if committees come and go than if the same ones keep reporting month after month. Then, too, many laymen excel in short-distance dashes rather than in cross-country endurance races. In any case, a committee should know exactly when to report. Also, except in matters of routine, the chairman of the committee ought to read his report, word for word. After approval, and adoption of the recommendations, the written report should go to the secretary. He in turn should record every such action, and not much else.

Here may follow reports from the membership secretary and the treasurer, each of them brief and terse. The docket may call for other items such as the selection of delegates to denominational or interchurch gatherings. These matters need a place among the agenda, but they call for regulation, to prevent a growing sense of ennui. Many a meeting drivels into trivialities after the middle of the hour. Interest may revive when the docket calls for unfinished business, and new business. After the minister has opened the way for others to present matters for consideration, he should feel free to bring up another concern. If it calls for much explanation, he may ask someone else to preside. Here again, a pastor needs to use horse sense. He should not trouble busy men about little things that he can handle alone. Neither should he move forward in any important matter without first consulting the brethren. For instance, he should ask their approval before he accepts an invitation that takes him out of the parish for a series of meetings.

At first the novice may wonder why new business comes up not long before adjournment. Perhaps the fathers wished to see that everyone remained through such a meeting. More probably they knew that any important proposal called for brief discussion, to insure clarity, and for reference to the appropriate committee. Except in an emergency, a wise chairman leads the brethren to postpone action on any important issue the first time it appears on the docket. For much the same reason Queen Victoria used always to sleep over an important matter before she made up her mind. Then she appears to have reached a decision in the spirit of prayer. A wise executive encourages others, also, to look before they leap. Often this means looking without the leap. "Wait on the Lord." He promises always to guide, but not exclusively between eight and nine o'clock on the first Tuesday of the month. Give Him time to do His perfect work.

Any such meeting ought to end with a feeling of satisfaction and uplift. After the brethren vote to adjourn, the pastor may lead in a few words of prayer. If he wishes others to order their petitions aright, he should set them an example. After a benediction he may encourage them to tarry for social enjoyment. The meeting itself, ordinarily, should last no more than sixty minutes. Then wives at home cannot blame the pastor for keeping their husbands out "until all hours of the night." If the budget at the parsonage will stand the strain, he and his wife may ask the brethren to hold their meeting once a year in the house next to the church. After they adjourn she can serve light refreshments. Better still, she may have present as her guests the wives of the brethren. Often a pastor and his wife ask how they can return many favors they receive in the way of hospitality. As a rule they can best do so by opening their home to strangers. They can also entertain the officers and their wives. Such an open door at the parsonage does much to make people love and esteem their pastor and his chief helpmeet.

Thus far we have assumed that any such body should convene once a month, and not oftener. In case of an emergency rules need not apply. In a large church the pastor needs skill and care in order to deal adequately with all the issues at hand. In a small congregation the docket for a given month may seem meager and uninviting. Even so, let the meeting take place according to schedule. After the brethren have dealt with everything on the docket, the pastor may lead in a discussion of some major concern. According to the season and the program for that part of the year he can open the way for a brief discussion of Christian education, evangelism, missions, or trusteeship. Without monopolizing the conversation, a man with a teaching mind can lead the discussion into profitable channels. Then he can have the brethren pray round the group, perhaps on their knees. While they still kneel, he can lead them in singing one stanza of "Blest be the tie that binds." After this he can pronounce the benediction of light (Num. 6:24-26).

THE CONDUCT OF A MEETING

The conduct of a meeting calls for preparation and resourcefulness. To every such hour a pastor should come with a rested body and a calm heart, not with tense nerves and a troubled look. Laymen enjoy meeting with a minister who looks happy. They have burdens enough of their own without having on their hands a leader who does not excel in apostolic optimism. The more important the gathering, and the more delicate the issues, the more the need for planning the earlier parts of the day so as to appear at the meeting in the full vigor of Christian manhood. However, if a funeral and other pressing demands keep a pastor busy all afternoon, the brethren will make allowances. In any case let him come to the meeting in the spirit of prayer.

Much the same principles obtain in presiding over a public assembly. In making his preparations the minister should try to envision the meeting step by step. Then he should let the spirit of the occasion determine the tone color of his leadership. Under God, that will depend largely on his ability to inspire confidence and respect on the part of those present. He should know how to keep things moving along with interest, and without haste or confusion. He should also school himself to guide the meeting and not to exploit his own oratorical powers.

Every minister who presides at public gatherings should learn how to introduce a guest speaker. One chairman embarrasses the stranger by fulsome flattery. Another presiding officer unintentionally deluges him with cold water. Any man who serves as a peripatetic preacher can testify that many pastors do not know how to make the visitor feel at home during the first few minutes before the sermon. Much the same feeling applies to the conversation in the study, before the two men go into the sanctuary. Many a pastor wonders why a certain guest minister flounders at first. The dear man may have to warm up after careless conversation in the study, followed by an infelicitous introduction.

Wherein lies the path of wisdom? Each occasion calls for something different, but the following suggestions usually apply. If the meeting calls for a bulletin, the introduction may appear there, and there only. Whether written or spoken, the words about the visiting brother should be few. The chairman should confine himself to facts. He should neither appraise the speaker's powers nor forecast the effect of the coming address. Rarely should the chairman refer to himself and the many times he has had intimate contacts with the distinguished guest. Neither should the chairman, as a rule, indulge in humor. Only a master can speak facetiously without hurting sensitive feelings or distracting attention from the subject in hand. In short, present the speaker, not yourself. Be brief. Bid him Godspeed and then let him go on his way rejoicing.

The chairman finds more difficulty in presiding over a gathering that permits free-for-all discussion, with more or less impromptu talks by members of the group. However, much the same principles still apply. Effectiveness consists in getting the hearty co-operation of the persons assembled, and in leading them to definite conclusions. These the chairman does not determine in advance, and then impose on others. Leadership, here as elsewhere, does not depend on sheer manpower. According to a well-known statesman, however, a certain ranking government official did not call men in to ask them what he should do. He summoned them together to tell them what they must do.

The right principles appear in a statement about presiding over a secular group. The writer, a distinguished physician, succeeded Sir William Osler in charge of the medical department at Johns Hopkins University. The discussion relates in part to committee meetings, but the suggestions have to do with presiding over a larger assembly:

Anyone who has attended many board or committee meetings knows how much depends upon the chairman for the efficiency and speed with which its activities are conducted. Members are sure to suffer when discussions are unnecessarily prolonged, when matters wholly irrelevant to the topic under consideration are permitted to be introduced, or when a presiding officer of arbitrary tendencies makes decisions without giving opportunity for adequate presentation of both sides of a controversial subject.

A chairman should be alert, courteous, and understanding. He should be well versed in the usage of deliberative assemblies, should see to it that the latter are observed, and should exhibit sound judgment, both in cutting short needless discussion and [in] prolonging debate when the occasion warrants it. He should possess "the flair that can pierce irrelevance and reach the core of essential facts." By promptness and decisiveness, exercised in a civil manner, a chairman can do much to expedite the transaction of the business.[1]

---

[1] Llewellys F. Barker, *Time and the Physician* (New York: G. P. Putnam's Sons, 1942), p. 238.

CHAPTER XIII

The Outlook on the Community

WE come now to a subject about which church leaders disagree.
To what extent should the local body try to influence the
community? How far should the pastor try to exert such an influence?
Whatever the answer, he should know the facts about the community. By this term we mean "a group of people living together." In
a rural district the community may signify "that area in which the majority of the people secure the majority of their services at the village
center." [1] In a residential district of a city the term may mean the
area surrounding the church. In a downtown church the community may consist of the whole city and its environs. However vague
the description, every church needs a map outlining its community.

In such a community, ideally, the church ought to serve as a
"colony of heaven" (Phil. 3:20a, Moffatt). In the Apostle's time the
Empire had determined to Romanize certain communities throughout
her domain. In such a center as Philippi or Corinth the plan might call
for the transportation of three hundred citizens from Rome. At the
new center they would establish homes, enter into business, and in
every other way attempt to Romanize the community. This ideal the
Apostle seems to have borrowed when he strove to Christianize those
centers.

Today, also, the church influences the community, often quietly
and unconsciously. For example, in 1916 Governor and Mrs. W. R.
Stubbs offered a prize of a thousand dollars to "the best city in Kansas in which to rear a family." After a careful investigation of the
communities that entered the contest, the committee gave the prize
to Winfield. From that time to this, the community has maintained
its concern about the welfare of young people and children. For in-

[1] For an able treatment, sociologically, see Rockwell C. Smith, *The Church in Our
Town* (New York and Nashville: Abingdon-Cokesbury Press), especially chap.
III, "Fitting the Church to the Community."

stance, says the city editor of the *Daily Courier*, "The summer activity program was one of the first in the United States, and has since gained nation-wide recognition, having been studied by national juvenile delinquency groups and recreation organizations."

For such an achievement no one group or agency can claim all the credit. In the eyes of the governor's committee the homes and the schools worked for the same ideals as the churches. Here we think only about the churches. According to a minister who served there at the time, all the congregations worked together, each in its own fashion. Ninety-eight per cent of the boys and girls in the community belonged to the church schools. The laymen regarded the community, not as a place to make a living, but as an opportunity to apply the principles of the Christian faith. What else can it mean to have a "colony of heaven"?

In a large city the difficulty may increase, but every church becomes either a community asset or a liability. It becomes either a contributor to community betterment, or else a parasite. For an example of wholesome influence by the pastor, rather than the church, study *George W. Truett, A Biography*.[2] In Dallas he exerted much the same kind of influence that Mark Matthews wielded in Seattle. Before the city fathers took any important action involving the public morals of Seattle, some of them would confer with Pastor Matthews. Also, if he objected to the showing of a certain motion picture, the manager would substitute something clean.

Every pastor about whom we have been thinking would have subscribed to the motto, "Let the church be the church." No one of them ever preached reform because he had no Gospel. Each of them loved his home community, and strove to make it a heaven on earth. As the leader of a church he co-operated with civic officials, public schools, libraries, social welfare agencies, and all the other forces that helped to make it easy for boys and girls to do right, and hard for them to go wrong.

When a minister comes into a community, he ought to get acquainted with the leaders in other forms of human betterment. In a

[2] Powhatan W. James (rev. ed., New York: The Macmillan Co., 1945).

downtown church this may mean one thing, and in a residential district another. Not every pastor needs to call on the mayor and the councilmen downtown, but every local leader ought to know the men and women who share with him the responsibility for the welfare of the community surrounding the church. If one of these representatives does his work well, the pastor ought to write a word of commendation. Without entering into partisan politics he can stand out openly in favor of every official or group that endeavors to make the community a good place to rear boys and girls.

As for ways and means, a church leader may follow one of two courses. Or else three, if we count the hands-off and do-nothing attitude worthy of mention. A certain minister joins societies, makes addresses, attends committee meetings, heads movements, and becomes known as a leading citizen, if not a live wire. He may try to represent the congregation everywhere, instead of enlisting lay members in local betterment. However, many a man of this type has enlisted lay representatives, instead of doing too much community work himself.

At first a young minister feels flattered when he receives an invitation to join a dinner club. After a year or two he may begin to wonder about the wisdom of such affiliation. If he can afford the time and expense, he may need such an outlet, socially. But he should not go on joining societies. Let the church remain first in his heart. In a city of 45,000 a young pastor recently withdrew from a civic club. By way of explanation he told another minister, "My membership cost me $67.00 a year, and took two or three hours out of every Tuesday, one of my best days for work. In as far as I have been able to judge, my belonging to the club never has helped me attain the ideals of our congregation. I have decided to let our business and professional men represent the church in such clubs."

Does this sound selfish? In some cases it might, but with this young man the step called for self-denial. He enjoyed those contacts, but he gave them up because he had found better ways of investing his time and energy, not to speak of money. On the other hand he inspired the men and women of the parish to work for the betterment of the city. He felt that a congregation ought to do more than congregate. It ought also to serve as a "colony of heaven." But the pastor should not attempt to do all the work. As an executive the head of a Roman colony depended on his three hundred citizen-soldiers. This point of view appears in the records about Maltbie D. Babcock at Baltimore. By going back of our own time we can see the principles without becoming confused by current trends. The appraisal comes from a prominent leader in social welfare work. One of her other volumes has become a standard guidebook in that field.

His creed and mine differed widely and I seldom heard him preach. But there was no public task with which I was associated that did not show the influence of his daily endeavor to apply the Gospel of Christ to the life of the city in which we both worked. . . .

Some clergymen who feel this "call of the city" fling themselves unselfishly into its life, but dissipate their strength by becoming directors of many boards, attending many meetings, and making many addresses on a great variety of topics. This was not his way.

Having in mind always that the exercise and development of the members of his own congregation in the Christian life was his highest duty, he set himself the task of studying first the needs of the city in which they lived; then the possibilities, both social and spiritual, of the many agencies created to meet these needs; and last, the aptitudes and capacities of his people.

The city was their workshop, and into it he fed them freely, associating them with every uplifting work that was going forward. Some of his men visited prisons and became volunteer probation officers in charge of individual boys. Others founded an equitable loan company for the poorer sort of borrowers. Many worked hard in municipal campaigns.

The women of his church visited families in distress, under the best guidance that he was able to secure for them, and gave efficient aid in countless hospital committees and in children's work. . . .

All the work that they did was religious work. They always so regarded it, and their first loyalty was always to their church and its leader. Sometimes it seemed to me, an onlooker, that he played upon the community as upon a great organ, drawing from it new and inspiring spiritual harmonies.[3]

[3] Mary E. Richmond, *The Good Neighbor in the Modern City* (Philadelphia: J. B. Lippincott Co., 1908), pp. 146-48.

What a tribute for a pastor to receive from the chief social worker in the home city! Without becoming a joiner, or doing community work directly, this man became a power for uplift in everything that concerned the moral welfare of Baltimore. Like every other parish leader, he could not keep all the adult members busy in the work of the congregation. So he encouraged many of them to discover openings in the larger life of the city. Partly for this reason his name still lives in Baltimore as one who made his congregation a power.

How different the attitude of many a pastor! In Louisville recently a minister told his people from the pulpit that if he had three hundred laymen ready for Christian service he could transform the city. Perhaps he quoted John Wesley, but without that leader's practical wisdom. When Wesley made such an appeal, he could carry out his part of the proposal. After the service in Louisville a layman went up to his pastor and offered to enlist three hundred workers. When the layman asked what problem the minister wished them to tackle first, he could not say. He had not supposed that anyone would take his sermon seriously! According to A. J. Gossip of Glasgow, "There is no more miserable object than a man pitchforked into a job too big for him, and conscious of his own incompetence. Most of us preachers are like agitators rousing dissatisfaction in men's minds, leaving them soured and unhappy, but with no constructive policy how things can be put right." [4]

THE NEEDY WITHIN THE FOLD

About one aspect of community betterment all church leaders ought to agree: the local pastor should feel much concern about needy members in the home church. He should resolve never to handle money for the relief of the poor, and ordinarily not to do that part of the work himself. Even so, he should help indirectly, if only by putting the matter on a basis that will gain the respect of experts in social service. As for the group in charge of relief, customs differ widely.

[4] Arthur J. Gossip, *The Hero in Thy Soul* (New York: Charles Scribner's Sons, 1930), p. 197.

The same principles apply to a separate board, a committee, a men's club, a group of deaconesses, or a class in the Sunday school. Whatever the title, some group of wise and tactful friends ought to have on their hearts the relief of God's poor in the congregation.

These friends may find a family or a lone church member in distress, but unwilling to accept financial aid: "We never have been paupers. We should rather starve than become objects of charity." The church representatives ought to admire this spirit. From the pastor they can learn how to deal with such a case, without hurting tender feelings: "We in the home church form a large family. If one of us were in distress, and you could help, you would want to act like a good neighbor. Please let us aid you in the spirit of Christian love." If they still refuse, the pastor himself may intercede. Ordinarily he should not appear in the picture. On the other hand, he can lead the congregation to provide all the funds needful for the relief of needy brethren. To no cause will Christians give more freely if they trust the friends who distribute this part of the Lord's money.

A case will show how these friends can help a worthy family maintain self-respect. A daughter serving as the sole breadwinner could meet all ordinary demands, but she felt helpless when her mother had to undergo a surgical operation. The pastor suggested to the proper group that one or two of them go to the surgeon and offer to pay half of his bill if he would cancel the other half. During the interview the surgeon thanked the two for such generosity, which was new in his long experience. Then he asked for the bill, which he tore in shreds. Those servants of the Lord did not feel that they had labored in vain, and neither did the surgeon. As for the hospital bill, the group did not ask to have it lowered, but helped the daughter pay it in full. All such facts should remain secret.

On the other hand, zealous almoners of the Lord's bounty may waste money in helping to make paupers. So might the pastor if he tried to administer these funds. Such churchmen forfeit the respect of social agencies. One of those experts, a member of a church, tells about "babies baptized seven times in different churches, of rent paid five times over, of Protestant fuel and Catholic groceries supplied, while the family earnings go in drink and in Sunday picnics." [5]

In order to forestall such folly the pastor should encourage the friends in charge to keep in touch with some reliable social agency. Except where they feel sure about the facts and the correct procedure, church representatives can learn much by talking things over at times with social experts. If the pastor and his associates co-operated sympathetically with these agencies, more of the experts might become active members of local churches.

Better still, both pastor and lay almoners should seek and follow the guidance of the Lord. In the most practical of all the epistles the sacred writer discusses matters of poor relief. Among other sayings pertinent here, let us single out two. "If any of you lacks wisdom, let him ask God who gives to all men generously and without reproaching, and it will be given him. . . . Religion that is pure and undefiled before God and the Father is this: to visit orphans and widows in their affliction, and to keep oneself unstained from the world." (James 1:5, 27, R.S.V.)

Suggested Readings

Christian Rural Fellowship bulletins, 156 Fifth Ave., New York 10.

Diffendorfer, Ralph E., *The Church and the Community*. New York: Missionary Education Movement, 1920.

Douglass, H. P., ed., *The Greater Cincinnati Church Study*. Cincinnati: The Council of Churches of Greater Cincinnati, 1947.

Douglass, H. P., and Brunner, E. E., *The Protestant Church as a Social Institution*. New York: Harper & Bros., 1935.

Leiffer, Murray H., *City and Church in Transition*. Chicago: Willett, Clark & Co., 1938.

————, *The Effective City Church*. New York and Nashville: Abingdon-Cokesbury Press, 1949.

Lynd, Robert S. and Helen, *Middletown; a Study in Contemporary American Culture*. New York: Harcourt, Brace & Co., 1929.

[5] Mary E. Richmond, *The Long View* (New York: Russell Sage Foundation, 1930), p. 116.

————, *Middletown in Transition*. New York: Harcourt, Brace & Co., 1937

McIver, Robert M., *Community*. New York: The Macmillan Co., 1924.

Morgan, Arthur E., *The Small Community*. New York: Harper & Bros., 1932.

Ogden, F. S., *Small Communities in Action*. New York: Harper & Bros., 1946.

Richmond, Mary E., *Social Diagnosis*. New York: Russell Sage Foundation, 1917.

Sanderson, Ezra D., *Leadership for Rural Life*. New York: Association Press, 1940.

Smith, Rockwell C., *The Church in Our Town*. New York and Nashville: Abingdon-Cokesbury Press, 1945. A study of the rural church.

Chapter XIV

The Appeal of Paid Publicity

STUDENTS of the church differ about the value of paid publicity. Neither side can win the argument, because the value depends partly on the character of the advertising, and more on the nature of the community. Over in London at St. Martin's-in-the-Field Dick Sheppard used publicity with telling effect. Taking a downtown church that was little known, he put it on the map and made it a power in the city. He insisted that the effectiveness of a downtown preacher, under God, depended on three factors: a striking personality, dramatic ability, and persistent publicity.

Nearer home every student of church life can think of a downtown congregation not one of whose members lives within walking distance. And yet throngs of worshipers attend the services every Sunday morning and evening, with lesser numbers throughout the week. Why? Partly because of publicity, all sorts of publicity, skillful and persistent. At the First Presbyterian Church in Pittsburgh, for example, cards of invitation and other forms of advertising show that the officers believe in such spending, and that someone knows how to prepare the copy. It draws people. If it did not, it might repel.

These methods do more for an evening service than for morning worship. Many people come to church in the morning because of habit. If they attend an evening service, or vespers, they respond to some appeal. Publicity also does more to increase attendance at a special service, or a series, than at regular times of worship. In a residential district the following rule may hold: Always advertise a special service, and never any other. For much the same reason a grocer calls attention to something new on his shelves, not to staples such as flour and sugar. He does not advertise the main part of his stock in trade, but promotes items such as seasonal fruits.

More than a few pastors and lay officers question the appeal of paid publicity. They agree with Ivy Lee, a well-known master of public

relations: "The best way to get good publicity is to deserve it." On religious grounds they ask why a church should adopt the devices of
a grocer. On the basis of sound business they wonder if church publicity accomplishes what its advocates claim. For example, in Rochester, N. Y., some of the churches depended much on newspaper advertising. For three months, because of a strike which lasted from
November 8, 1946, to February 8, 1947, the city newspapers suspended publication. During that period those church leaders could
see no lessening of attendance and interest. Some of them changed
their minds about the value of paid publicity.

What then shall the parish leader conclude? He should confer with
his officers and with them decide on a policy. If local custom bids the
pastor send in topics for the Saturday papers, he should comply. In
any case he ought to call on the city editor of each local paper, or
perhaps on the church editor. The pastor will find newspaper men
and women easy to approach, except during rush hours, before the
next issue goes to press. If the minister meets the editor as a friend, and
asks no favors, the two will find their relations pleasant and helpful.
Afterwards, a note of thanks occasionally or a lead about news will
make the editor think of the minister as a friend worth having.

In more than one city the editors never hear anything from Protestant pastors except complaints: "Why didn't you print what I sent
in?" "Why did you rewrite my news item?" "Why do you discrimi-
nate against Protestants?" If the minister went to the editor and
talked things over in a kindly spirit, the latter might explain: "Roman
Catholics handle these things differently. They have experts who
know what newspapers want, and how to prepare copy. Catholic publicity men keep us supplied with news items and cuts, many of which
we do not use. Often we have to limit local matter because we have
a surplus from elsewhere. When we need something to fill up space, we
can always lay our hands on a newsy item from the Catholics, well
written and ready for the press." Such publicity costs nothing in dollars and cents, but it calls for skill and care.

As for the radio, few of us question its value to a church that can
afford to send out the right sort of programs.[1] However, some ob-

---

[1] See Everett C. Parker et al., *Religious Radio* (New York: Harper & Bros., 1948).

servers believe that the radio, religiously, has begun to lose its appeal, and that even television may not keep it from assuming a smaller place in the religious life of tomorrow. The majority of us feel grateful for its contribution to the work of the Kingdom. Still we wonder about the effect on ninety-and-nine churches that cannot afford to broadcast religious services.[2] Even if they had the facilities, they might not know how to send out programs that would appeal. In radio, as elsewhere, the value of publicity depends largely on quality and timeliness. How can amateurs with little experience compete with highly paid professionals?

Enthusiastic radio preachers may overestimate the size of their "vast radio audiences." Those who command the largest hearing have found that people respond better to a special program than to the broadcasting of a regular service. At eleven o'clock if the pastor speaks over the air he may think chiefly either about the friends he can see in church, or about strangers who worship with him from afar. In either case, psychologically, he may feel a sense of tension, not to say bewilderment. He may decide to speak over the radio at another time, and have a service lasting only thirty minutes, or else fifteen. Someone, however, ought to hold radio services at eleven for the sake of the shut-ins.

OTHER FORMS OF PUBLICITY

1. *An outside bulletin board.* Almost every church needs some sort of board outside, to show the identity of the building and the name of the pastor. An architect can decide whether to have the board attached to the front of the edifice, or else put out on the lawn. In either event a lover of beauty will recommend a display in keeping with the style of the building. Such a board usually has permanent letters, and those not many. It aims to tell the basic facts, not to increase attendance.

Many a church makes use of a board with movable letters. In this case the copy ought to change once or twice a week. After each Lord's Day the outside pulpit may carry a brief sentence such as this: "Christ died for the difference between right and wrong." Or else

---

[2] See my *Preparation of Sermons,* chap. XIX, "The Helpfulness of the Radio."

the board may announce a special feature. Later in the week the chief notice may consist of the topic for the evening sermon. Stress only one thing at a time, and make that display striking.

Occasionally a bulletin board seems more of a liability than an asset. Even when new it looks cheap and flimsy. Later it lacks paint. The letters look dog-eared, and the copy crowded. If a passing autoist felt interested, how could he read what the display tries to tell? Then too the sermon topics may not appeal. For various reasons, many churches have done away with this kind of advertising.

2. *A bulletin board inside.* This form of publicity serves a different end. The person in charge does not try to attract people out in the community but seeks to inform those who come to church. Placed on the wall in the lobby or narthex a neat bulletin board can do much to promote missions, or any other cause dear to Christian hearts. The display needs to be in keeping with the architecture, attractive in appearance, with new copy every week. Such a board calls for a glass cover, under lock and key. The friend in charge needs a nose for news, a sense of beauty, a love of variety from week to week, and something of surprise power. In view of all these factors, church officers should think twice before they authorize a bulletin board inside the building.

3. *A literature rack.* Some person neat and tactful may accept the responsibility for a wooden rack with an assortment of booklets and pamphlets, fairly uniform in size and appearance. Ordinarily such printed matter goes out free of charge, but an occasional church asks for payment in a coin box near by. During three months in one summer, worshipers at the Fifth Avenue Presbyterian Church in New York City took from the racks 7,000 free copies of a pamphlet by the pastor, "How to Read the Bible." Not every congregation ministers to that many people in summer, offers such attractive literature, and feels able to give away that many pamphlets. Nevertheless, many another church would find a literature rack helpful—under careful supervision.

4. *A church bulletin.* Almost every congregation has some sort of weekly bulletin or calendar. If people take it home, and ask for extra copies to send through the mail, it must do good. Many church-

goers, however, do not find bulletins attractive, interesting, or helpful. The paper may look muddy, the cut of the church blurred, the printing hasty, and the proofreading careless. The bulletin of one congregation contains so much material, all huddled up, that it keeps people reading news when they ought to be worshiping God. In the next church scanty materials may seem like a few dry bones.

If either congregation wishes to do all things well, why not begin with the bulletin? Eggshell paper, white, usually serves better than glazed stock. If the front page includes a cut of the building, the entrance, or the tower, an artist can make a line drawing, or pen-and-ink sketch. An inexpensive bulletin may include a ready-made cut of the Cross, or of an open Bible. Some of the most attractive bulletins display no cuts. Partly because of this omission, the first page does not seem crowded.

If the Sunday schedule calls for two services, the order for the first one may appear at the top of page two, and for the other one at the head of page three. Then the notices for the day will come on the lower part of page two, and those for the week on the lower half of page three. The friend in charge should put certain kinds of material in the same places week after week. For much the same reason, a daily newspaper always runs the editorials on a certain page, with the lead article first. As for variety and interest, that comes through choice of materials and felicity in phrasing.

Occasionally the fourth page may show the names of the church officers, with the personnel of the various organizations. Such information proves timely before and after the annual meeting. At other seasons the page affords an opportunity to print something helpful for the hour of worship, and worth taking home to send through the mail. In this space the editor can put the names of new members, the number present at the Sacrament last Sunday, and anything else of interest to readers at home and elsewhere. He can also insert a brief item or two about the broader work of the kingdom.

All of this costs more than some churches can afford. Hence they secure made-up bulletins by the hundred, with pages two and three left blank. These the officers have printed with local copy, or else run off on a duplicating machine. The cut and the other boilerplate material come from the denominational publishing house, and often look more attractive than bulletins printed at home. The inner pages may not measure up to the imported matter. The value of the bulletin, therefore, depends much on the skill, foresight, and resourcefulness of the friend in charge. While the pastor needs to supply part of the materials, he should get someone else to do the work, both as editor and as operator of the duplicating machine.

5. *A newsletter.* In a large congregation every family, or lone member, may receive through the mail on Friday a newsletter of at least four pages. It may also serve as the bulletin on the coming Lord's Day. According to existing postal regulations the permit for this kind of second-class matter costs $25.00, and holds good permanently. The rules specify that all the contents be printed, not processed on a duplicating machine or reproduced otherwise, and that 50 per cent or more of the material be of general interest.

At first the congregation must secure and submit a list of paid subscribers, at a minimum rate of fifty cents apiece. After the first year the entire cost may come from the church budget. The newsletters go out in packages, according to geographical districts, and are weighed by the pound. A New Jersey church that sends out four hundred copies a week does so at an over-all mailing cost of nine cents. How that must delight the heart of the treasurer! For other regulations, intricate and at first confusing, consult the postmaster. To be sure about the matter, show him a copy of such a newsletter, and not a bulletin that has come through the mail. Sending out bulletins at a cent and a half apiece would quickly run into money.

Many of us regard the newsletter as the most effective sort of church publicity, at least within the community. Once a week a message goes out from headquarters to every member or adherent. The contents may concern the worship, the teaching, or the work of the church. Every issue ought also to include brief items about broader aspects of the Kingdom. All of this does not come automatically. It requires an editor with a vision of what Josiah Royce called "the world and the individual."

Such a policy accords with that of William Allen White in editing the *Emporia Gazette*.[3] Under his supervision it went to almost every home in that town and county. The paper called attention mainly to local achievements, minus the dirt of Main Street. The editor insisted on short articles, and on printing the names of people. At least once a year, and much oftener, if possible, the columns must include names from every family in the district. When the paper dealt with national or international affairs, the treatment had to show the bearing on people in that part of Kansas. In like manner a church weekly ought to become "person-minded," with little poetry, and that not long.

6. *A church magazine.* A large congregation may need a larger magazine, with ten issues a year, once a month except in July and August. The general program resembles that for the newsletter, with still more need for talent on the part of the editor. Any church with resources for such a venture should know how to manage it. As J. Pierpont Morgan once told a man who asked how much it would cost him to run a private yacht: "If you have to think about the cost, you cannot afford to own a yacht!"

7. *A special card.* In addition to the regular means of publicity, a series of evening sermons may call for a card about $3\frac{1}{2}$ by $5\frac{1}{2}$ inches. The printing all appears on one side, so that anyone can send the notice through the mail. These cards may assume all sorts of sizes, shapes, and colors. Ordinarily, white serves best. The men of the church, or some other group, distribute the cards to their friends, and not from door to door. The effectiveness depends much on skill in wording the copy, and on resourcefulness in getting cards to the right persons. In some cities no one can register at a downtown hotel on Saturday, or walk through near-by streets on Sunday evening, without receiving a printed card of welcome to the services in a church round the corner. And yet some observers wonder why that church attracts countless strangers!

8. *A personal invitation.* Better than any or all these methods is invitation by word of mouth. It may or may not accompany a printed card. Nine persons out of ten may not respond even to a spoken invitation. As in selling life insurance, however, if church members

---

[3] See David Hinshaw, *The Man from Kansas* (New York: G. P. Putnam's Sons, 1945), p. 88.

keep inviting people, results will follow. Of course the solicitors should approach persons who do not belong to churches in the community. Then too, the congregation must offer something worth coming to enjoy. Once again, "The best way to receive publicity is to deserve it."

9. *A pastoral letter.* Every local minister should write letters and cards day after day. In Cleveland Bernard C. Clausen advocates sending many such missives, each of them short and personal. In Baltimore, Maltbie D. Babcock used to do so repeatedly, especially after he had made brief pastoral calls. Once in a while, also, the minister can send a circular epistle to all the members of the congregation. These he ought to sign by hand. As with other pastoral contacts, the value depends much on love and care in writing the letter. Even so, the effectiveness may wear out if he sends letters often. A pastor may content himself with three a year, one after Christmas, another a few weeks before Easter, and a third near the beginning of active preparation for the ingathering of pledges.

All of these plans lie open to various objections, mainly two. The officers may feel that publicity worthy of the cause requires too much money. If they investigated, they would find that intelligent use of printing more than pays for itself. Because of increased attendance and interest, larger offerings more than make up the additional cost. Even if publicity did not attract people, or lead to increased giving, every businessman knows that an institution must keep in touch with its constituency. For this reason many big corporations keep sending attractive literature to all their stockholders. When shall we begin thinking of church members as stockholders in the most important enterprise on earth? Alas, some of our publicity makes the local church seem cheap and tawdry. Why publicize ugliness and twaddle?

A second objection looms larger. Unless the minister watches his steps, he may cease to serve as a prophet, and become a promoter. The man responsible for such a program as we have outlined may devote to publicity stunts more time and attention than to study, not to mention prayer. However, the pastor may discover in the church, or else have in the office, a friend who knows more about such things than the minister will ever learn. If he can enlist that person, the people may enjoy publicity full of human interest and a pastor full of the Holy Spirit.

Experience and observation have led to certain negative conclusions. Even if some forms of publicity appealed to people, the home church should not stoop to such means. They do not suggest the atmosphere of the mountaintop. These objections seem so obvious that they call for little discussion.

1. *Fans in the pews.* If people must use fans in lieu of air conditioning, the printed matter need not extol the merits of a funeral parlor.

2. *Paid advertisements in the church paper.* In most communities merchants respond to such demands, but not with alacrity. They look on these payments as cash contributions, with no option about the cause. Why let the church become a parasite? Develop a sense of self-respect! If the members cannot afford to defray the expense, let them do without a church paper. Above all, let there be no advertisements on the back of the Sunday bulletin. Keep away from the clink of the cash register at the butcher shop. "My house shall be called a house of prayer."

3. *Cards in store windows.* Merchants also object to putting display cards in front windows. What has a large piece of printing to do with the design and color scheme of a shop window? On the other hand, why let such a card appear in a window without design and color scheme, where it will be buried and not read?

4. *Handbills.* In many communities the laws forbid this kind of litter, which used to abound. Church people and other zealots would strew front porches with lurid posters printed on cheap paper. If they appealed to some persons, such posters repelled many others. To which side of people's natures does the church wish to appeal? The careful-housekeeper or the sloppy-sister side?

5. *Business blotters.* This way of advertising, too, has become less

common. It tended to cheapen the church. Especially after the blotters became soiled and stained, they did not commend the cause of Christ. If church officers wish anything of the sort, they can prepare a calendar, attractively printed and ready for use every day. A calendar does not suffer from smears of ink.

6. *Motion-picture notices.* The manager of the neighborhood movie house may feel willing to run a church notice on Friday and Saturday. Instead of helping the cause of Christ, such publicity may set the stamp of approval on a motion-picture concern. What congregation wishes to commend such an establishment today?

7. *Street-car advertisements.* Once again, the association seems scarcely Christian. Thoughts about mother, home, and heaven do not accord with the displays in street cars.

8. *Highway billboards.* Instead of adding to the number of highway horrors, the church ought to ask the authorities to abolish all such billboards. Anyone who journeys along the Merritt Highway, with its succession of overhead bridges, and never a billboard, can see why Christians ought not to disfigure the landscape. Only a moron would respond favorably to a religious appeal from a billboard near lurid signs about automobiles and hotels. What a way to body forth the light of the Gospel!

"Ye are the light of the world. A city that is set on a hill cannot be hid. Neither do men light a candle, and put it under a bushel, but on a candlestick; and it giveth light unto all that are in the house. Let your light so shine before men, that they may see your good works, and glorify your Father which is in heaven." (Matt. 5:14-16.)

Suggested Readings

Baus, Herbert M., *Public Relations at Work.* New York: Harper & Bros., 1948. Not religious.
Brodie, W. Austin, *Keeping Your Church in the News.* New York: Fleming H. Revell Co., 1942.
———, *Keeping Your Church Informed.* New York: Fleming H. Revell Co., 1944.
Dolloff, Eugene D., *Crowded Churches through Modern Methods.* New York: Fleming H. Revell Co., 1946.

Fortson, John L., *How To Make Friends for Your Church*, Association Press, N. Y., 1943.

Harral, Stewart, *Public Relations for Churches*. New York and Nashville: Abingdon-Cokesbury Press, 1945.

————, *Successful Letters for Churches*. New York and Nashville: Abingdon-Cokesbury Press, 1946.

Simpson, Gertrude W., *Working with Newspapers*. New York: National Publicity Council for Health & Welfare Services, 1945. 31 pp., large.

CHAPTER XV

The Comity with Other Churches

WE have been thinking about a church as though it stood alone. Now we must broaden the scope and look at its relations with other bodies in the same area. In all dealings with his own officers and people the minister needs to encourage friendly relations with sister churches of the various denominations. Otherwise he may become unpopular with ministerial brethren. The church he loves most of all may become a byword in the community. How then can he help to avert interchurch friction, or deal with it where it exists?

The more active a congregation, the more easily may it incur disfavor. The more effective the program and the more zealous the workers, the more the likelihood of causing interchurch jealousy and strife. A moribund congregation, or one about to breathe its last, creates few problems about comity. The body that ministers to all its own members, and keeps reaching out to win others, may run the risk of trespassing on posted ground. For example, a writer about visitation evangelism tells of personal workers who visited a certain home twelve times before they put the people on the dead list. All the while the workers knew that those persons belonged to another denomination. What a way to win the esteem of brethren in that other branch of Christ's Church!

Think of another case from life. In a city with a number of suburbs one of the central churches reports 1,800 resident members. The majority of them live in outlying districts, in each of which their denomination has a smaller neighborhood church. If all the members of the body downtown would unite with congregations near where they live, the central church would have to close its doors, or else go to a new suburb and start out afresh. Instead of moving their memberships, however, those people keep winning recruits in outlying districts. Hence some of the neighborhood churches look askance at that central body. They insist that it makes proselytes.

In one of those communities a neighborhood church of the same denomination cultivates its field assiduously. At times workers from the two bodies seem to compete. Then the downtown church must bear the blame. In another residential district a sister church of the same denomination does little or nothing, apparently, to gain recruits. Strange to tell, the members of this body resent the diligence and effectiveness of workers from the central church. How can the Kingdom of God come through congregations that dislike and distrust each other?

Among Protestants compulsory zoning scarcely seems feasible. No doubt we have started too many struggling churches. Since we have let them begin their work, we must accept them, much as they are, at least for the nonce. We cannot change human nature overnight, or compel Protestants to worship where they do not choose. In a residential district people patronize different physicians, some of them at a distance. On the Lord's Day some of these church people like to get in their cars and hie away from home. They want to worship with friends from elsewhere. The women, especially, have been cooped up all week. Now they desire something different. Even if shortsighted and wasteful, such a policy obtains in many a city.

Neither would church union solve all these problems, though often the right sort of mergers would help. Perhaps unfortunately, a change in church machinery and names does not transform members of local churches. In these matters, as in a family circle, the worst quarrels often spring up among sisters. In more than one city the central church gets along more amicably with other Protestant congregations than with those that have the same heritage and bear the same name. All of this presents no insuperable barrier to church union, or to local mergers. But such measures, especially if imposed from without, cannot quickly solve the problems now in view. Under God, the solution depends mainly on the pastor. What should he do to promote comity?

Let him encourage the workers to keep within their field. There they will find abundant opportunities for intensive farming. The field consists of those who already belong to the church, and those who do not belong anywhere, locally. If a member of the staff or a lay visitor discovers a person or a family that ought to unite with another church, this worker should immediately telephone the office of that other body and report the facts. Soon the ministers and the laymen in the city would conclude that this pastor and his people try to play fair. Such a reputation might seem unique. In any case, what else do we understand by church comity? In some manuals for pastors and laymen the word comity and the idea of local interchurch co-operation do not appear.

On the contrary, a closed-shop policy might go too far. If in any family the father and mother wish to change their church home, they have that right. They ought to worship and work wherever they think best for their children. If these friends already belong to a certain congregation, or denomination, other churches ought ordinarily to keep hands off. When the father and mother wish to transfer their memberships, they ought to take the initiative. If so, they should make clear to the pastor of their former church that they have yielded to no pressure from the minister and people in the new church home. As for folk who keep shifting memberships from church to church, they usually prove to be goats rather than sheep. In short, comity means the Golden Rule at work in the community.

THE EFFECTIVENESS OF UNION EFFORTS

Another question relates to union movements. To what extent should a church take part? Theoretically, almost always, and that with enthusiasm. In a pastoral experience of seventeen years I led the people to take part in such activities. Only once did I encourage them to hold back, for reasons I do not recall. Because of that refusal I have always felt a sense of shame. What a way for Protestants to lose friends and alienate people! Sometimes we smile at Dale Carnegie and his ilk, whereas we might learn from them the kind of horse sense that leads to teamwork. In a certain community, for example, four churches sent out workers to canvass the same community during four consecutive weeks—one week to each church!

Actually, nevertheless, union efforts may prove disappointing, especially after the novelty wears away. If a congregation holds its own services year after year at ten o'clock on Thanksgiving Day, with something special and attractive,[1] the people may form the habit of attending. If the church unites with half a dozen others, the numbers year after year will likely dwindle, and then the offerings will decrease. The same holds true, as a rule, with union meetings on Sunday evenings, and with evangelistic services extending over a week or more. After every one of the many union efforts in which the people and I took part during seventeen years, the lay officers and I felt that we could have accomplished more by expending the same amount of time, energy, and money in ways all our own. However, as a by-product, the laymen and I enjoyed getting to know the brethren in those other churches.

Every reader can point to exceptions that show the folly of sweeping statements. In the East End of Pittsburgh, for instance, Protestant congregations have been holding union services on Sunday evenings throughout the summer for more than thirty years, consecutively. During one season twenty-seven churches took part—belonging to eight denominations. Fourteen of those churches represented two sister denominations closely related in everything except willingness for organic union. If they love the Lord and love each other, sister churches can worship and work together. In this case note that the union meetings are held week after week, and year after year, in a popular assembly hall, not in a church. Also, the various denominations secure the ablest preachers in the country. In brief, let no one find fault with such union meetings.

Movements for local co-operation have become common. If the pastors in a community carried out all the projects that come down from headquarters—denominational and otherwise—some of these dear men might have time and strength for little else. With the spirit and the purpose of many projects the minister feels in hearty accord. But he wonders if the ecclesiastical statesmen who evolve such time-consuming plans have served as pastors long enough to know about the other demands on a minister. How can he personally do all that the statesmen expect in the way of attending conferences and taking part on committees or subcommittees? He wonders why he should not

[1] See my *Planning a Year's Pulpit Work*, chap. II, "Observing Special Days."

follow the counsel of Jethro. If a pastor succeeded in enlisting lay representatives, instead of doing the interchurch work himself, these people would learn far more about the work of the Kingdom, and he would not need to neglect the parish.

In the last analysis every such broad movement depends on the local church and its pastor. Wherever such movements have failed, as more than a few have done, the weakness has appeared in the local body. On the other hand, among ministers who have distinguished themselves as church leaders, few if any have also become known for zeal in attending countless committee meetings elsewhere.[2] However heretical the feeling, many pastors have decided that the Protestant Church needs another Reformation. Among other things good and high, such a movement would set pastors free for their work as leaders of their own flocks.

As for local meetings of church representatives, they would accomplish more for the Kingdom if they consisted largely of lay men and women. Meanwhile, the Kingdom of God cometh not through conferences that keep shepherds away from their sheep. Much the same principle holds in social service work. In that field one of the leading experts has called for a return to "the retail method of reform." [3] She insists that if you wish to change any part of society you must deal with human beings one by one. This sounds strangely like the ways of our Lord as He went about doing good.

RELATIONS WITH OTHER MINISTERS

Two parts of local interchurch work a pastor cannot delegate, at least not entirely, even to another ordained member on the staff. One part relates to attendance at stated meetings of church "courts," whatever the denominational title. Such gatherings the pastor as a loyal churchman ought to attend, regularly. He should also accept and carry out his share of the committee work. However, many a young minister may feel unable to do all that the older brethren

---

[2] See L. M. and M. S. Sweet, *The Pastoral Ministry in Our Time* (New York: Fleming H. Revell Co., 1949).
[3] See Mary E. Richmond, *The Long View;* also George A. Buttrick, *Jesus Came Preaching* (New York: Charles Scribner's Sons, 1931), chap. V, "The Individual."

ask. He rightly thinks that he should give himself largely to the home parish, especially during the first few years. Sometimes too he wonders why the genius of American Protestantism calls for increasingly complicated machinery and a multiplicity of meetings. Oh, for that Reformation!

Another aspect of a pastor's work has to do with ministers of neighboring churches. He should know them well, love them much, and work with them all. Whenever a new pastor comes to a church in the same general area, the minister and his wife should make a social call. Sometimes, however, a young pastor in a small church hesitates to intrude on the incoming minister of a large congregation. Even so, every pastor can follow this rule: Speak nothing but good about a brother minister. Another rule also holds: Whenever in doubt concerning a transfer of members from one congregation to another, confer with the other pastor. Show him the sort of courtesy an honorable physician accords another worthy follower of Aesculapius.

These ministerial contacts may bring abiding joy. When a pastor reaches middle age he may become a sort of father-confessor to young clergymen. In Buffalo a mature brother became known among the younger ministers as an apostolic friend and helper for any young Timothy or Titus in distress, or down in the dumps. By day or by night that older man stood ready to render first aid to any young friend in need, whether real or imaginary, desperate or trivial. During his latter years this father-confessor may have accomplished almost as much indirectly as by his own church work. In the words of a current book,[4] he put men back on their feet and helped to keep them there. He never became known nationally. If his name appeared on this page, many readers might wonder why. That name, nevertheless, stands high in heaven, and shines brightly in the hearts of pastors here below. "The teachers shall shine as the brightness of the firmament; and they that turn many to righteousness as the stars for ever and ever." (Dan. 12:3, A.S.V., margin.)

Every mature pastor should welcome an opportunity to cheer a

---

[4] Frederick K. Stamm, *Keeping Men on Their Feet* (New York: Harper & Bros., 1949), pp. 87-95.

disconsolate young shepherd. Bishop William A. Quayle [5] used to do so at times by telling about his early experiences as a pastor in Oklahoma. In those pioneer days he and his wife had felt tempted to envy any neighboring minister whose work seemed to be prospering. Then the future bishop made a discovery that led to a change of attitude toward interchurch relations. He found that whenever the worship and the work of neighboring congregations flourished, the worship and the work of his own church shared in the overflow. If many a pastor would learn this lesson he might avoid most of the heartaches that come from ministerial jealousies and interchurch rivalries. Of course he should lift all these matters to a higher level, and look on them more spiritually. Whether or not comity benefits the local church every minister ought to co-operate. This too we learn from Bishop Quayle.

Suggested Readings

Becker, Edwin L., *The Pastoral Unity Plan.* Indianapolis: United Christian Missionary Society, 1946. 42 pp.

Douglass, Harlan P., *Protestant Coöperation in American Cities.* New York: Institute of Social and Religious Research, 1930.

Dun, Angus, *Prospecting for a United Church.* New York: Harper & Bros., 1948. Favors church union.

Kincheloe, Samuel C., *The American City and Its Church.* New York: Missionary Education Movement, 1938.

Leiffer, Murray H., *The Effective City Church.* New York and Nashville: Abingdon-Cokesbury Press, 1949.

————, *In That Case,* Chicago: Willett, Clark & Co., 1937. Chap. VIII, "Inter-Church Problems."

Scotford, John R., *Church Union; Why Not?* Boston: The Pilgrim Press, 1948. Favors church union now.

Zahniser, Charles R., *Interchurch Community Programs.* New York: Thomas Nelson & Sons, 1932.

[5] For a taste of his quality turn to *The Pastor-Preacher* (New York: The Methodist Book Concern, 1924).

PART TWO

The Pastor as Organizer

CHAPTER XVI

The Arrangements for Evangelism

R ECENTLY a prominent clergyman in one of our largest denominations told a group of ministers: "You can divide the
Protestant churches of our country into two classes, those that believe
in evangelism, and those that do not." He excluded the Roman
Catholic church, which relies largely on preaching missions, radio
sermons, and other forms of evangelism. Also, he did not include
Anglo-Catholics, most of whom show zeal for winning converts.
Where does that leave many of us Protestants? Perhaps we should
sing: "We are all divided, not one body we."

Some of us think of evangelism at home and missions abroad as
close to the heart of New Testament Christianity. In fact, we find
in the Old Testament many a record of declension and revival. As
for church history, what else does it record? Probably those who hold
aloof from evangelism object to American revivalism, but evangelism
flourished long before Columbus discovered America. Revivalism
stressed mass movements and emotionalism, sometimes bordering on
hysteria.[1] The emphasis at times fell on machinery, money, and manpower. Revivalism may have suited the needs of pioneer days. If so,
the trend has moved away from semi-sensationalism, toward the
ideals of the New Testament.

The movement away from revivalism gained impetus from Horace
Bushnell. In 1847 he sent out the first edition of *Christian Nurture*,[2]
a work that seemed to stress Christian education instead of dealing
with adult atoms. Bushnell insisted that the chief opportunity of
the Christian Church to win recruits lay in her own boys and girls.
In a godly home such nurture ought to begin at birth, if not before.
"The child is to grow up a Christian, and never know himself to

[1] See F. M. Davenport, *Primitive Traits in Religious Revivals* (New York: The
Macmillan Co., 1917).
[2] See the latest edition, ed. by L. A. Weigle (New Haven: Yale University Press,
1947).

be anything else." To this doctrine many of us heartily subscribe, though not perhaps for Bushnell's reasons, doctrinally. We do him injustice, however, if we make him appear hostile or indifferent to evangelism. In the book now before us he discusses Christian nurture, but not to the exclusion of soul-winning among adults. Here follow some of his words: "There are two principal modes by which the Kingdom of God may be and is to be extended. One is by the process of conversion, and the other that of family propagation: one by gaining over to the side of faith and piety; the other by the populating force of faith and piety themselves. . . . What I propose at the present time is to restore, if possible, a juster impression of this great subject; to show that conversion over to the church is not the only way of increase." [3]

In Bushnell's day of rampant revivalism he thought it necessary to plead for Christian nurture. If he were living in New England now, he might do the reverse. He believed in both sorts of Christian activity. For instance, suppose that he called at a home where young parents had become concerned about the spiritual welfare of their two children, a boy of four and a girl of two. Bushnell might have discovered that neither father nor mother had accepted the Lord Jesus, and entered into the Christian way of living. What would that shepherd of souls have tried to do with those parents? He would not have expected them to engage in Christian nurture before they had any such experience.

Even if a large section of the Protestant church ceased to believe in evangelism, the rest of us would cling to the teachings and ideals of the New Testament, as illuminated by the experiences of the Church in later times. According to Professor C. H. Dodd of Cambridge University—a foremost New Testament scholar—the Apostolic Church gave the right of way to evangelism.[4] Both in the homeland and on the foreign field the apostles devoted themselves to evangelism. After they had won recruits, and led them to establish Christian homes, the apostles began to promote Christian nurture. "What therefore

[3] *Ibid.* p. 125. See also Bushnell's message, "Regeneration," in *Sermons for the New Life*, London, 1892, pp. 58-73.
[4] *Apostolic Preaching and Its Developments* (New York: Willett, Clark & Co., 1937).

God hath joined together, let not man put asunder." (Matt. 19:6b.)

Evangelism in the home church means the endeavor to present the claims of Christ and His Kingdom to every man or woman, boy or girl, in the community who is not now living for Him and His cause. Ideally the pastor and his associates ought to bring up everybody as a Christian from childhood. Actually personal workers in any community today find the majority of their neighbors without any visible signs of belonging to Christ. In the country as a whole almost half of our people do not profess any church allegiance, and many of those who profess do nothing more. Hence the fields stand waiting for the harvest by an evangelistic church.

An evangelistic congregation means one in which the pastor and all the lay workers have this cause near to their hearts. Every organization strives to enlist men and women, boys and girls, one by one, for membership in Christ's church. In some cases, as in the cradle-roll department of the church school, the evangelistic opportunity may come indirectly. Even so, visitors can present the claims of Christ to the parents of any little one whose name appears on the roll. The home department visitors can keep their eyes open for any non-Christian in a household where some of the people belong to the church. Indeed, congregational evangelism ought to seem as natural to church workers as the soliciting of life insurance by an agent as he goes about meeting friends who already hold policies.

In promoting evangelism the pastor encourages lay workers to look out for opportunities to present the claims of Christ. Ideally he thinks of every church organization and every church member as evangelistically-minded. Practically he may enlist some one group as the most active promoters of this cause. For instance, as we shall see, the men's brotherhood may need a project more or less its own. If so, the pastor may ask the official board to designate the brotherhood as leaders in winning the unchurched and the unsaved.

As for methods, the churches of our day rely chiefly on home visitation. This plan has become so well known, and so favorably, that it calls for no discussion. However, it suggests two observations.

The first has to do with the number of workers on each team.

Current practice calls for sending them out two by two. Wherever this plan works effectively the pastor should rejoice and continue to plan this way. However, he should know about another method. Sometimes one man deals better with another man, and a woman with a woman, face to face and heart to heart. Since the Spirit has blessed both ways of working, the pastor, or the evangelistic committee, should feel free to send a "team" to a home and a person to a person.

The second observation relates to the season for such activity. Often we think of it as extending over a week or two and then subsiding. In some quarters the movement continues a month or more, prior to Easter. Obviously the Christian Year calls for seedtime and harvest. More people unite with the church during the harvest season known as Lent than at any other time. But the pastor and his coworkers should never declare any closed season for evangelism. "Now is the accepted time; behold, now is the day of salvation." (II Cor. 6:2.)

Ideally work ought to go forward the year around. The Spirit of God can move on the hearts of men and women in July and August as surely as in February and March. Actually, as many a church operates, soul-winning proceeds more satisfactorily at some seasons than at others. In making plans for such a movement the leaders should take into account the climactic stages of the Christian Year. Those who do not belong to a denomination with liturgical forms of worship can take account of changing seasons with varied opportunities to set forth the crown rights of the Redeemer. Instead of concentrating all the activities in the period just before Easter, some churches also stress the time leading up to Christmas, and the weeks prior to Pentecost.

In various congregations it may not seem wise to employ these liturgical terms. Whatever the terminology, why not take advantage of rising tides in the hearts of men and women? During the Advent season any congregation can stress the work of evangelism in the home. Through December many persons look forward to Christmas as homecoming time. When they sing Yuletide carols they utter words like these:

O come to my heart, Lord Jesus,
There is room in my heart for Thee.

Cast out our sin, and enter in,
Be born in us today.

In keeping with these prayers set to music, plan to win for Christ and His Church every home where father and mother join with little ones in acclaiming the coming of the Redeemer.

Born to raise the sons of earth,
Born to give them second birth.
Hark the herald angels sing,
"Glory to the new-born King."

The Lenten season calls for evangelism still more intensive. At this time of year, if ever on earth, men and women think about their souls. Hence the call may come for individual evangelism. At a time when everybody within reach of church influence keeps thinking about the life, death, and resurrection of our Lord, conversions ought to increase. At this season, too, sickness and death abound. Without resorting to terrorism, present the only way by which "frail children of dust, and feeble as frail" can find the faith that conquers fear.

After Easter the church ought to think much about the glory of the living Christ and the power of the Holy Spirit. These truths lie close to the heart of the New Testament, and of present-day Christianity. Hence the season affords an opportunity for the pastor and the lay workers to present the claims of the Church as God's agent in blessing the world. With some such program every church may plan for these three special seasons of ingathering, instead of one, as in many a field today. On a farm in Kansas the person in charge prepares for three crops of alfalfa from a single field.

Evangelistic workers need instruction from the pastor. They ought to learn about the Christian home as earth's nearest approach to heaven; the Christian life as a new creation from above, and not merely turning over a new leaf; and the Christian Church as the visible representative of the Invisible Lord who wishes to reign in every heart He died to redeem. Evidently the promotion of evangelism calls for brains. The parish leader must have what Brooks terms "the mind's love for God." [5]

Evangelism leads to the winning of souls, with additions to church membership. The movement also results in the spiritual growth of the workers. Even if the minister could do all the soul-winning himself, he would show far more wisdom by sharing the privilege. If any pastor wishes to foster among God's people a love for Christ and the Church, with zeal for the coming of the Kingdom throughout the earth, let him enlist church members in praying for their unchurched friends and neighbors, and in leading them to the foot of the Cross, there to lay life's burden down and receive the joy that God alone can give, and nothing on earth can take away.

A leading divine in the Church of Scotland has pointed to the saddest fact about our generation. He declares that no one born since the turn of the century has witnessed a real revival in the Christian Church. So let us join in the prayer that often appears in the *Lectures on Revivals of Religion,* by Charles G. Finney:

> O Lord, revive thy work in the midst of the years,
> In the midst of the years make known;
> In wrath remember mercy. (Hab. 3:2.)

Suggested Readings

Blackwood, A. W., *Evangelism in the Home Church.* New York and Nashville: Abingdon-Cokesbury Press, 1942.

Bryan, Dawson C., *A Workable Plan of Evangelism.* New York and Nashville: Abingdon-Cokesbury Press, 1945.

————, *A Handbook of Evangelism for Laymen.* New York and Nashville: Abingdon-Cokesbury Press, 1948.

Dobbins, Gaines S., *Evangelism According to Christ.* New York: Harper & Bros., 1949.

Finney, Charles G., *Lectures on Revivals of Religion.* Chicago: Fleming H. Revell Co., 1868.

Homrighausen, Elmer G., *Choose Ye This Day.* Philadelphia: Westminster Press, 1943.

[5] See *Sermons Preached in English Churches* (New York: E. P. Dutton Co., 1910), pp. 22-42.

Jordan, G. Ray, *The Emerging Revival*. New York and Nashville: Abingdon-Cokesbury Press, 1946. Sermons.

Kernahan, A. Earl, *Adventures in Visitation Evangelism*. New York: Fleming H. Revell Co., 1928.

Meckel, Aaron N., *A New Day for Evangelism*. New York: E. P. Dutton Co., 1947.

Powell, Sidney W., *Where Are the People?* New York and Nashville: Abingdon-Cokesbury Press, 1942.

————, *Toward the Great Awakening*. New York and Nashville: Abingdon-Cokesbury Press, 1949.

Sangster, W. E., *Let Me Commend*. New York and Nashville: Abingdon-Cokesbury Press, 1948.

Shoemaker, Samuel M., *Revive Thy Church Beginning with Me*. New York: Harper & Bros., 1948.

Trumbull, Charles G., *Taking Men Alive*. New York: Fleming H. Revell Co., 1938.

Chapter XVII

The Conservation of New Members

CONSERVATION here means prevention of loss—plus much more. The project calls for prevention of soil erosion, and for increase of soil fertility.[1] In ecclesiastical terms, the subject concerns ways and means of receiving and training new members as permanent parts of Christ's Church. More than a hundred years ago Bushnell wrote on "The Out-Populating Power of the Christian Stock." This chapter in *Christian Nurture* has to do with boys and girls in believing homes, but the principle also applies to adults who unite with the church. If we could conserve all who come into the fold, whether young or mature, what a power the Protestant Church might become in America and far beyond.

Away then with soil erosion and soul depletion. According to conservative estimates many a congregation, year after year, loses at least half of this potential energy. For instance, a report comes from a young man in Maryland. He has served in a small village church long enough to get his bearings. Now he has begun to appraise the ideals with which he entered the active ministry three years ago: "We find it easy to secure new members. Year after year we welcome into the church nearly all the boys and girls in the Bible school. Through visitation evangelism we also reach and enlist men and women, especially among young married people with little children. But among the majority of our new members, whether young or mature, joining church seems to mean little more than turning a new leaf that gives pleasure only in passing. Despite all our accessions the work does not move forward spiritually. For example, church attendance does not increase. The people do not give so large a proportion of their income as in former years."

Wherein lies the difficulty? Regular attendance and liberal giving

[1] See Louis Bromfield, *Pleasant Valley* (New York: Harper & Bros., 1945); and William Vogt, *Road to Survival* (New York: William Sloane Co., 1949).

158

may not mean everything. Still they afford external marks of inward graces, or else lack of graces. In dealing with souls personally, a minister ought to condemn no one except himself. But in viewing the work as a whole he has a right to form tentative conclusions. With all charity many a pastor feels that more than a few church members have had no experience of redeeming grace, or that they have fallen from that high estate. Whatever the cause, or the explanation, many church members today do not sense the meaning and the importance of such affiliation. Herein lies the most immediate problem in many a church. How can the pastor lead in making this problem over into an opportunity?

By way of analogy, think about divorce, whether actual or only in the offing. In order to deal with this growing evil we must get down to the source. In each case it usually lies in conditions that have led to the marriage. In the breaking up of a home or in the loss of vital connection with a church, the remedy lies not in discouraging marriage or membership, but in making marriage or membership real. How then can the pastor help to prepare each applicant for church membership as carefully as he strives to prepare two young friends for marriage and the making of a Christian home?

The pastor himself ought to deal with every couple who desire him to perform their marriage ceremony. He cannot hope, single-handed, to prepare all the adult applicants for church membership, and afterward nurture them in the Lord. As an organizer, through conference with associates, he should work out a method, and then follow it year after year, with such improvements as time and experience suggest. For a working method we now turn to the Central Presbyterian Church of Rochester, New York. The pastor, William S. Meyer, has led in formulating a plan that would apply in any parish, large or small, with such modifications as local conditions require.

This congregation reports 2,255 members. During the past year 81 united on profession of faith in Christ, and 80 by certificate from other churches. In comparison with statistics in other churches, with different methods, the number of accessions may not seem large. At Central Church the stress falls on personal acceptance of Christ, and not on the number of persons who unite with the church. In each case the program for the reception and nurture of a new member of Christ's body extends over three years. This period coincides with the length of time Bushnell allows a father and mother to make a lasting impression on a newborn babe. So we may paraphrase well-known words in *Christian Nurture:* [2] "Let every pastor and his associates understand that more is done, or lost by neglect of doing, on a new member's churchmanship in the first three years of his affiliation than in all his years of discipline afterwards."

At the Rochester church the program of conservation calls for activity in four distinct stages. At every stage we shall assume that soul-winning, especially visitation evangelism, precedes conservation. These stages do not always follow in the order of time that appears below. For example, the work of enlisting new members in church activities ought to proceed side by side with other ways of working. For the sake of clarity, however, let us look at each of the stages as though it stood out by itself.

THE ADMISSION OF NEW MEMBERS

The prospective member comes to the pastor's office for a personal interview. There the candidate tells about his Christian experience. Even if he seems ready for admission, he agrees to attend church for at least a month before he presents a formal application. At the end of this interview the candidate receives an application blank, complete and detailed, showing what the congregation will expect of him as a member. All of this makes an outside observer think of the way a pastor ought to confer with a candidate for matrimony.

After a month or more the candidate for membership hands in the application, which he has filled out at home. Then he unites with the church in accordance with the customs of the denomination. Since this procedure is different from that in other bodies, we need not include a description. A wise pastor and his associates plan to make the rite of admission an event, and not an incident. After the ceremony of induction, as after a marriage service in the sanctuary, the new

[2] Third edition, London, 1872, p. 161.

member ought to feel that he has taken a momentous step Godward. A person soon finds that marriage means a beginning, not an end. Before the new member leaves the meeting with the officers, he receives from one or two of them literature about the meaning of the new relationship, and about the opportunities for service in the new church home. A little later he shares in the public welcome of new members. On the first Lord's Day of each month the morning hour of worship gives a prominent place to the recognition of all members received during the past four weeks. Here again, customs vary in different branches of the Church. Somehow or other each congregation as a whole ought to honor every new recruit and bid him Godspeed in the Christian life.

THE INSTRUCTION OF NEW MEMBERS

The plan likewise calls for the instruction of new members. Here again we shall think only about adults. The officers urge, though they do not require, every man or woman who unites with the church to attend the pastor's class. This adult group meets on Wednesday evening before the midweek service, and continues for ten weeks, consecutively. The instruction covers the usual ground: what it means to be a Christian; how a person grows in the Christian life; the history, organization, and program of the Christian Church; what every member can expect from the congregation, and what it expects from each new member.

The officers of the church school try to enroll the new recruit in one of the Bible classes. There the friend should continue to learn until he becomes a teacher in the school.

THE SPONSORS FOR NEW MEMBERS

Two of the church officers, representing different boards, accept responsibility for friendly concern about each new member. This relationship continues for three years, but not all the time so actively as at first. As in the transplanting of a shrub, life and growth depend largely on preparation of the new soil, and on nurture of the new life. At the Rochester church the pastor and his associates regard the first six months as decisive. Partly for this reason every sponsor receives a set of suggestions known as "The Assimilation Plan."

The nature of the plan appears from the statement about the purpose of the sponsor's first call. He should welcome the new member, become well acquainted, familiarize him with the church program, enroll him in a Bible class and in other groups, discover any talent for special work, assure him of the sponsor's continued friendship, and urge attendance at the pastor's class for ten weeks, unless special circumstances make attendance not feasible. Before he departs, the sponsor gives the new member two pieces of printed matter, "The Communicant Member," and "My Certificate of Church Membership." The other sponsor calls at another time. Before leaving he delivers a third publication, "Know Your Church." By way of encouragement each sponsor receives the following suggestions, as a part of the assimilation plan:

Make the call as soon as possible after you receive the assignment. If possible take your wife along in making the call. Be sure to get literature from the office, or the assimilation chairman. Report your findings to the church secretary, using the special card. At least once a month check up on the new member's "assimilation." Invite him to come with you to a church dinner or other special event. For three years share with the ministers in pastoral care and oversight.

At the end of the church year each sponsor receives from the office a letter asking for a report on the friends under his care. Near the end of the year, also, the officers of the congregation and their wives serve as hosts and hostesses at a dinner reception in honor of the persons who have united with the church since the dinner a year before. The cost of this banquet comes out of the church treasury, as a regular part of the budget. Those in charge spare no effort or expense in making the occasion a red-letter event in the life of the congregation.

THE ENLISTMENT OF THE NEW WORKERS

Meanwhile, the officers of the church have been securing information about each new member. They wish to know his past church experience, if any; his interests and his aptitudes. All of this they have the secretary put on the back of the application blank, which rests in her files. From the assimilation record she can secure and compile any sort of information that leaders of a parish organization need. The following items appear on these records: Sunday-school teaching, choir and which voice, piano playing, adult class, youth work, men's work, women's work, office in church, ushering.

Let us remember that this account does not follow the order of time. The work of enlistment goes on from the beginning of the contacts with a prospective member. Through all those other stages the work of enlistment continues. The officers try not to pester the new friend. Still they know that the sooner he begins to serve actively in one or more groups the more likely will he become a permanent asset in the congregation. He will belong to the church, as a full-fledged member of God's redeemed family. Consequently the leaders of the societies secure a succession of new recruits, and have in reserve a number of friends to fill posts as they become vacant. In no case do the two sponsors consider their work effective until they have enlisted the new member as an active worker in at least one organization of the local church.

THE MERITS OF THE PLAN

What a reflex influence all of this activity must have on each of those sponsors, and on his wife! According to the laws of human nature and divine grace, the man who puts most of himself into the work derives most benefit from church privileges. The exercise of his spiritual muscles creates in the sponsor a desire for the atmosphere and the food that he finds on the mountaintop with his Lord. Since the lay shepherding continues for three years, and includes the friendliest of contacts with more than one new member, each sponsor must have a host of joys like those of the minister.

This program, nevertheless, calls for a word of warning. According to the pastor in Rochester, the plan does not always work ideally. Sometimes, indeed, it fails. If so, the fault may lie with one of the sponsors, with the new member, or with both parties. But, as the minister insists, even if the plan proved effective with only 70 per cent of the new members, that would mean a higher percentage than the church could expect after any hands-off and do-nothing way of dealing with recruits.

Some such plan for conservation would operate in any church, large or small. But the pastor must have a vision, and be able to enlist sponsors who will labor as undershepherds year after year. This kind of work requires something more time-consuming than letters and telephone calls. It demands the expenditure of energy and thought, in the spirit of prayer. What else does it mean to serve as lay officers of Christ's church? When shall we begin to bestow as much care on the conservation of every new member as a nurseryman and his helpers lavish on a new cutting for a future boxwood tree?

In order to facilitate a beginning in soul conservation, draw up some such literature. Before you have anything of the sort printed, present it to the official board for adoption. The plan may call for four statements like these in Rochester: (1) Application for Membership; (2) Suggestions for New Members; (3) Suggestions for Sponsors; (4) Openings for Christian Service. In the application for membership the candidate finds the following, which he ought to study in the spirit of prayer, and then sign with his full baptismal name, much as a knight at the Round Table used to receive a commission from King Arthur.

My Covenant with God and the Church [3]

I. In uniting with this church I subscribe to the following declarations:
    A. Believing Jesus Christ to be the Son of God, I accept Him as my own personal Saviour, and acknowledge Him as my Master and Lord (Luke 12:8).
    B. Trusting in the Holy Spirit for guidance and grace, I shall seek to lead a consistent Christian life, honoring Christ in all my relationships (John 15:14).
II. As a member of this church I accept the following responsibilities:
    A. I shall strive to be faithful in my attendance upon its services (Heb. 10:25).
    B. I shall endeavor to render some form of Christian service (II Tim. 2:15).

[3] For permission to reprint this and other materials, with countless kindnesses, I am indebted to William S. Meyer.

   C. I shall give regularly by pledge to the support of the church and its benevolences as the Lord shall prosper me (I Cor. 16:1).

III. Desiring to have a share in the program of the local church and the advancement of the Kingdom of God throughout the world, I pledge to pay $———— per week, until further notice, and request that envelopes be provided for my convenience in making this weekly contribution.

Date ———————   Signature ——————————————

Chapter XVIII

The Dependence on Group Leaders

I N addition to all the activities so far, the up-to-date pastor may desire a band of group leaders. The plan works in various ways, according to the size and character of the church. The larger the flock, and the more shifting the constituency, the more pressing the need, and the greater the difficulty. On the other hand, strange as it may seem, the members and adherents of a large church, or one of medium size, may receive more attention and care than those in a small congregation.

In New Jersey the young pastor of a church with less than two hundred members sensed the need for keeping in close touch with the people. He found that he had not been dealing adequately with certain families. So he secured a map of the community and divided the parish into six units, geographically. Then he put the map on the wall of the study, with a red pin to show where each family lived and a green pin to indicate a prospective family. As a result the whole work of the parish benefited. The improvement did not come from the plan so much as from intensive cultivation of the field. At first, however, the minister did too much of the work himself.

During the six years of this man's pastorate the membership has more than doubled. Recently he has led in a planning conference, which resulted in a group system that merits study. Partly because of the growing community round about, and the large number of newcomers, the plan calls for twelve groups. Since the parish lies along the Atlantic seaboard, with many visitors in the summer, that season does not bring a letdown, or even a lull. The following statement appears in "Tower Time," a brochure celebrating the ninetieth anniversary of the church's founding:

Each group will have a chairman, a co-chairman, and other leaders as the need arises. All groups are expected to participate in the work of the whole year, but each group will assume responsibility for its month. Close contacts within the group are possible, due to the arrangement in neighborhood sections. We trust that new members will answer the call to service and take some of the burden from those who have borne it in the heat of the day. Thus a larger sharing of leadership and a wider distribution of responsibility will become a reality in our total church program. Certain main objectives should be in our mind as we begin:

1. Increased regularity of attendance at church services.
2. Increased sponsorship for church activities and the fellowship hour.
3. Visits in homes by groups.
4. Prompt information about illness or trouble, with expressions of sympathy and offers of help.
5. Fostering the material as well as the spiritual growth of the church.

In order to realize these objectives each group will be responsible for the following general services:

1. The chairman and co-chairman will co-operate with the deacons as hosts in the vestibule on Sunday mornings during the month of that group.
2. Visit promptly and give cordial welcome to new members of the church who are placed in that particular group.
3. Hold one reception for the entire group during the year.
4. Take notice, by appropriate expressions of Christian affection, of both joyful and sorrowful events in the homes of the group.

Experience here and elsewhere shows that geographical units serve better than any others. In Pittsburgh a congregation in a rundown area near the river comprised three hundred members. Geographically the terrain lent itself to the formation of six units. Each of them consisted of about fifty members, which seemed large enough. Ordinarily the number of units ought to remain constant. If the congregation grows, some units may need to subdivide, or swarm. Certain people will move away and others will come in. Wise leaders do not shift geographical boundaries often, even if a certain group waxes or wanes. For convenience the identifying numbers ought to remain constant. However, if the fourth unit becomes too large and unwieldy, it may subdivide into 4A and 4B. At Pittsburgh the plan helped in many ways, despite the fact that the young minister knew next to nothing about the group system. Hence he could introduce it in only a rudimentary fashion.

At Buffalo, as we have seen, an experienced pastor led to the formation of geographical units in a large church. Since the membership ran over 2,500, the plan called for fifty groups, each with a man and a woman at the head. The activities of these leaders included preparation for the quarterly celebration of the Sacrament. The congregation also observed this rite at other seasons, but the stress among the fifty groups fell on the quarterly Communion. Unless a member partook of the Sacrament at least once a year, either in church or at home—if physically unable to visit the sanctuary—he forfeited a place on the active roll. Before each quarterly Communion the male group leader would visit each of his members, about fifty in all, and deliver a token. This token the member presented at the church on Communion day. According to the plan, unlike that in the small Jersey parish, the male leaders consisted of the main church officers.[1]

Historically this plan may go back to the time of Thomas Chalmers in Glasgow. During his tenure of St. John's Church the parish consisted of twenty-five units. Each of them included from sixty to a hundred families, with two lay officers in charge. One of these had to do mainly with spiritual needs, and the other with physical. With these district leaders the pastor worked as diligently as though everything depended on him alone. Not only did the system prove a blessing to the people spiritually. It also led to the relief of the poor, through a wise distribution of charitable funds, and that in a community where poverty abounded.[2]

In our country the plan may call for only one male leader in each group, with a woman as the associate. The two should come from different households. The male leader represents the congregation more or less officially. The woman thinks of herself as a promoter of friendliness. In their different ways the two can bring the grace of God to bear on any situation that arises in the area. All of this coincides with the best teaching of our day about intensive cultivation of a field or an orchard, from which the husbandman expects a bountiful return.

---

[1] For the plans of a special group organization in a large metropolitan church see my *Pastoral Work*, pp. 219-21.

[2] See Thomas Chalmers, *Christian and Civic Economy of Large Towns* (Edinburgh, 1826).

In many a unit the effectiveness of the plan depends largely on the woman worker. Despite all our modern gadgets, or perhaps because of them, many a neighborhood includes lonely folk, especially among women. In a day when people move from district to district, and often from city to city, many of them feel uprooted. In a strange house and community displaced persons need more than a telephone and a radio, with an automobile and good roads. They long for friends like those back in the old home church.

This feeling obtains even among people to whom others look up with awe. In the book to which we referred earlier Mrs. George Marshall recounts her experiences in going hither and thither with the General. At Chicago, for instance, she found the people kind. Still she wrote wistfully: "I am not much of a joiner, but I received cards to join the Friends of Art, Friends of China, and finally Friends of Opera. When the last one came, I told my husband that what I would really like would be to have some friends of my own." [3]

As group leaders women often prove more effective than men. With some exceptions on both sides of the statement, women have more time for visiting, more tact in making friends, and more skill in human relations. They do not lose patience with shut-in folk who seem garrulous, or resent having to deal with endless details. The man in charge of a group may carry out his part of the assignment faithfully, but he finds that the lady colleague can handle a delicate matter where he would feel at a loss for something to say or do. In starting the system, therefore, secure as leaders of each group both a man and a woman.

THE ADVANTAGES OF THE SYSTEM

The group system affords advantages of many kinds. For example, it enables the church to secure information about members and prospects in any part of the field. Let us begin with sickness. Often the minister asks how he can learn about every case of serious illness. If he has alert group leaders, he may wonder how to take care of all the cases they report! In time he can get them to distinguish between cases that call for pastoral attention, and others that the group workers can deal

---

[3] Marshall, *op. cit.*, p. 19.

with themselves. In any event a church family should never feel that nobody in the congregation cares about their troubles, whether large or small.

One or the other group leader can learn about any kind of misfortune in the homes of the group. A husband fifty years of age may lose his job as a machinist and need help in securing work less taxing on his nerves. A wife may grieve because she cannot go to her mother dying in the Far West. A family may feel disaffected because the pastor has not called repeatedly. They tell the neighbors about the coldness of the church and the unfriendliness of the minister. Such persons may want coddling. Even so, every church includes families that need personal attention from month to month. These conditions the group leaders can report or else deal with themselves.

The plan also enables a church to keep in touch with changes of address, and with newcomers. In former days nearly all the members lived within walking distance, and remained in the same houses year after year. Now people move, sometimes because they must, and again because they can. Often they neglect to transfer their church memberships. If a family goes to another section of the city, the home church ought to ascertain the new address at once. If the friends remove to another part of the state or country, the church ought to know the pertinent facts immediately.

Statisticians report that since the outbreak of World War II 40 per cent of the people in our country have moved to other abodes. Among those who belong to Protestant bodies almost 50 per cent seem never to transfer their memberships. Hence they are lost to the Church at large. Ideally they ought to seek out the local sanctuary and apply for admission by letter. Practically they wait to find out whether or not they are wanted. Erelong they become church tramps. If they find no rest for their souls, and no friends in the new loneliness, these wanderers begin to give all churches absent treatment.

Much of the loss by removal group leaders could help to prevent. Before a family moves away they should ascertain the facts and notify the church in the new community. In that distant place other group workers ought to discover the newcomers at once, and help to make them feel at home in the unfamiliar church. No plan works ideally, but when failure comes, the fault ought not to lie with our church.

Group leaders can also discover prospects for the Bible school, and relay much other information that would otherwise call for a community survey. In capable hands the group system may work as intensively as the "block method" did under Mayor Hague in Jersey City. He devised ways and means of ascertaining facts about any man, woman, or child in that city. While a church might not adopt him as a model, the pastor and his aides ought to show themselves as faithful and resourceful as any political leader and his helpers. "The sons of this world are wiser in their own generation than the sons of light." (Luke 16:8b, R.S.V.)

The group plan likewise enables a church to promote any forward movement. If the workers have established friendly contacts throughout the neighborhood, they can relay information about missions, evangelism, or anything else pertaining to the Kingdom. Wise leaders do not overwork these facilities, which might lose their appeal. Neither do such leaders engage actively in the every-member canvass, at least not in their own areas. How could they carry on the regular group work if they became known as solicitors of money for the church?

An example will show the possibilities for the group promotion of a worthy cause. A church plans to hold services in the main sanctuary every night except Saturday during the week before Easter. The plan calls for two cottage prayer meetings in each geographical unit during the week before Palm Sunday. For these home gatherings on Monday and on Friday evening, the group leaders can make all the plans, locally, and carry them out, perhaps with no assistance from any other group. Hence the church members in each area of the congregation enjoy blessings that would accrue from restoration of John Wesley's class meetings.

In view of all these advantages, and others like them, why does the group system not command itself widely? For at least two reasons. First, it calls for an additional set of church machinery, when church leaders already find it hard to keep the present mechanism oiled and running smoothly. Someone, it may be the church secretary, must take charge of the clearing house. To her must come reports from all the group leaders. From her must go all sorts of information for these friends. In order to carry out her part of the plan, she must have talent, tact, and time. Otherwise the pastor may wonder why he ever added to the machinery another cause for headaches and heartaches.

Another objection relates to the choice of group leaders. Not every church officer knows how to serve as a lay pastor of fifty sheep. Not every friendly woman knows how to call on people in her neighborhood, and help keep the peace within her group. Someone must give time and thought to the selection of the group leaders. Both among men and women the list should include only such persons as love the Lord and His people, one by one. In short, every group leader should have the heart of a shepherd.

In full view of these difficulties, those who have tried the plan believe in it strongly. The larger the church, the more varied the constituency, the more does this way of working foster a family spirit. A group system worthy of the name brings the work and worship of the congregation to the heart of every family, every member, and every adherent. What an opportunity for intensive cultivation of the field!

Suggested Readings

Beaven, Albert W., *Putting the Church on a Full-Time Basis*. New York: Doubleday, Doran & Co., 1928. Chap. X, "The Church Service Corps."

Chapter XIX

The Pastor of the Church School

THE pastor ought to regard the church school as the most important part of the congregational life and work. To the school he should devote more time and attention than to anything else in the way of organization. To the school he should look for support and assistance in reaching every one of the eight goals that concern us throughout this book. Let us think of them once again, and note how each of them relates to the work of the school: evangelism, Christian nurture, household religion, church friendliness, community betterment, national missions, universal brotherhood, and world missions.

So much for the ideal. Now for the facts. In many a parish during the first few decades of the century, the church school seemed to be going backward. At best the picture became disconcerting, and at worst alarming. Recently the attendance at most schools has been improving, partly because of an increased birth rate. For a while many observers felt that if the trend continued the church schools in some cities might become extinct. More conservatively, the Church Federation at Indianapolis reports the findings of a survey in that churchgoing city. Since 1930, according to the Chamber of Commerce, the population of the metropolitan area has increased from 422,666 to 535,000. During the same period enrollment in Protestant church schools had declined 10.3 per cent.[1]

As for the causes, who can tell? Some blame the equipment. More than a few church schools have to struggle along with buildings that embody the old Akron Plan. Nothing could lend itself less to the present idea of departmental work. Others ascribe the low estate of the schools to poor curriculum materials. Hence one of the major denominations has prepared a system of new materials, at a cost comparable to that of promoting world missions. All the while observers have felt the need of teachers more adequately trained and more

[1] For the latter figure see *The Christian Century*, June 23, 1948.

fully devoted to their calling. In these and other respects our educational work must stand comparison with the public schools. When the church school flourished many of the pupils thought of it in comparison with a little white schoolhouse down in the dell. Now only a few congregations can afford equipment, curriculum materials, and teaching facilities comparable to those in the public schools.

On the other hand, the parish leader may face a problem of a different kind. If the Bible school, or the men's class, becomes active and efficient, it may enter into competition with public worship. In fact, the one may become a substitute for the other. Ideally the church school ought to serve as the main source of supply for worshipers of all ages, and as the chief way of recruiting people from the community. Actually few of the boys and girls who attend the church school worship God in the sanctuary. To this problem we shall return, since it affects the future of Protestantism. Once again, if the men's Bible class becomes a going concern, many of those who belong may show little zeal for the public worship of God.

Who can wonder that the pastor becomes discouraged? How can he shepherd two different flocks within the same fold? For all practical purposes, he thinks, the sanctuary and the building for Christian education might as well be located a mile apart, on two sides of a railroad track. "Oh, East is East, and West is West, and never the twain shall meet." In the past somebody has blundered. Perhaps more than one former minister has left the church school to sink or swim, live or die, survive or perish. But let not the present pastor lose heart. He will find the workers in the school, at least the majority of them, ready and eager to engage in teamwork. In time even the most serious of these problems should yield to the right sort of pastoral leadership, and become an opportunity. Meanwhile the situation affords a test of the minister's ability and resourcefulness. What then should a wise man do?

1. At first let him *accept what he finds*. Gradually he can prepare the way for any changes that seem necessary. Meantime he can win the friendship of the officers and teachers. If he finds workers who love the Lord, love the Book, love their pupils, and love to teach, he can become reconciled to many things that fall short of perfection.

We think of the church school too largely in terms of the public schools. We ought to make this part of our work distinctly Christian, and that calls for something different from the public school system of today. Why not in every community set up a church school as a model for the public schools?

2. The parish leader should encourage the church officers to *provide adequate equipment*. In some cases this may require the erection of a new building for Christian education. More often the work calls for the improvement of the present quarters. Especially in rooms set apart for little boys and girls, seek after quarters attractive, comfortable, and adequate for teaching. All of this the minister can help to bring about gradually. He should remember, however, that in more than one parish the slump in the church school has come after the change to first-class equipment.

3. Lead the officers to *provide for the school in the church budget*. Ideally the contributions from the school should go to benevolences. Then the budget of the congregation should provide liberally for the running expenses of the school. This the church leaders ought to do gladly, and not grudgingly. Let them secure and keep in first-class condition the best available curriculum materials, songbooks, and other supplies. How else can the church make clear what it thinks of the school?

On the other hand, as we have seen, believers in Christian education may not understand the facts about the budget. They may insist that it allots more money to music than to Christian nurture. They forget that 40 or 50 per cent of all the congregational expenses have to do with Christian education, mainly in the school. Think of the church edifice, the salaries, the expenditures for upkeep and maintenance, with the cost of heat, light, and power. Those critics might as well say that a father gives his teen-age children nothing more than weekly allowances for pocket money, whereas both father and mother love to give their young people everything they need. Then too the right sort of musical program really forms a part of Christian nurture.

4. Still working gradually and indirectly, the minister can help to *introduce new curriculum materials*, and new songbooks. He should give the preference to publications from his own branch of the

Church if they prove worthy. Nowhere else in Christendom, it seems, have we suffered more from cheapness and shoddiness than in outside lesson materials and songbooks for use in training boys and girls to love and serve God.

5. In a church of any size the pastor may persuade the people to *employ a full-time director of Christian education*. Then the officers will face the problem of finding, securing, and retaining such a leader with ability and charm. When times seem prosperous, the demand for such leaders outruns the supply. Many a graduate from seminary or training school does not have maturity and experience enough to direct the educational and social activities of a large church. Fortunately, the various denominations have begun to train young women for this kind of service. They will do much better work after a few years' experience under pastoral supervision. So do not yield to the craze for youth.

6. All the while the pastor should *work through the superintendent*. Or rather, the two should work together, with the superintendent publicly to the fore in matters educational. Gradually the minister can infuse new life and zeal into a discouraged superintendent. Even so, the facts may call for a younger man with a vision. The same applies to some teachers. But as long as a superintendent or a teacher remains in office, the pastor should accept the facts in the case. Ideally he should look on the superintendent as the most important and influential layman in the parish. When the time comes for the election of such a leader, the minister can do much to ensure the choice of a man sent from God.

7. In order to show concern about the school, the pastor should always *be present ahead of time*. He may not tarry in the building throughout the time for instruction. If he greets in person all the officers and teachers as they arrive, he can encourage them to come early. Better still, by presence and interest he can show the boys and girls how much he cares for them and for the school. In a small church, during a vacancy, he may have to serve temporarily as superintendent. Elsewhere for an hour, occasionally, he may have to take the leadership of a department, or teach a class. Ordinarily he can do more good by keeping both hands free. Then he can drop

into any department or group that needs a quiet boost. Fortunately he need not remain through the class session or departmental exercises.

8. At school gatherings and at other times the pastor can *win the friendship of the officers and teachers*. He may feel the need of a teachers' training class, but except as a last resort he should not serve as the instructor. Neither should his wife. They will find it better to wait until the proper leader comes to view. In a city area this kind of training may come through joining with workers from other churches in the community. All the while the local officers and teachers should feel free to consult with their pastor. When they come for advice or encouragement, they should find him thoroughly versed in the theory and practice of their art.

Think of a case from life. In a large school a teacher of six-year-olds came to the minister with a problem. She knew the accepted theories, and wondered why they did not work, especially when she used object lessons. She welcomed the pastor's suggestion that he visit the class next Sunday morning. He came in early, before the work started. To her amazement he left soon after it got under way. She saw encouragement in his smile when he said good-bye to the children and their teacher. Two days later she came by appointment to see him at the conference hour. There she caught a gleam of light that enabled her to become one of the most useful teachers in the primary department.

"Miss Green, quit worrying," he said. "You have good ideas and you make them clear to the boys and girls. Your object lessons interest them, and help to show what you want them to learn. When they come in early, you can see them look around and examine everything you have made ready. Why don't you time those object lessons?"

The teacher studied a minute or two. Then she saw the light. She resolved to keep all the exhibits under cover. She ought to present each of them when she came to the proper stage in the lesson. Better still, as an artist would say, she determined to mix all her colors with brains. She also decided to watch the minister as he taught in the midweek service and elsewhere. In short, she found the pastor ready to help, but not willing to interfere. What if every band of teachers had such a pastoral leader! Note how he led her to solve her own problem. He must have had a seeing eye and a teaching mind!

9. The pastor can hold up this ideal: *elect the staff of the school once a year*. Better still, he can lead to care in selecting the superintendent. Then the superintendent can nominate the other officers and teachers. In a large church he may serve as chairman of the nominating committee for the school. However the plan operates, the minister ought to see that every officer or teacher comes up for election once a year at a stated time. Otherwise the work may suffer from superannuated holdovers. Whenever a seminary professor asks local ministers for problems to use as case studies, he gets more than a few about superintendents and teachers who seem to have outlived their usefulness. Why not encourage rotation in such offices once a year? If so, be sure to re-elect every teacher called of God.

10. Once a year *have a recognition service* for the officers and teachers. Early in the fall, with the corps of workers all complete, set apart an eleven o'clock service in honor of Christian education. Unlike many another special occasion, this one need not become secular. The sermon may come from Dan. 12:3, as it reads in a marginal version: "The teachers shall shine as the brightness of the firmament, and they that turn many to righteousness as the stars for ever and ever." (A.S.V.) Those words hail from anxious and fearful days, more than a little like our own. The topic may be "What God Thinks of Our Teachers."

Such a service may help to put a school on the map. If the pupils, the workers, and the rest of the congregation are to see the importance of this work, the pastor must make ready for the recognition service with all his skill and care. After the message he can have the workers come forward and range themselves before the pulpit, or else around the altar. Then he can lead in a duplicated service of recognition, including a litany of dedication, and a hymn of commitment, such as "Lord, Speak to Me That I May Speak," with the benediction of light (Num. 6:24-26).

11. Help to *put "school" back into the church school*. This proposal calls for still more ability and work on the part of the minister. Gradually he can lead the laymen to plan for an educational insti-

tution worthy of its name. Meanwhile it may attempt to do almost everything but teach. Teaching takes time every Lord's Day. So do opening and closing exercises, with many other things that prevent instruction of the pupils. For this idea in a fuller form see chapter V in *The Educational Work of the Church*, by Nevin C. Harner.

Professor Harner brings out into the open what many of us have long been thinking. Not being experts in the field, we have kept quiet, perhaps too quiet. We welcome his suggestion that for members of the school above twelve years of age there be only ten minutes of worship and forty-five minutes of teaching. In some adult classes the proportion seems to be the other way round. And yet we wonder why many people come only to the school or to morning worship, and not to both. Why do we make the school hour a replica of public worship? Let the school be a school!

12. In a large church *lead to a change in organization*. It may call for a body known as the board of education, or the council of Christian education. This body operates under the official board of the church. The council includes representatives from all the educational interests of the parish, and strives to correlate their activities. Such a plan may call for a children's division, a young people's division, and an adult division. Ideally this last should include the work of the women's association. Actually those friends may insist on remaining separate. For a much fuller discussion, with a diagram, turn again to the book by Professor Harner, chapter III.

These suggestions may not apply to a small church with only one room for religious and social purposes. Even there the minister ought to become an enthusiast for the school. He should look on Christian education as an inseparable part of work for the Kingdom—on a level with evangelism and missions. A Kingdom-minded minister cannot speak or pray without revealing enthusiasm for all these enterprises. Little by little he can lead the church into holy discontent with Lilliputian plans for the most important work in the world. Why attempt to serve God with a one-room cabin in a community where every farmer keeps dairy cows in a better building? Why not erect an edifice to show the community what it means to put God first?

Meanwhile the pastor can serve as the advisory coach of all the teachers and officers in the church school. When Woodrow Wilson went to teach at Wesleyan University he never had played a game of football. Still he coached the team and infused them with his own spirit. George Pierce Baker did much the same with Harvard debating teams. Parodoxical as it may seem, the most important person in the growth of a church school—more important even than the superintendent—may prove to be one who never teaches a class or otherwise seems to lead. As a lover of Christian education the pastor-coach stands on the sidelines and cheers the workers on to many a victory for God.

Suggested Readings

Bower, William C., *Christ and Christian Education.* New York and Nashville: Abingdon-Cokesbury Press, 1943.

Chave, Ernest J., *A Functional Approach to Religious Education.* Chicago: Univ. of Chicago Press, 1947.

Crossland, Wayland, *How to Build Up Your Church School.* New York and Nashville: Abingdon-Cokesbury Press, 1948.

Cummings, Oliver D., *Administering Christian Education in the Local Church.* Philadelphia: The Judson Press, 1936.

Eakin, Mildred M. and Frank, *The Church-School Teacher's Job.* New York: The Macmillan Co., 1949.

Elliott, Harrison S., *Can Religious Education Be Christian?* New York: The Macmillan Co., 1940.

Harner, Nevin C., *The Educational Work of the Church.* New York and Nashville: Abingdon-Cokesbury Press, 1939.

Hockman, William C., *Projected Visual Aids in the Church.* Boston: The Pilgrim Press, 1947.

Murch, James D., *Christian Education and the Local Church.* Cincinnati: The Standard Publishing Co., 1943.

Rogers, W. L., and Vieth, P. H., *Visual Aids in the Church.* Philadelphia: Christian Education Press, 1946.

Sherrill, Lewis J., *The Rise of Christian Education.* New York: The Macmillan Co., 1944.

Slattery, Margaret, *A Primer for Teachers.* New York: Harper & Bros., 1942.

Smith, H. Shelton, *Faith and Nurture.* New York: Charles Scribner's Sons, 1941.

Vieth, Paul H., ed., *The Church and Christian Education.* St. Louis: Bethany Press, 1947. Working bibliographies.

CHAPTER XX

The Other Work with Boys and Girls

IN many a community today the most alarming problem relates to boys and girls. Juvenile delinquency abounds, and the age level has been getting lower. In one state the most recent scandal of the kind involved boys eleven and twelve years of age. All of them came from homes more or less Christian, at least in name. No one of them could plead lack of money as an excuse for committing robbery, and for attempting to commit murder. In view of such facts, by no means rare, lovers of boys and girls have concluded that the home, the church, the public schools, and various other agencies should work together to safeguard and train these men and women of tomorrow.

Here we can think only about the minister and his plans for this kind of leadership. Through personal contacts with boys and girls he can derive many of life's choicest satisfactions. As he watches over their growth in favor with God and men, he should give thanks for a large share in the development of these coming men and women. If some of them go wrong, however, he may ask whether or not he and his workers have done all in their power to shepherd the lambs. Especially among boys out over the community, the minister ought to accept much of the responsibility.

In northern New Jersey a group of ten lads began to assemble a sort of arsenal. Two of them stole, and the others talked continually about committing burglary. Before they got launched on a career of crime, those lads had to appear before the judge. In order to keep them from going to the state reform school, a young pastor intervened. When the judge asked if he would serve as their parole officer for the next three years, the young man may have gulped. Even though none of the boys belonged to his fold, he accepted the responsibility. Now that three years have gone by, he reports that the ten lads have gone straight, and that all but one give promise of becoming useful citizens. Ideally the pastor should have enlisted laymen to serve as big brothers. In this case he had to make a decision almost at once. Then too he knew that the lads wanted him and not laymen of his choosing.

Within every field the work for boys and girls ought to start long before they begin to seem incorrigible. According to *Christian Nurture*, a book to which we have often referred, such pastoral concern ought to start with the birth of a baby, and even before. In the pulpit and everywhere else the minister can hold up Christian ideals about marriage and the home. Directly and indirectly he can lead young married folk to prepare their hearts for the coming of the first little baby. When shall we church folk abandon our hush-hush ways of dealing with an expectant mother and her unborn babe? What could be more holy than a child of the covenant about to be born into a Christian home? As for little ones elsewhere, some of them seem to be damned into the world.

The pastor can do much with young parents. Even in the most worldly-minded home he may discover concern about the little ones. Except among older boys and girls, nowhere will he find a richer field for pastoral evangelism. If two young parents wish to rear their children in ways pleasing to God, both father and mother need to know Christ as personal Saviour and Lord. This type of soul-winning has become known as home evangelism. Often it means that "a little child shall lead them" (Isa. 11:6c). Those prophetic words call for a broader application, about the crisis of our civilization. But that crisis itself has much to do with the home. So if any minister would do his part in remaking the world for which the Redeemer died, let him become like the Lord Jesus, a lover of little boys and girls, and of the parents—both parents.

The pastor can help much by inculcating Christian ideals of the home as the most important spot on earth. He can encourage every wedded pair to set up a family altar on their marriage night, and to have words of grace before every meal. If father and mother, taking turns, pray with a little one at the bedside, both parents need to live all day in the spirit of the prayers at eventide. In addition to all of this at home, boys and girls need other forms of Christian nurture.

THE NURTURE OUTSIDE THE HOME

Every pastor should wish to see the boys and girls at morning worship. He may organize a league of young worshipers, or something of the kind, with awards to everyone who attends throughout the year. Most parish leaders prefer to rely on machinery already in motion, including personal contacts with parents and children. The effectiveness of any work among boys and girls depends far less upon methods [1] than upon love for these young friends, one after another. In public worship the leader should make the hour attractive to boys and girls old enough to attend the public schools. If he can interest and inspire them, especially by encouraging them to reach up for something beyond their grasp, he can help to prevent many a moral shipwreck in years to come.

If boys and girls take part in only one religious service on the Lord's Day, let that one be morning worship in the sanctuary. There let the minister lead them close to the heart of God. Except in a Christian home, nowhere outside the sanctuary can they so surely form lifelong habits of devotion. They should also attend the church school. There they may spend sixty minutes, or even seventy-five. In church they should have to tarry little more than one hour. Between the two services they can have a breathing spell. At the public schools these lads and lasses spend five hours a day, five days in the week, without injury to health or nerves.

The leaders in the sanctuary and the church school ought to make their two hours and a half of God's time even more absorbing than longer hours in the public schools. No one else on earth has such an appealing subject as the friends who introduce boys and girls to "fairest Lord Jesus, ruler of all nature." At one of the largest churches in New York City workers with boys and girls keep them in the edifice for three hours every Sunday morning, though not in the

[1] See my *Preparation of Sermons*, chap. XXI, "The Message for Boys and Girls."

main sanctuary. Such a plan leads them to think of the Christian religion as "the chief concern of mortals here below."

In many churches the program also includes junior and intermediate "Christian Endeavor," perhaps under other names, more alluring. Here again, the value comes from the spirit and the skill of the leaders, not from the labels. The junior society may include boys and girls old enough to attend the grade schools. The intermediate group may consist of young folk old enough for junior high. In either society the leaders should make the programs differ both from the morning service and from the church school. Since the morning service stands for worship, and the church school for teaching, the third hour may call for expression. If so, how can boys and girls express what they have yet to experience? At least they can learn how to voice their desires—both in song and in prayer. They can also repeat in concert golden psalms and hymns, with classic prayers of the Church, such as the well-known collect of Chrysostom.

This kind of group may become the cell out of which will issue church leaders for tomorrow. Thirty-five years ago a young minister went to serve as pastor of a city church down near the river. From brethren who ought to have known better he heard that the work down there had been going back for years, and that the church ought to close its doors. However, he found signs of life and hope, especially among the young people. Under the leadership of a woman who loved them, one by one, a group of teen-age young folk learned to voice ideals by which they would live as men and women. Today that church stands and shines as a beacon light. More than a few of the officers and other leading workers have come from that society. What a blessed way to prevent the abandonment of a church in a community that needs the Gospel!

Conditions may also lead to troops of Boy Scouts and Girl Scouts, with younger bands of Cub Scouts and Brownies. In such a case the work calls for wise leadership. Not every man who likes boys has character and honor enough to serve as their hero. To take an extreme case, the leader may promote homosexuality. More likely he wishes to have week-end hikes that interfere with keeping the Lord's Day and with attendance at Bible school and church. The same holds true with the leader of girls. She ought to have all sorts of charm, and use it for the glory of the God from whom it comes.

With leadership of the right sort any of these groups may call for commendation. In the community as a whole, however, the program at church and school may keep a boy or girl busy almost everywhere except at home. If so, the leaders of community life ought to co-operate with parents in reducing the social load. Then boys and girls could live more at home and escape strain on their nerves. The program might call for fewer hours at the church, and more with mother and father. Why should boys and girls move every week on a merry-go-round not of their own choosing?

For some such reasons a congregation may settle down to a three-point program for boys and girls. The plan may call for morning worship, church school, and junior choir. Under a full-time minister of music these young friends can secure first-class training in choral music. Once a month they can render a special selection at the morning service. For years a plan somewhat similar has operated in the Protestant Episcopal Church, which has drawn many of its clergymen from the ranks of choir boys. The newer way also enlists girls, and provides training for wee tots in a cherub choir. After a while such a program ought to result in a singing church. As in everything else about church work, the value depends largely upon the leader of the musical training, and upon the adult support he receives.

THE PASTOR'S CLASS

At first glance the program of choir work may seem to break down just when boys feel tempted to give up church. When their voices begin to break, and they become self-conscious, they must drop out of the junior choir. At this juncture, or else before, the plans may call for a pastor's class, which often goes under the heading of a communicants' class. The former name seems preferable; it shows that the pastor wishes to become well acquainted with these young friends, whereas the longer name would suggest that he required them all to unite with the church. He and the lay officers hope that the class will lead to such applications. In each case the decision ought to come at the end of the class sessions, and not at the outset. Before any boy decides to join the church, he ought to feel sure of personal faith in the Lord Jesus Christ. In the heart of a decent lad such a discovery may come without such a cataclysm as rent the soul of the jailer at Philippi.

In a large church the numbers of boys and girls may call for two classes of the same general age. If so, the pastor may deal with the boys, and his wife with the girls, who average a year younger. If the staff includes a director of Christian education, or an assistant pastor, either of them may conduct such a class. But the senior minister should prefer to do this work himself. At the end of a year or a lifetime he may discover that nothing on earth has brought more abiding satisfaction than the privilege of leading boys and girls to discover in Christ their Saviour and King.

Ideally the pastor's instruction ought to extend over two or three years. The classes should continue from the opening of the public schools in the fall to their closing in the late spring, with the customary holiday periods. Some such schedule obtains in certain branches of the Church, especially in those that spring from Holland, Germany, and the Scandinavian countries. In most of our churches, unfortunately, the minister has taken on so much other work that he must rest content with classes running eight or ten weeks. The period usually comes during Lent, so as to culminate at Palm Sunday. Then for the first time the boys and girls can enroll publicly under the banner of King Jesus. Pastors here and there run classes, also, during the autumn, so as to have an ingathering at Christmas time.

If the minister wishes the pupils to regard the class as important, he should prepare as carefully as for the pulpit. After the first year or two he may fall into a rut, but if he prepares afresh every season, week by week, he can deal with the same old truths in novel ways. He should make attendance on the class cost something, though not too much. He may hold it on Friday at four o'clock, instead of during the time for the church school. In a rural district he may teach on Saturday afternoon when parents come to shop at the village center. He may require each boy or girl to purchase a book that costs twenty cents, and to prepare work as assigned. All of these details he can settle after conference with the lay workers who know most about boys and girls.

The class work should relate to Christ and His Church, with stress upon the sacraments. The instruction ought also to include some Christian ethics. In his epistles, after Paul has shown the truth about Christ and the Church, he stresses the resulting duties. Today no one of us would make ethics a substitute for doctrine, or doing good an alternative to faith. But neither should we ignore what the New Testament teaches about Christian duty. In view of the facts about juvenile delinquency, with widespread immorality, the times call for teaching about the way young Christians should live in a world full of filth. When at length the instruction leads to confirmation, perhaps under another name, the ceremony ought to stand for Christian belief and Christian conduct, because of Christ-filled hearts.

What Charles E. Jefferson has written about a man's pulpit work should also apply to his teaching of boys and girls year after year: "Measure your success as preachers not by the size of your congregation, which may after all be only a huge ecclesiastical jellyfish, drifting aimlessly and uselessly through the social sea, but by the stature and girth of the manhood which you develop in individual believers, by the orderliness and serviceableness and Christlikeness of the separate disciples whom you build into the Christian brotherhood."[2]

Suggested Readings

Applegarth, Margaret T., *Missionary Stories for Boys and Girls*. New York: Harper & Bros., 1948.

Chaplin, Dora P., *Children and Religion*. New York: Charles Scribner's Sons, 1948.

de Schweinitz, Karl, *Growing Up*. New York: The Macmillan Co., 1928.

Eakin, Mildred and Frank, *The Pastor and the Children*. New York: The Macmillan Co., 1947.

Ellenwood, James L., *Just and Durable Parents*. New York: Charles Scribner's Sons, 1948.

[2] *The Building of the Church* (New York: The Macmillan Co., 1913), p. 115.

Hopkirk, Howard W., *Institutions Serving Children*. New York: Russell Sage Foundation, 1944.

Manwell, E. M., and Fahs, S. B. C., *Consider the Children—How They Grow*. Boston: Beacon Press, 1940.

Norsworthy, Naomi, and Whitley, M. T., *Psychology of Childhood*. New York: The Macmillan Co., 1938.

Sherrill, Lewis J., *The Opening Doors of Childhood*. New York: The Macmillan Co., 1939.

Sweet, Herman J., *Opening the Door for God*. Philadelphia: The Westminster Press, 1943.

Thorpe, Louis P., *Child Psychology and Development*. New York: Ronald Press, 1941. Secular.

CHAPTER XXI

The Program for the Young People

I N many a church today the officers feel concerned about the young people's problem. If the pulpit becomes vacant the congregation may demand a young minister, in the hope that he will enlist young people. The situation calls for a leader young at heart, if not in years. Not every mature pastor knows how to reach young people, but neither does every young minister know how to lead in such work. What a problem! Or rather, what an opporunity!

A case will bring to view some of the principles. In a small town of central Ohio the United Brethren church had the best young people's work in that part of the state. The president of the Church Federation in Columbus arranged for the minister to tell city pastors the secret of his effectiveness with young people. In the address he said that he could not claim the credit. He gave it all to the young people themselves. As a young man he had come to the field and found this part of the organization at a low ebb. He knew little about young people's work technically. But he discovered that he needed most of all to love them, trust them, and, under the right sort of lay leadership, let them do much as they pleased.

Every pastor ought to learn some such lesson. Treat young people as people, not as problems. Deal with a young man as a man, not as a blushing boy. Look on a young woman as a woman, not as a giggling girl. Remember your own plight as a teen-age lad, striving, as the Apostle says, to put away childish things. How did you feel? Shy and self-conscious! What did you want? To be treated as an adult and not as a child! Think of the way our Lord dealt with Peter. Another type of leader would have chided him for childishness, but the Lord expected him to act like a man. Largely through such expectancy the Master transformed young Simon into a leader with power.

This kind of love in action goes under the name of sympathy, or empathy. At a divinity school the professor of Christian education asked each member of an elective class to write a paper on the subject: "What to Tell a Teen-Age Group about Jesus." Most of the students wrote about His manliness, His courage, and so on. A more mature member of the class, a mother of growing boys, handed in a paper about Christ's sympathy with young people. The professor gave her an "A" and had her read the paper before the class. At home her husband later asked why she had chosen that subject, and she replied: "When you reached the age of seventeen what did you want from people at church? Loving sympathy! You felt that nobody understood you, or cared for you. So did I feel that way. How do we older people treat teen-age boys and girls? We laugh at their attempts to act like men and women. Think of Booth Tarkington's *Seventeen!* No, think about Jesus! When once you get a group of young Christians to know that He cares, you can lead them to do anything the Lord wishes. Why do we talk about our own young people as a problem? We older folk constitute the problem; they provide the opportunity."

That mother never has looked on her sons as a problem. She has seen one after another go into the ministry or other full-time Christian service. Some of us men need such practical wisdom. At a national gathering of a large denomination male speakers repeatedly referred to Negroes, and always with something praiseworthy. Thank God! Those friends need the kind of sympathy they receive from the Lord's people, whether South or North. But whenever a platform speaker referred to young people from our own homes and churches, he referred to them as a problem. If our Lord had dealt that way with Peter, would he later have preached at Pentecost?

THE VARIETY OF METHODS

The Christian philosophy about young people works in various ways, according to the field. In another congregation of central Ohio the pastor found the teen-age group indifferent to the church school and the sanctuary. They looked on the whole concern as "the old folks' church." The forty-five members of the governing boards, all men, included not a person less than forty years of age, with the average nearer sixty. When the officers awoke to the seriousness of the problem they determined to treat their young people as honored members of the Lord's household. As soon as feasible the "church fathers" began to put younger persons in posts of leadership. In still other ways those church leaders showed how much they thought of their young people. In time that problem resolved itself into an opportunity with all sorts of fascination.

Sometimes a church demands too much from young folk in the way of attending meetings. In other days many of them would come to church school and morning worship, Christian Endeavor and evening service. In an occasional parish such a program still works. Young people who occupy themselves in other ways all week, and feel lonesome on the Lord's Day, may enjoy a sort of merry-go-round, including a free-for-all singspiration after the evening service. Let no one make light of such a program. Out in Hollywood, with all its reputed worldliness, a large congregation enlists several hundred young people for all sorts of religious activities on the Lord's Day and throughout the week. This church sends scores of its young men and women into the ministry and other forms of full-time Christian service.

A less ambitious program calls for emphasis on either the morning or the evening of the Lord's Day, not on both. If some of us had to choose, we should prefer the former, including the Sunday school and morning worship. If young people form the habit of regular, enthusiastic attendance at the morning service, they will likely continue active in church life all their years. But if not, then not! Where the Sunday school deserves its name, and does not become a replica of morning worship, young folk ought to enjoy both hours. At the morning service the program would call for uplift and inspiration, both in the other parts of the worship and in the preaching. Inspiration here does not mean froth, or a string of anecdotal illustrations. Do not treat young people as morons.

More than a few ministers prefer a procedure almost the reverse. The stress falls on the young people's service in the evening, and on the hour of worship that follows. If this program works effectively, it ought to continue. But in most fields the plan meets with difficulties. The evening service, or vespers, may have gone on the rocks, and the young people's meeting into the doldrums. This word means "a state of listlessness, or ennui, or tedium." In such a case the pastor and his advisers may need to take stock before revising their plans. If the situation calls for a young people's gathering on Sunday evening, be sure to make it go.

The facts locally may call for a change of organization. At the turn of the century such groups usually belonged to the Christian Endeavor Society. If this plan still commends itself to the young people of a church, the minister ought to feel grateful. As a coach he should never break up a winning team. Theoretically an interdenominational movement has much in its favor. It tends to keep the home society from becoming provincial and self-centered. But if this plan has lost its novelty and appeal, why not try another system? This calls for affiliation with societies in the same branch of the Church. At first glance this may look like going backwards, but why should it seem more selfish for young people to organize denominationally than for the women's missionary society?

The effectiveness of the young people's work depends far less on the name and the affiliation than on the leadership and on the program. In many societies the sort of pap that used to serve has ceased to attract young people with brains and force. In order to insure a program with activities worthy of young people who wish to think, secure as advisers a young man and his wife with charm and tact, and a love for young folk. These lay leaders can guide the young people in sending delegates to conferences in summer, and in planning worth-while meetings all the rest of the year. In almost every denomination the publishing house affords a wealth of literature. Among Congregationalists, for instance, the Pilgrim Press at Boston sends out attractive literature for young people. The local leaders must know how to use literature in making a program and in planning meetings.

Experience has shown the wisdom of keeping young folk of high-school age in a group by themselves. They have difficulties and needs more or less their own. If at times they seem indifferent to the call of the church, remember the claims of the public schools. High-school teachers require all sorts of homework, some of which young people postpone till the weekend, which may mean Sunday night. As for social diversions, not to say distractions, they abound all week. Hence it may prove hard to gain the attention of these teen-age friends. If they keep coming to the Sunday school and morning worship, that may be all their parents deem expedient. Meanwhile these men and women of tomorrow need the friendly oversight of both church and pastor. Nobody but God knows how many temptations young people face these days.

Young folk beyond high-school age have different needs. Especially in a downtown church, these friends between the ages of eighteen and twenty-five may feel lonesome, and exposed to all sorts of allurements. In lieu of spacious homes they must survive in cramped quarters. At church they need a home away from home, with opportunities to meet young people of both sexes. In days of peace the church ought to do for young folk what it did for soldiers and sailors during the war.

In a downtown church at Richmond, Virginia, such conditions led to a young people's forum, over which the minister presided. At the sanctuary earlier in the afternoon he conducted a vesper service for people of all ages. In the church house at six o'clock the young people took charge for the next two hours. They let some of the older folk attend and partake of light refreshments, which the young people served at cost. But during the forum proper every person beyond twenty-five years of age had to sit in the balcony and refrain from speaking. In this case older folk could be "seen but not heard."

The young people themselves suggested most of the subjects and took part freely in discussions under the leadership of the pastor. The subjects ranged over wide areas, with the main stress on doctrine and on ethics. One week they would consider the Christian attitude toward war, or else the relations between the two sexes. The next week they might deal with the meaning of doubt, the use of Sunday, or the problem of race relations. If they became deeply concerned about an issue, they might vote to continue the discussion for another meeting or two. Needless to say, this undertaking called for a minister with ability, resourcefulness, and a touch of humor. In the case before us the attendance averaged more than two hundred young people. The meetings ran through the main part of the year. In the South few leaders would dare to continue such a program through the summer, unless the young people could assemble on the church roof.

Over in London, at the City Temple, Leslie D. Weatherhead sponsored a still more ambitious program.[1] Before the church building was destroyed by bombs the attendance ran as high as four hundred young people. The aim, frankly and openly, was to secure and deepen communion with God in Christ. A glance at the list of subjects would show that the appeal did not come from the sort of inane "inspiration" that has sometimes marked young people's meetings nearer home. We can pay our young people no higher tribute than to assume that they wish to deal with difficult subjects in a Christian spirit.

In that Friday evening fellowship at City Temple the question at times would be devotional. For example, "When you pray, 'Be with me, Lord, today,' what do you really expect to happen? Does it happen? If not, why?" Here opens up a vista of God's Providence. What an opportunity for bringing out the relation between doctrine and experience!

Again the group would take up a theme directly theological. For six weeks they discussed this question: "How can the death of Christ two thousand years ago have relevance for our lives now?" At other times the discussion would relate to a perplexing text, a problem of biblical interpretation, or the meaning of inspiration. Again the group would consider the opposition a young man meets when his friends find out he is a Christian.

Successive meetings followed a simple order. The gathering would begin with a few moments of silence and a brief prayer, led by the pastor. Then he would open up the subject suggestively, pointing out certain lines of thought, but not answering any question he raised.

[1] See *This is the Victory* (New York and Nashville: Abingdon-Cokesbury Press, 1941), pp. 260-62.

Soon the young people would divide into seventeen groups, averaging twenty persons or more. Without seeming bossy each group leader would keep the discussion in line with the topic. The best leader, as a rule, proved to be shy rather than talkative. Such a person would make a good pastor, able to listen with appreciation, and eager to bring out the best in everybody else.

During the meeting of a section, the scribe would take down the findings, but not the questions. His work called for ability to select the significant and omit the trivial. In large measure the value of each group depended on the skill and the tact of the leader and the scribe. Naturally every group needed a substitute convener, with an assistant scribe. According to the account at hand, the fun began later in the evening, when the young people came together and started to discuss the findings of the various groups. All of this must have required generalship on the part of the presiding minister.

In view of a problem soon to come before us, we ought to note another aspect of the London plan. In this young people's work, as in everything else at City Temple, the leader of any activity must be a full-fledged member of the church. This means a person who has given the officers credible evidence of a personal Christian experience. Work among young people ought to depend on Christian leaders, and move on a Christian level. Within these limits Dr. Weatherhead thinks that young people should feel free to discuss any kind of subject, if sufficiently large, interesting, and profitable today. Whatever the topic, they should approach it from a point of view distinctly Christian.

In view of all these facts, what shall the parish minister conclude? In young people's work elsewhere he can see much of value. But before he begins to think about adopting such ways and means at home, let him feel sure about the facts locally. Then he and the lay advisers can begin to consider ways and means. Among the various proposals thus far they may select here and there. No one standardized plan can lead to a prefabricated structure adapted to the needs of young people in any church. On the contrary, the pastor who loves them can guide in planning how to solve their problems in a way pleasing to Christ.

THE QUESTION ABOUT DANCING

Before a pastor has served long in a field he may face the question: "Shall we permit dancing in the church parlors?" The issue may assume one of two forms, which call for different answers. In one case the young people already dance on the church premises. Another issue of the same kind relates to card parties, with various devices known as petty gambling. This last problem, however, likely concerns mature women rather than young people. All these matters remind us that in many a church today ethical issues loom larger than doctrinal matters.

If the young people already dance in the church parlors, the pastor may deem it wise to say and do nothing, at least for the present. However, he should lead the officers to forbid any form of indecent dancing, or gambling. All of this the parties concerned should accept in the spirit of loyalty. But many people in the church these days do not think of dancing itself as necessarily evil. If the minister does not agree with the prevailing opinions and practices in such a field, he should not become the pastor. However, if he must accept the appointment, he ought to proceed cautiously as a reformer.

In a Protestant church not even the minister ought to serve as parish pope. What right has he to decide whether or not young people shall dance at home and elsewhere, and whether or not women shall play cards? According to Arthur J. Gossip: "It is seldom that a man has the right to lay it down in the pulpit that on a debatable question of the day he has the mind of Christ, and that whoso differs from him parts with the Master." [2]

In most parishes today young people never have danced on the church premises. If so, the pastor may keep the matter from becoming an issue. If it arose, he might have to take a stand, and that publicly. But if he loves the young people, and if they love him, he can keep the matter out of court. When they come to him before they present a petition to the official board, he can persuade these young friends to wait awhile. If, occasionally, some of them dance in the church parlors without permission, he need not counsel drastic action. In a

[2] *In Christ's Stead* (New York: George H. Doran Co., 1925), p. 36.

certain sense, the church was made for young people, and not young people for the church.

A wise minister does not preach about the matter, but he should pray about it in secret. Lovingly and cheerfully, when with young friends, he can explain the spirituality of the church, and the holiness of the building. If they ask about the harm in dancing where they feel free to engage in various games, he may tell them, "It is hard to put your finger on what makes a matter right or wrong. One thing I know: If we authorized such dancing we should lose the respect of people in the community whose esteem we value highly. Also, we could not appeal to other people of that kind when they moved to town."

Some of the young people themselves do not believe in such a use of church premises. They notice that church dancing on Saturday night does not attract young people to worship on Sunday morning, or make them feel an interest in any religious program. About all of these matters opinions differ, sometimes sharply. But anyone who visits many churches and watches their influence will find that few of our ministers and missionaries come from congregations that permit dancing in church parlors.

As with other matters of right and wrong, this one springs from roots unseen. If in any church the young people want to dance in the church-school building, the minister and other officers may ask each other: "Wherein have we failed? Why have we not trained our sons and daughters to believe in the spirituality of the church? Have we provided them with all the opportunities they need for social enjoyment?" If any minister finds the answer to such questions, he can change this young people's problem into an opportunity for service.

THE ROOTS OF THE MATTER

Now let us dig down in quest of the roots. We have been looking at the surface of the problem, and thinking about it from the standpoint of prudence. At times we may have seemed to keep fiddling while Rome burns. Really we have been getting our bearings. What shall we conclude about the remedies for such ills? What do our young people need? In sooth, what do they not need, in the name of Him who toiled as the young Carpenter of Nazareth, and later enlisted as leaders young men of promise? [3]

Our young folk have grown up in a generation cursed by global wars. They dread the outbreak of a still more hellish conflagration. More than a few seem determined to enjoy their fling before the curtain falls. Some have yielded to cynicism and despair. Countless other young folk, sincere and high-minded, know not what to believe, whom to follow, or how to live. They mull about in a state of unrest and ferment, of which their elders may not dream. In many a circle a happy young man or woman who can find? And yet we prate about youth as being free from cares and fears!

Unfortunately the youth movement in our time has developed outside the churches. In Germany, Italy, and Russia, after World War I, leaders of the movement either ignored the Christian Church, or else plotted her ruin. In Britain and in the United States the movement now finds expression almost everywhere else more than in the church. In college and university, for example, many young folk oscillate between irresponsible mirth and cynical despair. What do they need? No cheap and easy panacea will reach and cure such deep-seated ills. They need God! "Is there no balm in Gilead? Is there no physician there? Why then is not the health of the daughter of my people recovered?" (Jer. 8:22.)

In God's will these disillusioned young folk should find William James's "moral equivalent of war." They need what Josiah Royce has termed *The Philosophy of Loyalty*.[4] His volume looks on religion and life as the "will to believe in something eternal, and to express that belief in the practical life of a human being." "Loyalty is never [mere] emotion." It means "the willing and practical and thorough-going devotion of a person to a cause," as that cause is embodied in a leader. In five different ways this description of loyalty lends itself to our thinking about the needs of young people both today and tomorrow. They ought to have:

[3] The next two paragraphs owe much to addresses at Montreat, N. C., by Bishop Fred P. Corson of The Methodist Church.

[4] New York: The Macmillan Co., 1908, pp. 17, 357.

1. *A cause.* Many a young man or woman cries out in desperation: "Give me a cause worth living for, and worth dying for!" The supreme Lover of young people replies: "Seek ye first the Kingdom of God." In terms of ethics, not eschatology, He means doing the will of God, and seeking to have it done, here on earth as it is done in heaven. According to Paul, our chief interpreter of Christ's teachings, the Kingdom of God means the reign of "righteousness, peace, and joy in the Holy Spirit" (Rom. 14:17*b*). Hence the Kingdom includes all things good and high that young people ought to strive after here below. In time they should also learn to think eschatologically.

Locally the Kingdom ought to stand embodied in the church and its pastor. No one institution or person can claim a monopoly over the doing of God's will in the community. Still we can think of the Kingdom, locally, in terms of the church and its minister. In view of such an ideal the pastor and the lay officers may have to do some ecclesiastical housecleaning. Every church needs something of the kind at least once a year. Does the program lead young people to look at the church as the center of all their hopes and dreams? The women of the congregation have taken missions as their special concern, and the men ought to take evangelism, or trusteeship. Do the young people, also, look on the church as the focal point of all their Christian idealism? If not, why not? Let the Kingdom become their cause!

2. *A leader.* In our day young folk yearn for a leader in action, rather than a philosophy of life. Both in Europe and in America they have risen up to follow every leader whom they have trusted. Often they have met with disillusionment. They have seen idols crash, with feet of clay. To whom then shall they turn? To the Lord Jesus Christ, supreme Lover of young people and of the Church. In Him alone they can see the fulfillment of their ideals. In Him too they can find the authority they crave. Today as in Galilee of old the Lord of Life speaks to young men and women: "All authority in heaven and earth has been given to me. Go therefore" (Matt. 28:18*b*, R.S.V.).

At the church these lovers of heroes and hero worship ought to see their ideals embodied in the pastor and his wife. In these two friends young folk ought to behold, not busyness and fussiness about machinery and methods, but radiant personalities that show the meaning of Christianity today. Even if no longer young in years these two church leaders ought to keep young at heart. In the examples given in this chapter so far, not a pastoral leader of young people could have qualified as young. On a broader scale, over in Europe not a secular leader of young people began to be so until he had reached middle age. Why then do we insist that a church secure a leader with little or no experience? Why not find one who has already excelled and still keeps young at heart?

3. *A teacher.* In order to prove worthy of the Kingdom, and of Christ as Leader, young people must have instruction. Some of them already battle with doubts,[5] and others will do so before long. Every one of them needs to stand up for what he believes. "Always be prepared to make a defense to anyone who calls you to account for the hope that is in you, yet do it with gentleness and reverence." (I Pet. 3:15, R.S.V.) On the other hand, if we let young folk drift along, we may have another generation of religious illiterates.

Not only do they need to know the Bible, and how to use it in everyday living. They ought also to know the meaning of the Christian Church, with something about its growth. Otherwise, when a young man or woman falls in love with a Roman Catholic, the Protestant will appear to poor advantage. Why do we trouble about such "minor concerns" when the world faces critical issues? Because a marriage of this kind often ends in a fiasco. How can the Kingdom of God come in a household where husband and wife differ about their faith and the rearing of their children?[6] Our Lord never looked on marriage as a minor matter.

4. *A Master.* When young people unite with the church they should understand what it means in terms of self-discipline. The Church of Christ stands for purity between the sexes, for self-control in the use of God-given energies, and for self-denial when enjoyment of things not wrong in themselves would interfere with the largest

[5] See Henry van Dyke, *The Gospel for an Age of Doubt* (New York: The Macmillan Co., 1907).

[6] See *If I Marry a Catholic,* a pamphlet by Leland F. Wood (New York: The Federal Council of Churches of Christ in America, 1945).

possible contribution to the Kingdom. The home church should lead young people in a crusade for a better community, a better country, and a better world. We older folk should appeal to their strength, not to their weakness. In the name of Christ let us ask them for large things, and hard—for self-discipline and self-sacrifice, in the spirit of the Cross.

Young people know the meaning of giving up pleasure in order to win athletic prizes. Some of them have read *My Life Story*, by Joe Louis,[7] perhaps the ablest heavyweight fighter of all time. During the depression the Louis family in Detroit went on relief. When young Joe first began to earn money in the ring, he sent the Federal Government a check for $269, a sum that must have seemed enormous to him and his mother. He knew that she had worried about having been on relief. To win that money, in what seems to us a brutal way, he had to deny himself. He says that a fighter in training cannot play baseball, or even golf; keep late hours; ride a horse; drink, smoke, overeat ("The more work your stomach has to do, the less the rest of your body wants to do"), eat hot dogs, or anything else hard to digest.

In contending for Christ how can any young person set lower standards than those of a prize fighter whose ways sometimes appear not Christian? Negatively, the rules for a young Christian may differ from those of Joe Louis. Positively, the Lord Jesus calls for the worthy use of every God-given power and resource. As with an older person, the Christian regime calls for "making the most of the time, because the days are evil" (Eph. 5:16, R.S.V.). Hence the Apostle counseled young Timothy: "Take your share of suffering, as a good soldier of Christ Jesus" (II Tim. 2:3, R.S.V.). All of this a young Christian ought to do, "not by constraint, but willingly." Strange as it may seem to outsiders, a young believer can find all sorts of satisfaction in denying himself, taking up his cross daily, and following the Christ of Calvary (Luke 9:23).

5. *Enlistment.* In the home parish some of the ablest young people should enlist for full-time Christian service, as ministers, missionaries,

[7] New York: Duell, Sloan & Pearce, 1947, pp. 16, 104-5.

or wives of such workers. The majority will hear the call of God to engage in "secular pursuits." Thus they will follow the ideals of young Wilfred T. Grenfell in London. At the age of fifty-four he wrote in his autobiography about his Christian experience as a layman:

> Feeble and devious as my own footsteps have been since my decision to follow Jesus Christ, I believe more than ever that this is the only real adventure in life. No step in life do I even compare with that one in permanent satisfaction. I do not feel that it mattered much whether I chose medicine for an occupation, or law, or education, or commerce, to justify my existence by working for a living, as every honest man should do. But if there is any one thing about which I never have any question it is that the decision and adventure to follow the Christ does for a man what nothing else on earth can do. It develops all that makes a man Godlike.[8]

Looking back, think of the Kingdom as the cause, of Christ as the Leader, of the pastor as the mentor, of discipline by the youth himself, and of enlistment for service. What a way to transform a young people's problem into a Christian opportunity! How else could the pastor and his wife use their time more profitably than by leading in such a program?

First of all, therefore, set the young people an example of radiant Christian living in the midst of a busy world. However large the staff of full-time workers, the pastor dare not neglect the young people. However small the congregation, however few the young folk, let him bring them one by one into right relations with the Lord Jesus Christ, and with His Kingdom. What a glorious opportunity!

Suggested Readings

Bro, Margueritte, *Why Church?* New York: The Friendship Press, 1947.
Burkhart, Roy A., *Understanding Youth.* New York: The Abingdon Press, 1938.
Evans, Louis H., *Youth Seeks a Master.* New York: Fleming H. Revell, 1941.
Garrison, Karl C., *The Psychology of Adolescence.* New York: Prentice-Hall, 1940.

[8] *A Labrador Doctor* (Boston: Houghton-Mifflin Co., 1919), p. 429.

Harner, Nevin C., *The Youth Work of the Church*. New York and Nashville: Abingdon-Cokesbury Press, 1942.

Harris, Erdman, *Introduction to Youth*. New York: The Macmillan Co., 1941.

Maus, Cynthia P., *Youth and Creative Living*. New York: R. R. Smith, 1932.

Thom, Douglas A., *Normal Youth and Its Everyday Problems*, New York: D. Appleton-Century Co., 1932.

Wickenden, Arthur C., *Youth Looks at Religion*. New York: Harper & Bros., 1948.

Youth in Action. London: Society for Promoting Christian Knowledge, 1939.

Chapter XXII

The Promotion of World Missions

THE discussion of missionary promotion ought to include much about work among women, and vice versa. Ideally the cause should appeal to men as much as women. Actually the promotion in many a church rests largely with women. At first this may seem unfortunate but soon a pastor learns to thank God for missionary zeal among women. The cause tends to make them world-minded. Hence they look on Christian missions as God's alternative to global wars.

Such women never forget that the promotion of missions, under the guidance of the Spirit, depends mainly on the local church. In many a field this part of the work seems more effective than any other. Think of an inspirational gathering once a month, with a number of mission-study groups also meeting monthly, perhaps oftener. The entire program finds its rallying point in missions. The enthusiasm reaches out to include everything else in the home church, from Scripture reading and united prayer to old-fashioned friendliness and community betterment.

The missionary enterprise might appear under the heading of Christian education. Year after year the denominations send out missionary textbooks and teachers' manuals. The women of any live church become acquainted with world conditions, and with the programs of various denominations, notably their own. The whole enterprise shows how Christian education leads to Christian action, and Christian action increases the thirst for Christian education. If this account seems sketchy, remember that we must deal with such matters only as they concern the minister.

In a normal church the work of the pastor outside the pulpit resembles that of a superintendent in the public schools. The latter has nothing to do with training girls in athletics. But whenever they compete in a public game he sits on the sidelines and cheers them to victory. So the pastor supports the women's missionary work. He never interferes. He feels free to commend, but not to find fault. A wise man lets women leaders and their followers know that he believes in them, and that he thanks God for all they keep doing. He also welcomes any opportunity to confer with those who seek his counsel and support.

An example will show how a missionary-minded pastor can promote the cause without interfering with anyone in office. This man noticed that one of the ablest women in the congregation needed something to do, single-handed. He discovered she did not feel adapted to committee work, but that she would enjoy promoting the use of missionary books. Through the pastor and others she could secure the nucleus of a missionary library, most of it biography. All of this she herself suggested, and the pastor approved. But first he secured the endorsement of the leader in the women's association. Then the lay worker assembled her books.

Erelong the minister saw that his friend kept circulating those volumes among the homes of the parish. In his calling on the sick and on others he saw here and there standard works about Mary Slessor, and Christina Forsyth, Bishop Patteson and Albert Schweitzer. Soon the minister decided to catch up on this part of his own theological training. He found that such reading about missions influenced his prayers and his preaching, with his pastoral work and church planning. From year to year he witnessed an increased budget for missions, and a new concern about volunteering for full-time service. How much of all this he should ascribe to a conference or two with that one worker, heaven alone can tell.

THE PASTOR'S PROMOTION OF MISSIONS

How else can the minister promote the cause of missions? First of all, by saturating his soul with facts, facts, facts, as they have to do with men and women missionaries full of zeal for the Kingdom. Then he will begin to select missionary hymns. Especially when the sermon has little to do with the progress of the Kingdom, he can have the people sing "Hail to the brightness of Zion's glad morning," or "Jesus shall reign where'er the sun."

A minister's love for the world appears also in his prayers. Without turning devotions into homilies, he can guide the people into adoring the God of the whole earth; confessing their sins of failure to love and help their fellow men, near and far; and praying for the coming of the Kingdom throughout every land for which the Saviour died. Whether or not he uses liturgical forms, the man at the altar can order the prayers so that they will have to do with the work of the Kingdom.

In a large church on the West Coast the pastor takes a minute of every morning service to read the names of missionaries on the prayer calendar for the day. Thus he encourages the people to use the calendar in family devotions. Also, without serving as editor and censor of the church bulletin, or newsletter, he can lead to the insertion of interesting items about missionaries near and far. Knowing that the bulletin or newsletter may go to the ends of the earth, he can help to make it missionary-minded. Such promotion calls for skill and care in the use of facts. After reading in the bulletin a missionary item of fifty words, a visitor at a city church handed in a check for a hundred dollars to further the cause in view. If such results appear but seldom, so do missionary items that bring such results.

What about missionary sermons? When a certain young man went out from the seminary, he planned to deliver such a message once a month. But after the second missionary discourse he had to stop. He did not know enough about missionaries, and he had never learned how to prepare such a message. He soon found that laymen did not enjoy his efforts. In fact, they referred to most missionary sermons as dull, tame, and boresome. This kind of pulpit work may do more harm than good. It misrepresents the most thrilling adventure in the world today.

That young minister determined to make all his preaching missionary in spirit. He found that from New Year's Day to the following Christmas he could preach about any subject as it related to the progress of the Kingdom. He began to draw illustrations from missionary biography. Without using such facts profusely, he could interest the boys and girls who attended morning worship. Instead of dealing with missions as something off by itself, of interest only to women, he showed that the cause concerned every man in God's House. Through facts about Grenfell and Schweitzer, Kagawa and Sadhu Sundar Singh, the pastor appealed to the young folk. What a field for pulpit work about heroes and hero worship!

If the church program calls for a junior sermon, it affords an opportunity to present facts about missionaries, one at a time. Such a working method appears in a book by Hugh Thompson Kerr, Sr., *Missionary Story-Sermons.*[1] In this kind of message the pastor needs to use imagination. He should put himself in the place of a ten-year-old boy, look at the world through his eyes, and lead him to catch a vision of truth and duty as embodied in a doctor up in Labrador or over in Lambaréné. Such a preacher may follow the custom of Henry van Dyke. As a writer he resolved never to tell a tale without a moral, and never to tag a moral on a tale.

From time to time a minister ought also to preach a full-length sermon about missions.[2] How else could he present many parts of the Bible, especially the Book of Jonah and the Book of the Acts? In central Indiana a visiting brother brought such a message on the Lord's Day before March 15. Near the end of the sermon he drew out blanks for the past year's income tax return. Pointing to the section concerning gifts not to exceed 15 per cent, he said: "If you believe in world missions, show your faith by your works. Write out a check in keeping with your income last year." That afternoon the chairman of the financial board, who never had given a penny to missions abroad, made up part of the arrears by sending a missionary check for $5,000. As a rule, however, numerical returns appear gradually and in small amounts.

The minister can promote this cause during his work as a pastor. For example, early in the summer he learns that one of the lay officers has begun to convalesce after an attack of measles. From the physician the minister secures permission to call on the layman and chat with him out in the garden. Up until this time the pastor has not been able to arouse this man's concern about missions. In fact, the two have not become well enough acquainted to look on each other as friends.

[1] New York, Fleming H. Revell Co., 1915.
[2] See my *Planning a Year's Pulpit Work*, pp. 181-84.

Hence the minister determines to see this layman every weekday after the other pastoral visits. Largely because of these informal chats, and the layman's reading that then began, he became an enthusiast for missions at home and abroad. A real case!

Gradually a missionary-minded pastor can lead the church officers to share his enthusiasm. He may have little difficulty with the men who feel responsible for the spiritual interests of the church. But he may have to labor patiently and tactfully with those who manage the temporal affairs. In terms of government, these men might rank as isolationists. Through their womenfolk at home, and the boys and girls as they become enthusiastic about God's work in the world, even the most hard-headed and hard-boiled officers may begin to share the minister's enthusiasm. Few men who love the Lord can resist the climate of a church where the pastor and his teammates have a program for making the congregation missionary-minded.

Any such program ought to include the church school. As we have seen, all the offerings should go to missions at home and abroad. Then the support of the church school becomes a part of the church budget. With the right sort of teachers and officers, the boys and girls will soon begin to think of the Kingdom enterprise as the way the Lord works in a world where millions of little ones never have heard His name. Now that the public school, the radio, and the newspaper have taught boys and girls to think about every part of God's one world, the church school can capitalize on this growing concern about geography and international affairs.

For example, ever since the outbreak of World War II many a household has felt concerned about the South Pacific. In the church school young folk and others can learn about James Chalmers. Why did he go out from Scotland to New Guinea, and later die there as a martyr? Because as a lad in the church school at Inveraray he had learned about missions, and about the needs of cannibal tribes in the South Pacific. From that time to this, streams of life have been flowing from missionary-minded Sunday schools, where boys and girls have learned to pray for workers in the South Pacific. "The thoughts of men are widened with the process of the suns."

In like manner the men's brotherhood and the young people's

society should become missionary-minded. Without some Christian cause beyond itself, a young people's group may become self-centered. The meetings for uplift may consist largely in exhortations to each other, or in lamentations about the small attendance. But if the group assumes the support of a missionary in Africa or India, new life will come from beyond the seas. The society will begin sending delegates to summer conferences. As soon as the young people become mature enough to hold church office, they will support the pastor in making the program of the entire congregation missionary-minded.

Such a program calls for a school of missions every twelve months. The season of the year ought to depend on local conditions. In most cases the logical period comes after Easter. Earlier in the year, perhaps after Thanksgiving, the church has been stressing steward-ship. Between Christmas and Easter everyone has been thinking about evangelism. Now the time has come for still another Christian em-phasis. Both the new members and those of long standing need to learn about the adventure of missions. Indeed, they should regard evange-lism and missions as inseparable, much as they think of light and warmth as proceeding from the same sun.

After the initial school of missions the leaders have an entire year to make ready for a more effective school a year later. In all such planning the missionary committee of the official board should take the initiative, but the leaders of the women's society may do the real work. In conference with the pastor these friends need to decide which of two plans they will follow. One leads to an intensive effort throughout the evenings of a single week, except on Saturday. The other plan calls for a missionary gathering once a week, perhaps on Wednesday, for six or eight weeks in succession. In most places leaders find it easier to maintain and increase enthusiasm for one week than for two, and for six Wednesday evenings than for eight or ten.

Each way of working has its advantages and its advocates. In any church the leaders ought to adopt one plan or the other, instead of shifting back and forth. However, they may look on the first year as experimental. After the initial school the leaders can decide on a certain plan, more or less permanent. Then the improvement from year to year will come through more skillful preparation in the light of experience. If the school runs six evenings the same week, beginning on a Sunday, or six Wednesdays in succession, a different group in the congregation may volunteer to serve a supper at cost each evening, except on the Lord's Day. In such a case the schedule may run as below. If those in charge think it wise to have a brief address, they can lengthen the period for the opening devotions, and perhaps omit the get-together time near the end.

> Fellowship supper 6:00-7:30
> Devotional period.................... 7:30-7:45
> Class sessions........................ 7:45-8:30
> Findings conference 8:30-9:00

The value of the school depends largely upon the ability, the preparation, and the charm of the teachers. Hence the committee may deem it wise to hold only a few classes. If they count on an enrollment of a hundred, or perhaps a dozen more, the leaders may offer only four classes. One of them may deal with missions abroad, a second with missions at home, a third with stewardship, and a fourth with missionary heroes. This last group may consist exclusively of young people. The other courses stand open for election. If the teachers all seem gifted and popular, the three adult courses should enroll numbers approximately equal. Then the teachers have classes large enough to generate enthusiasm and small enough to permit discussion.

When at length the congregational year has gone by, what will the minister remember most pleasantly? Nothing except evangelism and the pastor's class may bulk so large as the school of missions. For that, and for all the rest of the promotion work, the minister will give much credit to the lay leaders, and all the glory to God.

Suggested Readings

Carver, Wm. O., *The Bible a Missionary Message*. New York: Fleming H. Revell Co., 1921.

Corey, Stephen J., *The Preacher and His Missionary Message*. Nashville: Cokesbury Press, 1930.

Fleming, Daniel J., *Bringing Our World Together.* New York: Charles Scribner's Sons, 1946.

Glover, Robt. H., *The Biblical Basis of Missions.* Los Angeles: Bible House, 1946.

Harner, Nevin C., and Baker, D. D., *Missionary Education in Your Church.* New York: Missionary Education Movement, 1942.

Latourette, Kenneth S., *The Christian Outlook.* New York: Harper & Bros., 1948.

Laubach, Frank, *Teaching the World to Read.* New York: Friendship Press, 1947.

Montgomery, Helen B., *The Preaching Value of Missions.* Philadelphia: The Judson Press, 1931.

Mott, John R., *The Larger Evangelism.* New York and Nashville: Abingdon-Cokesbury Press, 1944.

Sailer, T. H. P., *How to Lead an Adult Missionary Discussion Group.* New York: The Friendship Press. 16 pp.

Soper, Edmund D., *The Philosophy of the Christian World Mission.* New York and Nashville: Abingdon-Cokesbury Press, 1943.

Van Dusen, Henry P., *They Found the Church There.* New York: Charles Scribner's Sons, 1947.

Van Kirk, Walter W., *Christian Global Strategy.* New York: Willett, Clark & Co., 1945.

Chapter XXIII

The Activities Among the Women

THE work among women may bring the pastor heartsease or headaches. The choice lies mainly with him and his wife. If they adopt a friendly attitude, without seeming bossy, he may rely upon the women for more assistance than from any other group. On the other hand, if he and his wife, or either of them, attempted to boss women workers, more than a few might rebel. Under God, harmony and effectiveness depend on the ability of the minister and his wife to win and hold the friendship of women. Ideally he should thank God because these women "have labored side by side with me in the gospel" (Phil. 4:3*b*, R.S.V.).

The causes of thanksgiving lie near at hand. Many church women have more time and ability for such work than their pastors can utilize. Also, more than a few have objectives in line with the program of the church. In almost every congregation organized work among women has to do with missions, friendliness, and stewardship. Neither among men nor young people, as a rule, do these objectives stand out so clearly and boldly as among women. Partly for this reason, in an average church the work among women goes forward more surely and steadily from year to year than that of any other group.

In various churches the work among women proceeds under different names and functions in different ways. In a certain field a young pastor found he could rely most surely on one of the women's Bible classes. In the next church he got most help from the women's missionary society. In a third congregation he might have depended chiefly on the women's guild. Of course he tried to treat all the women's societies fairly, and give each of them a large opportunity for service, with due recognition. All the while, down in his heart, a pastor may find it hard not to favor a certain society, large or small, composed of women ready to pray and work with him and his wife as teammates and friends.

A case from life will show how a group may operate. In a church more than a hundred years old, and set in its ways, some of the women worked in two societies. The large majority, especially among newcomers, had nothing to do with either group. One of the newcomers, a woman of middle age, asked for an appointment with the minister. To him she explained her dilemma: "My work in school keeps me busy all morning, but not in the afternoon. I need something to do, work that I can enjoy. Tell me how to use my time and my car for Christ and this church."

The pastor thanked her for coming. After he had thought about the matter for a while, in the spirit of prayer, he saw the light. He knew of her ability to teach the Bible, and win friends among strangers. Without voicing any criticism of existing work among women, he told her about two needs in the church. The newer women needed someone to show them how to use the Bible and how to win friends. Acting on his suggestion, the teacher went to the superintendent of the church school and asked permission to organize a women's Bible class for newcomers. With his approval she began to visit and gain recruits. Soon she had other women calling with her, and with each other. Gradually that class became a force in every constructive movement throughout the community.

Such a pastor's way of enlisting women workers one by one has much in its favor. It reaches those not previously active, and sets them to work meeting present needs. In another field a woman discovered a need for visiting among the sick, the shut-ins, and the lonely. Soon she and her women friends began to branch out into the best kind of home evangelism. In still a third parish, with more than a thousand members, the pastor has repeatedly refused offers from the official board to secure a male assistant, fully ordained. The minister prefers to rely on unpaid women who know how to call on behalf of the church, and how to win friends in the name of the Lord.

In each of those parishes, however, the pastor and his wife felt the need of a plan more constructive and far-reaching. The functional approach led to an increase of machinery. That in turn might result in overlapping and in overlooking. Especially among women, activities that overlap may lead to friction. Overlooking may mean that some women have no place in any society. For instance, when a certain woman moves into the community, two or three of the organizations may plead for her support, though she has time and energy for only one. In another case all the societies may ignore the existence of the stranger. In either event, what a waste of womanpower!

A BETTER WAY OF WORKING

A better plan envisions an organization that includes all the women of the church, with the adherents. Instead of relying on hit-and-miss methods, with groups more or less competitive, the proposal calls for a single organization with as many group activities as local conditions require. This way of working has become common among various denominations. In one case the organization operates as "the women's society," in another as "the women of the church," and in a third as "the women's auxiliary." The smaller units often become "circles," a term that corresponds with "cells," but without any suggestion of furtiveness.

This movement among women has become perhaps the most noteworthy contribution of American Christianity to the organization of the local church. In some of its features the plan resembles that of Woodrow Wilson for teaching in a univesary. When a class of two hundred men engaged in the study of political science, or European history, he saw the need for their coming together as a whole, and later for their dividing into smaller groups, which he termed "precepts." So in work among women, as it operates in the South and elsewhere, once a month the society as a whole meets in the church parlors for an hour more or less inspirational. On another day the circles gather in various homes, for activities more directly informative.

A case will show one of many ways in which the plan operates. A young pastor went into a church with eight hundred members. Approximately 10 per cent of the women belonged to the missionary society, with an equal number in the ladies' aid. A few zealous sisters worked in both groups. Neither band functioned actively, or appealed to newcomers, especially among young matrons. The majority of women in the parish felt little concern for the program of the home church and less for the cause of the Kingdom at large. The apathy extended also to community betterment and to home missions.

Fortunately the leaders of the two groups felt dissatisfied with their methods of work. Gradually, with encouragement from the pastor, they prepared the way for a new plan. The first year it worked well and the second much better. From that time onward, under three different ministers, the plan has commended itself more and more as an effective way of enlisting practically all the women of the church for Christian service—building them up in grace through the exercise of spiritual muscles, and promoting the work of the Kingdom through the church. However, if the pastor and his wife, or either of them, had tried to impose that plan without waiting for enthusiasm to develop among the women themselves, the proposal would have fallen like a dud.

In one of its countless forms the plan starts as follows. In May the existing societies vote to disband. Before they do so, each group selects three of its members to serve on a joint nominating committee. The officers ought not to constitute such a committee, because some of these workers may become leaders in the new society. When the joint nominating committee comes together, it selects officers for the new society as a whole. Since the organization does not as yet exist, the committee may ask the official board of the church to elect the nominees. Needless to say, the effectiveness of the plan depends largely on securing the best available leadership.

Early in June the new officers meet to plan the work that will start actively in September. They arrange the time and place for the large inspirational meeting once a month. Then they determine the number of circles, and how often each circle should meet, also designating the day. Most important of all these arrangements, they select a leader for each circle, being careful to distribute the leaders geographically, and to have adequate representation of each former society. If the rolls of the congregation include two hundred women, with forty adherents, the officers may decide to start with eight circles, or perhaps only six. They wish each group to be large enough for inspiration and small enough for intimacy. They disregard geography and rely on alphabetical destiny. Now let us watch the assignment of the church women to various circles.

With the circle leaders grouped around her, the new secretary of the women's society reads one after another the names of two hundred and forty women. These the president assigns in course to the circle leaders. To each of them in turn the secretary gives a card showing the name and addresss of the circle member, with any other information needful, such as the facts about church membership. The card should include nothing confidential. Anything of that kind ought to go by word of mouth and not on paper. When the secretary has read the whole list of names, each leader should have in her group approximately thirty or forty persons, distributed through the alphabet. On this basis the new plan begins to operate when the public schools open in September.

In June a year later the officers increase the number of circles. They find, for instance, that business women and girls need a circle all their own, so that they can meet at night. As for the other circles, the membership changes from year to year. Consequently no group becomes a clique, and no sister need feel strange among women in any part of the church. Needless to say, leadership of circles affords opportunities for resourcefulness. Also the work provides a training school for future officers of the main society.

The women's association meets once a month. In summer the program may call for one or two gatherings on the church lawn or at a capacious garden, late in the afternoon. Whatever the season, the leaders strive for inspiration and friendliness. The program committee should work as hard and well as in any women's club. The monthly meetings usually prove interesting and, in the right sense, entertaining. The officers rightly feel that they should spare no expense, either for importing speakers or providing modest refreshments. At every meeting they aim to present certain aspects of Kingdom work at home or abroad.

In a parish where women can secure help in their homes, the circles may meet once a week. Elsewhere these smaller groups come together monthly. The program may call for a Bible reading, with prayer, and for mission study. The discussion plan gives everyone an opportunity to take part, while all remain seated and converse informally. The leader for the hour strives to keep the discussion within bounds, and moving forward to something definite. After adjournment, the plan calls for refreshments, the lighter the better. Especially among women, nothing promotes a feeling of camaraderie more surely than a cup of tea or a glass of fruit punch. In some circles, however, the menus become so elaborate that women with limited budgets hesitate about having such groups meet in their homes.

The circle plan opens the way for all sorts of ingenuity. If some of the homes cannot accommodate a group, two or three women go together and invite the friends to meet in one of the social rooms at the church. There they prepare the tables and the food as carefully as for honored guests in their homes. If the plans call for a luncheon, they prepare for the program to follow in an adjoining room. The circle meetings take countless forms, so that they often become as interesting as any other social groups in the community.

Each circle may select some project for special work. One may prepare small surgical dressings for a mission hospital; another, large dressings; a third, operating gowns for surgeons and nurses; a fourth, bedgowns for patients. Another group may work for the local hospital, or make layettes for a visiting nurse when she finds expectant mothers unprepared. A different circle may knit sweaters and socks, scarfs and mittens, for a missionary in Alaska. Women who have hitherto worked in the ladies' aid or some such group find an equal opportunity under the circle plan.

THE ATTITUDE OF THE MINISTER

The pastor ought to know what the women do in their union meetings, and more or less of what they accomplish in the circles. He should also keep informed about women's work in other congregations with a Christian philosophy and a forward look. Otherwise he could not serve as friend and counselor of the leaders in the women's work. The young pastor may need the following advice:

1. At least for a while, *accept what you find in the way of women's organizations.* Harmony and good will mean far more to the Kingdom than improvements in machinery, if a change would lead to

bruised feelings. Many women tend to be conservative about church changes. Especially as they grow mature—a pastor never refers to any woman as "old"—they want things to remain as in the days of their girlhood.

2. When at last a change comes, *let the women take the credit for the achievement.* Sooner or later some of them will return from a summer conference or from visits elsewhere all aglow with zeal for a unified society with a number of circles. If these women feel sure of backing from the minister and the official board, they will begin to promote the cause. However, they should advocate the change, not because it will please the pastor and the board, but because it will benefit the women of the church and promote the work of the Kingdom. In short, never attempt to boss good women or let your wife become a lady pope. No one can repeat such advice too often!

3. *Be alert about the choice of officers,* especially the first year under the new plan. Here again the pastor and his wife need not volunteer advice or otherwise interfere. But they should welcome every opportunity to confer with the nominating committee about a certain woman as a potential leader. Indirectly the minister can suggest the wisdom of rotation in office. After a term of two years—or it may be only one—no officer except the treasurer should succeed herself. Since the new plan calls for a succession of leaders, the pastor may have an opportunity once a year to use all his persuasive powers with a woman who suffers from an inferiority complex. If he helps the nominating committee persuade the right women to serve as officers, and as leaders of circles, he can leave the work in their hands for the coming year. What a pleasant way to avert headaches and heartaches!

4. Plan to *attend every gathering of the women's society.* Be present fifteen or twenty minutes before the meeting opens, or after it adjourns. Do not tarry for the program. Only an exceptional minister can do so without embarrassing women who take part. If all the circles meet on the same afternoon, according to the usual practice, the minister can arrange to be present at two of them on a given day, one before and the other after the program. These visits he counts a

privilege, as a part of his pastoral opportunity. As for matters of organization, he need not trouble about what he has committed to skillful hands.

5. *The pastor's wife should attend all the general meetings* of the association. She need not hold any office, or serve as chairman of any committee. In time she ought to become the friend, and even the confidante, of every officer or circle chairman. When things go awry, as they often do, she can show affection and sympathy for a leader who otherwise might lose heart. The wife can throw her arms around the sister as they laugh or weep together. In a small church, where her husband attends all the circles several times a year, she may go to one. In a large congregation, she and he can apportion the circles between them. In her case, however, attendance may call for remaining through the circle meeting, and then enjoying the social hour that follows. Again, what a pleasant way to promote the work of the Kingdom.

6. The next caution may seem needless. Even so, a pastor ought to *beware about frequent conferences with an attractive woman.* Not without reason do current novels about young ministers present the matter of sex. The best of such recent fiction, *The Bishop's Mantle,* by Agnes Sligh Turnbull,[1] tells about the temptation of a young hero. If all of this seems modern, think of the tales about Abélard and Heloise, or about Henry Ward Beecher. At the age of sixty-three, at the peak of his fame as the world's foremost pulpit orator, Beecher went through the most infamous trial in the history of Christendom. He apparently established his innocence on the charge of adultery, but he never had learned to deal discreetly with women. In almost every age of the Church more than a few clergymen have made shipwreck of their ministry because of inability to confer with women, one by one, for the glory of God. "Therefore let any one who thinks that he stands take heed lest he fall." (I Cor. 10:12, R.S.V.)

[1] New York: The Macmillan Co., 1947. See also Nelia Gardner White, *No Trumpet Before Him* (Philadelphia: The Westminster Press, 1948); Elsie Oates Barber, *The Wall Between* (New York: The Macmillan Co., 1946); Dorothy Walworth, *Nicodemus* (Boston: Houghton-Mifflin Co., 1946); and James Street, *The Gauntlet* (New York: Doubleday & Co., 1945). A descending series!

WOMEN'S WAYS OF EARNING MONEY

The pastor may incur enmity through opposition to the women's schemes for raising church money. How should he feel about a church supper for gain, or about anything else of the kind, such as a yearly bazaar? Before a young minister and his wife take a stand, they ought to know the arguments in favor of such practices.

1. *The community argument.* People in many a community need opportunities for getting together socially. Household help has become difficult to secure and almost impossible to pay. Many a weary housemother welcomes an opportunity to eat with her family away from home at a rate her purse can afford.

2. *The financial argument.* The church needs the money. The walls inside call for a coat of paint, and the floor requires a new carpet. Since the congregation ministers to the community, especially the children, people in the neighborhood should help to keep the equipment in first-class condition. Nobody asks outsiders to give for missions.

3. *The domestic argument.* Such affairs enable some women to contribute. Unfortunately, more than one husband controls the family purse. He pays the grocery bill and may not object to his wife's baking a cake for the church. He might balk at letting her give an extra dollar. What an ungodly way to manage a home and treat a wife!

4. *The social argument.* Working together in the church kitchen and dining room, women get to know one another. Not all of them shine as daughters of Mary, who can speak in public, and preside over meetings, always with grace and charm. Daughters of Martha feel more at home when they don gay aprons and wait on tables. Even in a city church they far outnumber the daughters of Mary.

On the other side, the pastor ought to remember:

1. *The spiritual aspect.* Ideally, Christians ought to give all the money necessary to maintain the church. They should think in terms of the tithe, plus free-will offerings. Then the treasury would never run low, with walls unpainted and bills unpaid. Wherever a church includes a considerable proportion of tithers, women need never resort to other means of raising the Lord's money. Tithers declare that

no other method of financing the church has ever received the approval of Holy Writ.

2. *The financial aspect.* Practically, other ways of securing money for the church may not work. Congregations that largely depend on methods other than straight giving do not always keep their finances on a sound footing. On the contrary, church after church has found that it prospered financially and spiritually after it began to raise all the Lord's money by giving, with the tithe as a working standard, though never compulsory.

3. *The domestic aspect.* Some of the best women in the congregation may not want to earn money by working outside the home. They do not feel above cooking meals and serving tables, but at home they find abundant opportunity for that sort of satisfaction. As for friendliness, they prefer to show sisterly love by putting on street clothes and by going out to call. Then too they think that most ways of raising money do not conform to present-day ideals of household management. One of them, with a record as a businesswoman, commented, "The women in charge of a sale for our church asked me to donate a homemade cake. I had neither the time nor the materials, and I offered to give a dollar. They insisted on my making a cake. So I dropped my work, changed my dress, went downtown on the street car, and brought home the ingredients. The materials cost me a dollar, not to mention my time and street-car fare. Then the cake sold for sixty cents! Do you think God wishes us to run His church that way? 'The Lord loveth a cheerful giver!' "

4. *The community aspect.* We may leave this to the imagination.

What then shall the pastor conclude? Shall he side with the daughters of Martha or with the daughters of Mary? With neither! Let him serve as pastor of the whole congregation. Sooner or later the women will settle this matter among themselves. Give them time! Perhaps they will agree on a compromise, by cutting down the number of such events. Meanwhile the pastor and his wife may sympathize with those who prefer to give church money rather than earn it by serving suppers and holding bazaars.

Very well! Let him proceed slowly, cautiously, and tactfully. In the pulpit and elsewhere he can advocate stewardship, with the tithe and free-will offerings as the working norm. He must never find fault with women who adopt other methods of showing devotion to the cause. If they prepare a church supper, or hold a rummage sale, he and his wife should attend, take part, and spend money according to their ability. After all, those women break no laws of God or of men. Why not retain their friendship and esteem? Any pastor and his wife who have tried the opposite course have learned to follow the more excellent way of Christian charity and forbearance.

All the while he can promote friendliness. If the people need more frequent opportunities for social enjoyment, he can encourage various groups to arrange get-together evenings, with light refreshments. If the resources of the congregation permit, he can ask the official board to provide money for a church hostess, who will put such matters on a business basis, and leave the women more largely free to enjoy each other while they work together for the glory of God.

In one church the women had raised large sums every year by serving church dinners. At last one of them suggested that they try a supperless supper. Instead of coming together to prepare an evening meal, and then serve it to members of their families, the women were to bring as afternoon gifts what they otherwise would have spent in preparing the supper. If anyone felt a sense of relief because of freedom from manual labor, she might double her gift. Perhaps because of novelty, that supperless supper brought in as much money as the women had earned at any previous meal. The next day all the women agreed that they had enjoyed the social gathering more than at any former time, and that afterward they had not felt worn out by an overdose of domestic drudgery.

In short, never force such an issue. Begin with the women where they are, spiritually and financially. If they insist on serving church suppers, the heavens will not fall, and the earth will not shake. Neither will the Kingdom come in power and glory through a church that relies largely on nonreligious methods. Little by little, then more and more, change the climate of the congregation. Then the women themselves will determine to do the Lord's work in ways that have come down from the Apostles. Once again we turn to the best motto for many a local church: "Seek ye first the Kingdom of God and his righteousness; and all these things shall be added unto you" (Matt. 6:33).

Suggested Readings

Ady, Cecilia M., *The Role of Women in the Church*. London: Press and Publications Board of the Church Assembly, 1948. Anglican.

Bacon, F. D., *Women in the Church*. London: Lutterworth Press, 1946.

Bowman, Leroy E., *How to Lead Discussion*. New York: The Woman's Press, 1934.

Chiang Kai-shek, Madame, et al., *Women and the Way*. New York: The Friendship Press, 1939.

Hiller, Margaret. *Leadership in the Making*. New York: The Woman's Press, 1936.

Lotz, Philip H., *Women Leaders*. New York: The Association Press, 1940.

Matthews, Winifred, *Dauntless Women*. New York: The Friendship Press, 1945. Biographical sketches.

Novotny, Louise M., *Women and the Church*. Cincinnati: The Standard Publishing Co., 1940.

Reed, Marie, *Leadership Today*. New York: The Woman's Press, 1939.

Wallace, Helen K., *Stewardship in the Life of Women*. New York: Fleming H. Revell Co., 1928.

CHAPTER XXIV

The Problem About the Men's Club

A S a rule the work among women goes far better than that among men. Only an occasional church can point with satisfaction to its men's club or brotherhood. In most congregations, whether large or small, the men's work either languishes or lapses. The same holds true among most denominations. In contrast with women's organizations, men's societies look small and disheartening. All the while both clergy and laity feel the need of Christian activity among laymen.

As time goes on, this need may increase. According to experts at the Metropolitan Life Insurance Company and in the federal government, within the next twenty years our country will have three times as many men over fifty years of age as we had in 1920.[1] On the other hand, except in prosperous times, men beyond fifty years must retire from many kinds of work. Once let loose they find it hard to secure employment. In view of such facts, what should the church do about its men's club?

During World War II more than a few men of mature years served on rationing boards. Day after day, without compensation, and amid all sorts of abuse, oldsters rendered service as devoted and efficient as that of young men at the front. After the coming of peace, so-called, those older men slipped back into what they call the "G.A.R., The Grand Army of the Retired." In making plans for the enlistment of other men, why does not the church employ the executive leadership of these mature laymen, with their abundance of leisure and wealth of idealism? In any such case the pastor ought to show concern.

Here and there a visitor finds men's work that shows what is possible under ministerial leadership. Year after year a certain brotherhood enlists the men of the congregation, with others from the community,

[1] George Lawson, ed., *New Goals for Old Age* (New York: Columbia University Press, 1943).

and keeps them actively engaged in various kinds of service. During a year's sojourn in the United States Dr. Emil Brunner, world-famous theologian from Switzerland, spent a number of weeks in North Carolina. Nowhere else in America did he witness anything that impressed him so much as the activity of men in certain congregations. Never had he seen anything of the sort on the Continent. Elsewhere in our country and in Canada he could have found such activity, but not in the large majority of churches.

Why does men's work not flourish in nine churches out of ten, perhaps in nineteen out of twenty? Why does it rarely equal women's work, either in extent or in power? Someone may reply that in the United States only 29.2 per cent of Protestant church members are men. But such a low proportion does not obtain in a church with a vigorous men's program year after year. In such a case the number of men often equals that of the women, both in statistics on the roll and in attendance at worship. In another community a church may become known as "a women's society" or even "an old ladies' home." The friendly observer asks, "Why?"

Other factors enter into the case, some of them beneath the surface. One thing stands out in the open. Religiously the men's club may have no reason for existence, with a local habitation and a name. Other church boards and agencies have in charge all the work that matters. The men's club meets for the sake of meeting, and spends its time discussing how to interest those who remain away. The picture may seem dark and overdrawn, but it represents the "work" where it languishes into lasting futility. In Bible days, when a husbandman owned such a tree, he would say to the servants: "Cut it down; why cumbereth it the ground?" (Luke 13:7c.)

By way of contrast think about one of those congregations that impressed the visiting churchman from abroad. The men come together once a month to promote the work of the Kingdom through the church. Of course they enjoy social gatherings, but only as by-products of endeavors to extend the Kingdom throughout the community and to the ends of the earth. Just as the women's association has taken as its province the promotion of missions and friendliness, the men of the church have assumed responsibility for evangelism and

brotherhood. No society can flouish year after year with a picayun-
ish program. Avoid the "Lilliputian heresy!"

What course then shall the incoming pastor follow? The answer
must depend on the milieu. If he finds no organization among men,
he need not make haste to demand such an additional piece of machinery. He may decide that existing groups can take care of all
needs. In any case he ought to wait awhile before he acts.

For example, take a rural community where farmers earn their live-
lihood as dairymen. This kind of work calls for early hours at bed-
time, so as to arise at four o'clock in the morning. Social outlets come
largely through the grange, and that in the afternoon. In such a
community the church ought to consider the needs of its men, but
not in a program that calls for gatherings after dark. If men have
free time, it comes during the day, especially on Saturday. Failure
to alter church methods with changing conditions may account for
a part of the decline among rural churches. Such failure in turn has
come largely through lack of adequate leadership.[2] Fifth Avenue programs do not fit the needs of men at Cream Ridge.

Take another case, also from life. In a residential district of North
Jersey the majority of the men commute to the city across the river.
That means leaving home about seven in the morning and returning
about six in the evening. More than a few others travel away from
home five days in the week, and sometimes six. At the end of the week
they feel all worn out. If you were pastor of such a church, would
you expect these men to maintain a brotherhood as a going concern?
Many a pastoral leader can echo the words of a Baptist minister in
South Carolina: "Every year I find it harder to reach the men of the
church between Sundays." He does not mean that they feel a lack of
concern, but that their mode of living has changed.

In view of such conditions more than a few churches have reluc-
tantly decided to dispense with the men's club. This way of working
calls on the church officers to plan for missions and evangelism,
Christian education and old-fashioned friendliness, with anything
else they find needful. The church officers should give special atten-.

[2] See Arthur W. Hewitt, *Highland Shepherds* (Chicago: Willett, Clark & Co.,
1939).

tion to the men's Bible class. In a congregation of any size two classes for men work better than one omnibus group. Two groups can deal with two different kinds of subjects, and use two different ways of teaching. One class may engage in discussion, under a leader who knows how to listen and how to steer, without saying much. At the end of the period, however, members should feel that they have arrived somewhere. The other class may consist of men who want a straight lecture. However unwisely, 50 per cent of the men may prefer this kind of teaching. Why not give them what they want?

As for social activities, the church officers and the leaders of the men's class, or classes, can provide anything needful. However, they ought to understand that even the Rotary Club and the Kiwanis find the need for something more than entertainment—for example, relief of crippled children, or support of a tuberculosis hospital. Only an exceptional church, with costly equipment and a paid staff, can compete with these dinner groups, and with the country club, in the way of entertainment. But groups of men who come together in the church for spiritual reasons have an incentive that few of them can find elsewhere.

Shall every church relinquish the idea of having a men's brotherhood? By no means. The cases that have come before us may prove to be exceptions, rather than the rule. If the incoming pastor finds a men's club, or a brotherhood, he need not throw up his hands in despair. Rather should he get in touch with other congregations where this part of the work flourishes, and then learn why. He may discover two facts, which belong together. Fact one, the organization of the men's group resembles that of the corresponding work among women. Fact two, the men band together to promote Kingdom enterprises as large and inviting as those of the women's association. How simple all of this sounds!

"The men of the church" should include all the male members and adherents old enough to vote. The work does not call for circles. Otherwise the plan resembles that among women, but the activities ought to differ. Since the women promote missions, what should the men do as a body? Unless the official board entrusts them with something equally important and interesting, how can those spiritual overseers expect this part of the Lord's work to flourish? Every men's group must have a sufficient reason for existence—something large, high, and permanent. Something directly relating to the Kingdom of God.

Two possibilities emerge. Fortunately the two go together. Accompanying them can go the promotion of friendliness. With men as with women, Christian friendliness flourishes best among those who work together in a common cause, prompted by love for Christ. Why not enlist the men for evangelism and community betterment? In other chapters we have looked at both concerns. Nowhere have we adequately considered the question: Which group ought to take charge of the movement for evangelism and for community betterment? Why not the men's brotherhood? Enlist the men of the church for these enterprises:

First, bringing to Christ every man or boy in this community who does not belong to some church.

Second, striving to make the community a colony of heaven, so that God may have His way in every part of the common life.

Third, as a by-product, leading the men of the church and community to become a brotherhood, bound together by Christian love.

For an example of men's work on a much larger scale, turn to Louisville. In a Methodist church the pastor's sermon one day led to action, which deserves the widespread commendation it has received. After a pulpit appeal for service, an oil man, George Stoll, determined to enlist other laymen. He felt that the men of all the Protestant churches should work together. Starting in 1941 and continuing until today, he has become responsibile for the leadership of three hundred men, two hundred and twenty-five of them active.

This "Committee on Institutions" works under the Louisville Council of Churches. The committee functions in twelve different ways. Five have to do with penal institutions: the police court, the state reformatory, the county jail, the city workshop, and the criminal court. Four concern themselves with child care: the children's division, crime prevention, the juvenile court, and the boy's club. Three busy themselves with public health: the general hospital, the state (mental) hospital, and the home for the aged and infirm.

To guide in these activities the general committee has set up four ideals: awareness of the facts in the case, support for every worthy effort, service to the people of the institution, and prevention of anything untoward. Before these workers undertake any movement they strive to ascertain the facts. They read the best books on the subject, confer with experts at home and elsewhere, and study local conditions. All the while they co-operate with the persons in charge of each institution, and never publicly utter any unfavorable comment. When these workers find institutional conditions that need correction, they go to the official in charge. If he co-operates, as he does with alacrity, they give him the credit. These laymen also strive to work with all the social agencies in the city.

Disinterested observers report that this layman's movement has gone far to transform the institutional life of Louisville. Through recent years the movement has kept growing, and has proved that it meant no flash in the pan. The leaders feel free to call on pastors and other clergymen for counsel or help. In the main the laymen themselves formulate the program and carry on the work. They have adopted various slogans, such as "every member a minister, and the clergyman a coach." Better still, the literature bids each committeeman utter this petition ten times a day: "Thy Kingdom come." According to the warden of the state reformatory: "These men listen sympathetically to our problems, and lend constructive advice and assistance when possible. They do not make destructive criticisms, or try to run the prison. On the whole these men are the civilian eyes, ears, and mouthpiece of this institution." [3]

Not every community needs this type of organization. But every inhabited area ought to have Christian laymen aware of local needs, and awake to such opportunities for service. In view of these ideals let us notice certain features about this layman's movement in Louisville:

1. *The impetus came from a pastor* and his sermon. During the hour of worship a layman caught a vision like that of Isaiah in the temple. Then the layman determined to enlist others for the betterment of the community.

[3] See *The Layman Helps the Warden,* a booklet by George Stoll (Louisville: Paul's Workshop, 1947), p. 37.

2. *The pastors stand ready to advise or help,* but laymen formulate the plans and do the work.

3. *The program throughout has been distinctly Christian.* The laymen represent the Protestant forces of Louisville, and strive to make the city Christian.

4. *The workers co-operate with existing social agencies* and with the heads of institutions. The program calls for constructive help, not for destructive criticism.

5. *The movement has resulted in toning up institutional life,* in betterment of institutions, and in quickening local concern about the underprivileged.

6. *The churches have felt the reflex influence* of all this activity. From it they have gained new inspiration for other kinds of Christian service.

7. *The people of the city have learned to respect the churches* and their ministers.

8. *Observers have seen an object lesson of how to enlist laymen* in practical work for the Kingdom.

9. *The same principles would apply elsewhere.* Think about the larger concerns of the nation and the world. Let the church rear and train the right sort of laymen. Let the minister inspire them to help change the existing order.

10. *"Let the church be the church."* According to President John A. Mackay of Princeton Seminary, "It is not the business of the Church to create a new social order, but to create the creators of that new order."

Suggested Readings

Agar, Frederick A., *Enlisting Laymen.* Philadelphia: The Judson Press, 1928.

Calkins, Raymond, *How Jesus Dealt with Men.* New York and Nashville: Abingdon-Cokesbury Press, 1942.

Gorham, Donald R., *Understanding Adults.* Philadelphia: The Judson Press, 1948.

Powell, W. E., *Understanding Adult Ways.* St. Louis: Bethany Press, 1941.

Sherrill, L. J., and Purcell, J. E., *Adult Education in the Church*. Richmond: John Knox Press, 1939.

Stoll, George, *The Layman Helps the Warden*. Louisville (241 E. Walnut St.): Paul's Workshop, 1947. 42 pp.

Verkuyl, Gerrit, *Qualifying Men for Church Work*. New York: Fleming H. Revell Co., 1927.

Weir, Wm. F., *Giving the Men a Chance*. Chicago: privately printed, 1931.

Westphal, Edward P., *The Church's Opportunity in Adult Education*. Philadelphia: The Westminster Press, 1941.

Chapter XXV

The Raising of the Annual Budget

T HE chief test of a church leader's ability may come in connection with raising the annual budget. A pastor may meet this test in one of three ways. A certain minister says: "Keep your hands off. Leave all that to laymen." Another protests: "A pastor ought practically to control the finances. I manage almost everything, except that I never take part in a canvass." A third, more representative, takes a stand between the two: "Have nothing to do with church money directly, and everything to do with it indirectly." This man deserves the name of church organizer.

When a minister goes into a new field, he should accept the financial program he finds in operation. After he becomes familiar with the parish, and acquainted with the officers, he may lead to better plans. However, if the officers already feel dissatisfied with their methods of raising the budget, he should stand ready to advise with them before the next canvass gets under way.

The time for the ingathering of pledges depends on the date for closing the church books. If the new year, financially, begins the first of January, the ingathering may come soon after Thanksgiving. In many communities this time of year suits well. The weather keeps favorable and sickness does not abound. Drives and campaigns for charitable causes either come earlier in the autumn or else nearer the spring season. Then, too, if the ingathering takes place early in December, evangelism can have the right of way from Christmas until Easter.

In certain fields, however, the ingathering needs to come in March or else in September. Very well! Whatever the date, the pastor and the lay workers have almost twelve months to prepare. They need all this time. Suppose that the activities of the year have led up to the annual meeting. At this assembly the governing board may nominate a layman to head the work of ingathering almost a year later. With him

may serve a commitee representing various agencies of the congregation. In a large church this committee may consist of fifteen members,
most of them men. In a smaller body fewer people can do the work,
with no subcommittees.

THE WORK OF COMMITTEES

The situation may call for four subcommittees. If so, one of them
may prepare a list of all the prospective givers. This subcommittee
hopes to secure from every member or adherent a pledge for current
expenses and for benevolences. Ideally the plan calls for giving week
by week in an envelope. If a man insists on writing a check in advance, either by the month, the quarter, or the year, the officers
ought to acquiesce. They know that more than one individualist
thinks it easier to give a hundred dollars at a time than to pay a dollar a week. Women and children, on the other hand, usually prefer
to contribute by the week (I Cor. 16:1-2). In any case the officers
ought to discourage the ever-present Lilliputian heresy, which leads
to little gifts to our great God.

The program likewise calls for a subscription, perhaps in bulk,
from every nonresident member who wishes to remain in good standing. What a word! "Standing!" Ideally everyone who removes from
the bounds of the home church ought to unite with one near at hand.
Actually many nonresident members neglect to transfer their memberships. If the church back home insisted on their continuing to contribute as long as their names appeared on the roll, this policy might
result in occasional payments. More probably long-distance members
would ask for their church letters, and join where they ought to attend.

Another subcommittee may draw up the yearly budget, for adoption by the official board, and perhaps by the congregation. The
minister probably believes in the double budget. This calls for duplex
envelopes, with two treasurers, and with accounts in two banks. He
may also believe in a fifty-fifty ratio between current expenses and
benevolences. Such a program tends to exalt missions at home and
abroad, and to keep people from becoming self-centered. If the lay
officers prefer the single budget, the pastor should not force an

issue. If the people have been giving at the rate of 85 per cent for current expenses and 15 per cent for benevolences, he may content himself for a time with suggesting a ratio of 75 over against 25. As the church becomes missionary-minded, he will see increased giving for benevolences, with no diminution in payments for current expenses.

The making of the budget calls for time and care. In such planning the committee begins with the budget for the current year. If the cost of living has recently risen 10 per cent, the planners try to arrange for a corresponding increase of salaries, beginning with the sexton. They also provide generously for all current expenses, and for reduction of any church debt. In the budget as a whole they set up an amount they expect to reach. Nothing financial heartens officers and people more than the knowledge that they oversubscribe the budget year after year. Nothing discourages them more than the feeling that they must fail to reach the goal. In time they will also learn to rejoice if subscriptions for benevolences increase more rapidly than those for current expenses.

The budget soon to appear may serve as a working basis. It keeps away from the customary terms, "for ourselves" and "for others." The first heading sounds selfish, if not sinful. A congregation of Christian people should minister to the entire community. Why suggest that any donor will receive adequate returns for every dollar he invests in Christ's work here at home? Also, a budget committee may need to omit some of the items, and perhaps add others. In a congregation with dual boards the committee should ascertain the desires of one group about current expenses and of the other about benevolences. In short, a co-operative enterprise!

KINGDOM WORK AT HOME	KINGDOM WORK ELSEWHERE
Salaries	Missions overseas
Church school	National missions
Church music	Church extension
Debt reduction	Christian education
Interest on debt	Evangelism
Insurance, fire and liability	World peace
Fuel, water, light, and power	Ministerial Training
Improvements and repairs	_____ College

Pension fund   _____ Hospital
Pulpit supplies   _____ Orphanage
Contingent fund   American Bible Society
                                      Special fund

The raising of such a budget ought to relieve the people from a succession of special appeals. Nobody should object to an emergency offering, occasionally, as when a sister church loses its building in a fire, or when a famine develops in China, because of a flood. Otherwise experience shows that repeated appeals interfere with plans for raising the budget. When people subscribe to the work of the Kingdom through the church treasury, they should not have to support the same causes in countless other ways. Unfortunately many people estimate the amount of their giving by the number of appeals they receive. Whether or not they respond, they grow restless if the pastor and the bulletin keep pleading for gifts to special causes. Wise officers encourage systematic giving rather than high-pressure propaganda.

A third subcommittee may have charge of publicity, or promotion, all relating to the approaching canvass. This work comes to a head on the day of ingathering. However, the promotion ought to begin long before, and continue throughout the year. In co-operation with the pastor, and with the editor of any church publication, the subcommittee ought to educate the people in the meaning and scope of stewardship. This group can also lead the members of the church to know the financial program, and to feel that the work deserves liberal support.

A fourth subcommittee may select and train the men who will solicit or receive subscriptions. These friends ought to be hand-picked. In some congregations women also serve, but as a rule men ought to do this work. If the plan calls for their going out two by two, a veteran may team up with a novice. In the course of ten or twelve years almost every able-bodied male member should have served on a team. After such an experience he will know more about church finances at first hand, and he should look on all such matters intelligently. The busier a layman elsewhere, and the stronger his influence, the more does this work call for his active service, at least during one time of ingathering.

The subcommittee may need to work tactfully in securing a man's consent to serve. In a certain community two solicitors for the Y.M.C.A. spent an hour with a well-known surgeon. At the end of that time they had secured his pledge for ten dollars. They had also aroused his interest. A year later he consented to serve on one of the teams, and he increased his own pledge. Within a few years he became the largest contributor. One term he served as president. Why? Because two businessmen whom he respected and liked had dealt with him tactfully, and had allowed him time to become concerned about the cause.

THE SECURING OF PLEDGES

For the sake of clarity we have delayed until now the consideration of a matter that calls for decision early in the ecclesiastical year. What method should the church employ in securing subscriptions for the annual budget? Theoretically the officers may choose one of eight different plans. Practically they may consider only two or three, but the minister ought to know about each of the others.

1. *The every-member canvass.* This plan has become so widely known that it calls for little explanation or comment. Basically it commends itself as sound. In a church with five hundred resident members the program culminates on the day of ingathering. The pastor may bring a message about the motto text for the year: "Seek ye first the kingdom of God, and his righteousness; and all these things shall be added unto you" (Matt. 6:33). Then forty men come forward while the people stand to sing "O Zion, haste, thy mission high fulfilling." The minister charges them briefly and pronounces the benediction of light (Num. 6:24-26).

These twenty teams may eat together at the church, or else go singly to their homes. At two o'clock they all start out from the church. Each member of a team has a typewritten sheet listing the friends he is to visit and their addresses. A sheet of this sort is less likely to be mislaid than a small card. Opposite each name the team member can write beforehand a few hieroglyphics. From them he can tell how much each person subscribed a year ago, and whether or not this friend has paid his pledge up to date. If such information were written out clearly, it might fall into the wrong hands and prove embarrassing.

Within two or three hours the teams ought to complete their rounds and return to report. At the church house the chairman of the main committee, or the secretary, should await them to receive subscription cards and thank the canvassers. As a matter of fact, a team may not find all its prospective givers at home. Even so, the reports at the end of the afternoon ought to indicate that some team has called on every man or woman, boy or girl, on the list of five hundred persons. Here we must allow for an occasional exception. Perhaps one per cent of the names on the church roll should not appear on the list, because these friends have no income.

Later in the day, or at least during the week, the two men on the team should visit the persons not at home early on Sunday afternoon. At the morning service on the next Lord's Day the chairman should be able to announce that his associates have seen every person on the list, and have secured pledges large enough to oversubscribe their budget. Then the people should rise to sing "Praise God from whom all blessings flow." Does all this sound idealistic? Perhaps so, but it sets forth what some of us have witnessed, year after year. In St. Paul the senior minister of a large congregation reports that 87 per cent of all the persons on the church rolls subscribe through the every-member canvass, and then pay through weekly envelopes. This time-honored plan still works in the hands of officers who love the Lord.

2. *The consecration of gifts.* In St. Louis the members of a well-known church prefer an altar service. After a period of intensive cultivation comes the day of ingathering. The pastor delivers a special sermon, in which he may or may not appeal for money. He may deem it best to speak about the vision of God's Kingdom at home and overseas. At the culmination of the service the people come forward with pledges, laying them on the altar, or the Communion table. Before the people depart from the sanctuary, the minister leads in a service of consecration. The fact that the pledges lie on the Communion table, or at the altar where people kneel to commune, shows that they regard these offerings as holy unto the Lord.

3. *The Lord's Supper.* In some congregations Holy Communion precedes the reception of pledges. The officers strive to secure attendance by all the people at the celebration of the Sacrament. In the atmosphere of the mountaintop they present their subscriptions. As for the manner of presentation, customs vary. One method calls for handing them to the officers at the head of each aisle as the worshipers in silence depart from the sanctuary. In another church officers receive the pledges on collection plates, which they pass after the Sacrament. Those who have employed such methods report that they work admirably under the right sort of leadership. Other observers question the wisdom of combining the Lord's Supper with anything like the raising of money. Why need all churches follow the same practice? "Where the Spirit of the Lord is, there is liberty." (II Cor. 3:17*b*.)

4. *The volunteer plan.* This method also assumes various forms. One of them calls for a special time of ingathering. On a certain Lord's Day, after morning worship and throughout the afternoon, various teams, two by two, wait in the social rooms of the church, or in alcoves of the church-school building. In a number of booths, lettered according to the alphabet, church members can meet with the teams, either to secure information or to fill out pledge cards. This plan affords an opportunity for questions and explanations.

As with each of the other methods, this one requires a follow-up. If certain members do not come to the church with pledges, teams must visit their homes. Sometimes the follow-up proves disheartening. The most generous givers respond to the first appeal with alacrity. Persons with a grudge or a grievance wait to be coaxed. Even so, a tactful team can do much to change the outlook of any family that has begun to feel aggrieved with the church or its pastor.

5. *The combination method.* To many of us this next plan seems the most nearly ideal. At a well-known church in New York City a "member-after-member" visitation precedes the day of ingathering. During the week before this high day visitors go into every home. Two by two they make a friendly call, present the budget, and reply to questions. Before leaving they hand out pledge cards and assure the friends of a hearty welcome in the sanctuary on the coming Lord's Day. All of this, let us assume, proceeds in the spirit of prayer. On

the day of ingathering the program may call for a formal consecration service. This method combines the advantages of friendly visitation in the homes and formal consecration in the church.

6. *The continuous pledge.* In a few congregations the officers let the subscriptions run from year to year. If the original pledges were made in prosperous times, they feel glad not to see reductions during days of depression. In isolated cases this plan seems to work effectively, but it does not call for adoption elsewhere. At least once a year every member of the church ought to face this question: "How much more should I contribute to the work of the Kingdom?" Even in bad times people who keep growing in grace find ways of increasing their pledges.

At a large church in Rochester the officers ask for some kind of increase every year. One time they call for volunteers to double their subscriptions. A year later the officers appeal for a straight increase of 10 per cent. Next time the budget may include a new item to encourage larger individual gifts. In the Lord's work never seem to be satisfied with anything short of perfection! On the other hand, if you expect increased giving, you must have a program that arouses enthusiasm.

7. *Solicitation by mail,* or by telephone. This method, too, falls far short of perfection. It affords the other person too easy an opportunity to say No. A life-insurance agent welcomes every chance to call on each patron at his home. The agent never mails a receipt if he can deliver it in person. As for the telephone, it seems even worse than the mail. Few people think about God when the telephone rings. In short, no ecclesiastical engineer has yet devised a cheap and easy way to transact the financial part of the Lord's business. It calls for a person-to-person approach.

8. *The community canvass.* Many of us know about this next plan only by hearsay. It calls for something akin to world-wide Communion, or the week of prayer. Suppose that all the churches of the community, or even the country, would set apart the first Lord's Day in December as the time for gathering in the pledges. Then all these bodies could combine to promote stewardship. Locally the churches

could work together, each in a fashion all its own. " 'Tis a consummation devoutly to be wished!"

So much for the eight methods. With the pledges all in hand, and the budget oversubscribed, the men on the committee may voice their thanks to God, and breathe a sigh of relief. In a sense, however, the work has only begun. Some group needs to follow up the pledges through the coming year, to see that they are paid in full and on time. Ordinarily the church treasurer does this work singlehanded, perhaps half-heartedly. A first-class treasurer may not have the temperament or the time to deal properly with delinquent subscribers. He may think more about extracting money at the moment than about preserving good will permanently.

The treasurer can help much by mailing receipts at the end of every quarter, or every month. If all the families and all the lone members get such receipts, no one can object when he hears from the treasurer. There in black and white the subscriber can see the status of his account with the church. If he continues being delinquent, he should expect a friendly call from a member of the finance committee. When church people pay their pledges in full and on time, they tend to think of the institution as a going concern. If they fall into arrears, they may begin to feel disgruntled. So say experts in every line of business or professional finance.

In order to stimulate the payment of pledges the officers may set up a roll of honor. In the newsletter at the end of the year everyone may read the names of those who have paid their subscriptions in full, up to date. In an occasional church such a list also tells the amount each person has pledged, and the sum each has paid. This kind of publicity may result in large receipts, but it runs counter to the spirit of Christ. "When thou doest alms, let not thy right hand know what thy left hand doeth: that thine alms may be secret; and thy Father which seeth in secret himself shall reward thee openly." (Matt. 6:3-4.)

THE BUDGET AT THE PARSONAGE

The ability of the pastor to lead in church finance may depend in part on the management of money in the parsonage. There the size of the salary may constitute a major problem. Both the husband and his wife, with the children, ought to dress neatly. He must purchase books and maintain an automobile. They must often entertain, and also at times secure a baby sitter. Then comes the need of saving for the children's education, for life insurance, and for emergencies. Who can wonder that they find it hard to live within their means?

Every such household needs a budget. On it the first item should be the tithe, most of which should go to the church and its societies. In the name of both, the wife can subscribe to the annual budget, giving half the amount to current expenses and half to benevolences. Otherwise how can they expect the people to give this way? Of the money that remains each month—after deducting the tithe—half may go to the wife and half to the husband. Then he can keep up the insurance, arrange for savings, take care of medical and dental bills, maintain an automobile, pay for the fuel, and finance the yearly vacation, with any other major expenses. As for the wife, anyone can see what she has to accomplish with her half. For an account of such a happy home with limited means read *My Boyhood in a Parsonage*, by the financier Thomas W. Lamont.[1]

Now for a few negations:

1. Both husband and wife should *beware of running up bills* and contracting debts. They ought also to refrain from installment buying. Let them pay as they go. If they cannot pay, let them not go.

2. They should *never ignore a debt*. Sometimes a minister carries over obligations from college and seminary days. He may incur debt in buying an automobile, or in financing the arrival of the first baby. If he owes money in a number of places, he should clear up the small debts first. Then he can make a businesslike arrangement about a major debt or two. This means going to the person or persons concerned, making a frank statement of the facts, and offering to pay interest until the debt is liquidated.

3. The minister should *never lend money*, or endorse a note. Why run the risk of losing both money and friends?

4. He should *never borrow*, except from a bank, or from someone back at his home.

[1] New York: Harper & Bros., 1946.

5. The husband and his wife should *never hint for a ministerial discount*. As for a clergy permit, most pastors accept it without a qualm. Few, however, write to express thanks.

6. Likewise they should *never hint for free professional services*. Plan to pay the doctor and the surgeon. If either of them declines to accept compensation, express thanks orally and in writing. You may amaze the dear doctor!

7. *Never receive a favor without making acknowledgment*, preferably in writing. Some church members receive few letters or notes, and they treasure those few, especially from a pastor whom they love.

8. Never *invest in a local enterprise*, however alluring.

9. In short, *never forget the promise in Matt. 6:33*. Untold hosts of pastors and their wives have found that God still takes care of His own.

10. *Never hesitate to preach about money* as a means of grace. If you and your wife set a worthy example, financially and otherwise, the people will do their part in supporting the work of the Kingdom. This includes the care of the church and the friends in the parsonage.

Let us not close on a negative note. An experience in the early ministry of Spurgeon shows how he secured all the money needful to carry on a rapidly expanding work in London. Largely because he had chosen a good wife, he learned to trust God for money, both at home and in the Tabernacle. Only the Lord knows how much he led people to give for the support of the church, the orphanage, the pastor's college, and other causes dear to the heart of Spurgeon. At the beginning of their married life he and his bride had agreed never to incur a debt. One day not long after, in a time of stress he exclaimed:

"Wifey, what can we do? I must give up hiring the horse, and walk to New Park Street every time I preach." Mrs. Spurgeon knew that he had neither the time nor the strength to do that walking. So they laid the matter before the Lord. "That night," she afterwards wrote, "or the next day, I am not sure [which], a letter was received containing twenty pounds for our own use, and we never knew who sent it, save that it came in answer to prayer." That gift enabled them to meet the emergency, which called for exactly twenty pounds. Then the wife commented, "I do not remember ever afterwards seeing him painfully anxious concerning supplies for any of his great works. He depended wholly on the Lord, his trust was perfect, and he lacked nothing." [2]

Suggested Readings

Cashman, Robert C., *The Business Administration of a Church*. Chicago: Willett, Clark & Co., 1937.

————, *The Finances of a Church*. New York: Harper & Bros., 1949.

Crossland, Weldon, *How to Increase Church Income*. New York and Nashville: Abingdon-Cokesbury Press, 1947.

Cushman, Ralph S., *I Have a Stewardship*. New York and Nashville: Abingdon-Cokesbury Press, 1946.

Gamble, Charles W., and W. W., *How to Raise Money*. New York: The Association Press, 1942.

Leach, Wm. H., *Toward a More Efficient Church*. New York: Fleming H. Revell Co., 1948, Chap. V, "Adequate, Democratic Financing."

Long, Roswell C., *The Stewardship Parables of Jesus*. Nashville: Cokesbury Press, 1931.

————, *More Stewardship Parables of Jesus*. New York and Nashville: Abingdon-Cokesbury Press, 1946.

Rolston, Holmes, *Stewardship in the New Testament*. Richmond: John Knox Press, 1946.

Versteeg, John M., *When Christ Controls*. New York and Nashville: Abingdon-Cokesbury Press, 1943.

[2] *Op. cit.*, vol. II, p. 184.

CHAPTER XXVI

The Provision for Church Records

A LL the discussion thus far shows the necessity of church records, accurate, complete, and up to date. To his amazement an incoming pastor may not find even a working list of the members, with their addresses. One or more of his predecessors has shirked this part of his official duties. The pastor himself ought to keep none of these records, save those that have to do with him personally. These latter do not concern us here, as they fall under the heading of pastoral theology. When a man accepts a call to the active ministry, he ought to determine by God's grace that he will lead to adequate records wherever he serves. How else can he hold the esteem of a local physician or merchant?

In order to excel in this part of his lifework a pastor needs to study the matter. Let him begin by learning the laws of his denomination. What sort of records does his branch of the Church require? How many of them ought to go into permanent volumes, securely bound? Even if he owes no allegiance to a higher church body, a wise young pastor makes rules for himself. First he ought to know how a system operates in a church like his own, and about the same size.

Some layman in charge of permanent church records will gladly show them to a young minister, and explain them in detail. If he hesitates to do so, probably he does not keep good records. In that case try another church. Also make an appointment with the secretary, if such there be, and have her show how she keeps more or less temporary lists at the office. Do not waste either person's time by dallying and asking pointless questions. On the other hand, probably neither of them has ever received such a request. Everyone likes to display the right sort of handiwork.

A visit to the denominational bookstore will also help. Here an expert salesman can show sample books and cards that conform with the requirements of the denomination, and with the desires of skilled secretaries. In any case of uncertainty, denominational officials stand ready to advise, but they should not have to bother with matters of detail.

At the same time a pastor should be sizing up the local situation. Not only may he find the records inadequate. He may even discover that they lie. Partly for this reason church statistics for the country as a whole may mean little or nothing save aggregate guesswork. For example, think of a case from life. A congregation boasted of having 1,200 resident members. When the minister died suddenly, after having served many years, the interim pastor urged the governing board to revise the rolls, so that the incoming man could know where he stood. The proposal met with this response, which indicated the prevailing sentiment of the board: "If we pruned our rolls, we should have to put four hundred names on the inactive list. Think how that would reflect on the memory of our former pastor."

What about the incoming man? How can he shepherd four hundred sheep that have become lost in the wilderness? Think of the effect on a governing board that knowingly reports falsehoods. In carrying out any reform, however, they ought to show Christian charity and forbearance. They should strive to bring every one of those four hundred wandering sheep back into the fold. Under a different figure our Lord tells about the fruitless fig tree: "Sir, leave it alone for this year until I have dug around it and fertilized it. If it bears fruit after that, well and good; if not, you shall cut it down." [1]

To facilitate careful husbandry the governing board may adopt for its own guidance—not for publication—some such statement as the following. Of course both the wording and the spirit ought to accord with the rules of the denomination. Few of them would interfere with some such action as this: "Our active membership consists of professing Christians who attend our services, if physically able, and contribute to our budget, if financially able." In carrying out such a working rule the officers need to exercise kindness and patience. In case of doubt or uncertainty they should keep a name on the active

---

[1] Luke 13:8, Charles F. Kent, *The Shorter Bible*. Copyright 1918 by Charles Scribner's Sons.

list. In general they should include only the names of those who attend with some degree of regularity, and contribute with some degree of liberality. Church membership would mean more if it cost more, both in time and in cash.

Why insist on such pruning? For much the same reason that the keeper of an orchard uses pruning shears. He wishes to increase the fruitfulness. By cutting away dead wood he gives the live branches an opportunity to bear more fruit. On the contrary, if he neglected a tree, he might watch it expand at the expense of fruitfulness. A prudent man does not judge a church or a tree by its size. He knows that either one might become twice as fruitful if half as large. So why not resolve to live in the Book of the Acts and not in that of Numbers? In order to carry out such a policy, think of the permanent records.

THE PERMANENT RECORDS

A designated officer, or perhaps the clerk or secretary of the governing board, keeps the permanent records of the congregation proper. In a congregation with an office secretary or two he may or may not delegate part of the clerical detail. In any case he holds himself responsible, especially for keeping any bound volume or volumes up to date. If at the church or in a business office he has access to a fireproof safe, he may prefer to keep the permanent records there. In short, he should guard them as a jeweler does with diamonds. Now let us think more in detail. As a rule each of these permanent records appears in a chronological order.

1. *A roll of members.* Each entry shows the full name of the person, the date of admission to membership, the manner of admission, and any other items of permanent interest. If the friend comes by certificate, the entry shows the name and location of the church that granted the letter. If a young woman marries, this new fact is entered. When a person dies, this calls for an additional item. Consequently the book may not remain a model of symmetry. The recording officer strives for clarity and for ease of reference.

2. *A list of baptisms.* In most churches the rules call for a separate list in the bound volume of all persons baptized, with the date of each ceremony and the name of the officiating minister. In some churches,

however, this information appears only on the regular roll of members. The former plan seems better. In bodies that practice infant baptism there may or may not be a separate section for this purpose. In either case the entry for each infant should include the names of the parents, showing whether one or both belong to this church, and in some bodies, the names of the sponsors or godparents.

3. *Marriages.* Whenever a minister of the church marries two persons, the facts ought to appear on the church records, permanently. Years later either he or the person in charge of the records can testify under oath about the facts in the case. The record may include the full names of the persons married, the date, the place, the name of the minister, and the names of two witnesses, or perhaps three. However, in most cases the record contains fewer items. As for a "marrying parson," he should not perform any ceremony on which he can not pronounce the blessing of Christ and His Church.

4. *Funerals.* Here the record runs much the same.

In a church of any size these records may call for two bound volumes. The one includes the roll of members, and allows ample space for possible later entries after each name. The other volume records the facts about baptisms, marriages, and funerals. In some bodies it seems proper to employ bound volumes with loose-leaf devices. If so, the man in charge should never remove a sheet except for immediate transfer to another bound volume.

THE OFFICE LISTS

At the church office the secretary needs many of these data. In fact, her cards of membership ought to duplicate the entries in the permanent records, with any other relevant facts, such as numbers showing geographical groups. These lists appear on cards which may be obtained from denominational sources. If the pastor prepares his own, he will find that 4 by 6 inch cards hold more data than 3 by 5. The names appear as a rule in alphabetical order. Especially in our time of countless moving vans in daily use, the secretary needs to watch out for current changes.

In a church with no full-time secretary the pastor and his wife may keep these lists. Perhaps he can find a former businesswoman, now married, who feels free for such work two afternoons a week. If so, she ought to receive compensation, and it should come from the church treasury. Among farmers, however, it may prove hard to show the necessity for such an outlay. Anyone who knows the following facts should see why the minister ought not to do the work without help. On the other hand, when he has a salaried assistant, the pastor should know how to insure the right sort of working lists, up to the minute, neat, and accurate.

1. *Membership roll.* In alphabetical order each card shows the facts we have noted. How many other items ought to appear no one from without can determine. One minister with an inventive turn has devised a system of cards with punch holes here and there, so that in a minute or two a wide-awake secretary can ascertain which young woman can play the piano and teach in the junior department of the church school. In an average church such a complicated and costly system would only add weights to shoulders already overburdened.

2. *Family lists.* Another drawer of cards may show the names and addresses of all the church families, with the names of the various members in each household on a single card. If the office equipment includes an addressing machine, with the necessary mailing lists, the person in charge may get along without any other list of families. Somehow or other the lists should make it possible to reach every household or lone member by mail, and still not spend needless money for postage. Any such list ought to show the group number of each family, the members of it who belong to the local church, and any other data of the kind needful.

3. *Reserve list.* Some churches maintain a list of passive members whom the officers are striving to restore to the active list. Meanwhile these persons belong on a "suspended list." After a time determined by local or denominational rules their names may appear again with the active members or else be dropped. Here again officials need to act with discretion and charity. Somehow they should act in accordance with the facts.

4. *Non-resident members.* These names show which families or lone persons have removed from the bounds of the congregation. Ideally they should transfer their memberships at once. Actually this may

call for time. Meanwhile their names ought to be in easy reach and yet not be included among the resident members.

5. *Former members.* When a member of the church takes his membership to another church and is there received, is dropped from the roll because of lost interest, becomes permanently lost to view, or else dies, the cards about him are all removed from the lists above, and one card is placed in the list of former members. In years to come the facts about any such person ought to be available at the office, and quickly. These same facts also appear in the permanent records, but usually in a form not so easily accessible.

6. *Constituency roll*, or prospect list. Except for the membership roll, the other lists do not compare in importance with the cards showing the names and addresses of the persons whom the church and the minister hope to win for Christ and the church.[2] In some denominations church law requires the maintenance of such a record. Everywhere else prudence calls for the preparation of a list showing the name of every unchurched man or woman, older boy or girl, throughout the community, for whose spiritual welfare the Lord holds this church responsible. Since evangelistic work now proceeds mainly through lay visitation, and that by households, the list may chiefly comprise family units. If so, each card ought to indicate the facts needful for the worker. Also, either the card cabinet or the room ought to remain locked whenever the room is not in use for church business.

THE OTHER RECORDS

The church treasurer or treasurers ought to keep the financial records as accurately as in a business firm. Otherwise some of the people may begin to grumble. Indeed, they may even withdraw from the church because of carelessness or mismanagement in such details. All the while the person or persons in charge may have the best of intentions, and may try to do the work properly. When an irate subscriber wants to check up on the record of her past year's giving, or when an auditing committee prepares for its annual report, a treasurer needs

[2] See my *Evangelism in the Home Church* (New York and Nashville: Abingdon-Cokesbury Press, 1932), pp. 106-9.

something more tangible than good intentions, and more complete than notes scribbled on the backs of used envelopes.

The same principle holds true in the church school, and in every other part of the local organization. Each secretary ought to keep accurate minutes of the business transacted, and each treasurer ought to have a businesslike record of every dollar received or disbursed. All of this ought to come about in time, if the pastor holds up the ideal of doing the Lord's work decently and in order. Anything worth doing for God is worth doing well. What else does it mean to become a good and faithful servant in charge of minutes or money? In time the various societies will begin to use care in choosing secretaries and treasurers. They in turn will respond to tactful coaching. They may even look forward to the annual meeting when they will appear with visible evidences of work well done for the King of Kings.

All the while the pastor can serve as the moving spirit. By personal example and by unconscious influence he can encourage the lay workers to keep the Lord's business on a worthy level. By carelessness and slackness he could help to demoralize the entire working force of the parish. And yet he might look on himself as "spiritual," because he cared little about doing the Lord's business well enough to command the respect of laymen who excel in the arts of trade and commerce. What other enterprise on earth begins to compare in importance with that of King Jesus and His Church?

How about the minister who hates business detail? "If any man will come after me, let him deny himself, and take up his cross daily, and follow me." (Luke 9:23.) What else does it mean to become a Christian, and a Christian minister? If anyone becomes a master in this part of his life work, he may begin to enjoy seeing all the records in the parish shipshape. Whether he enjoys this part of his work, or merely endures it as drudgery, let every minister determine, if need be, to take up this cross daily, in order to serve "the God of detail."

Suggested Readings

Blackwood, A. W., *Planning a Year's Pulpit Work*. New York and Nashville: Abingdon-Cokesbury Press, 1942. Appendix, "Storing the Fruits of Study."

Brand, Norton F., and Ingram, Vernon M., *The Pastor's Legal Adviser.* New York and Nashville: Abingdon-Cokesbury Press, 1942.

Cashman, Robert C., *The Business Administration of a Church.* Chicago: Willett, Clark & Co., 1937.

Cashman, Robert, *The Finances of a Church.* New York: Harper & Bros., 1949.

Foote, Henry W., *The Minister and His Parish.* New York: The Macmillan Co., 1923. Chap. V, "The Parish Records."

Greene, J. N., compiler, *My Pastoral Record.* New York and Nashville: Abingdon-Cokesbury Press. Planned for a pastor's lifetime.

Leach, William H., *Protestant Church Building.* New York and Nashville: Abingdon-Cokesbury Press, 1948. Pp. 137-43, "Building for Administration."

CHAPTER XXVII

The Plans for the Yearly Meeting

THE annual meeting may resemble a family feast or a free-for-all fight. More often it becomes a matter of long reports, statistical and dry, like "clods untroubled by a spark." Hence the attendance dwindles from year to year. How can the minister help to make the annual meeting an event in the church life, and not merely an interruption in a busy week? How can he encourage the making of a program that will cause the people to anticipate the meeting with pleasure, and look back on it with delight?

Why not? The friends at the home church have been engaged in the most important work on earth. As promoters of the Kingdom they ought to take stock at least once a year, and give thanks to God for His blessing on their labors. Fortunately the persons in charge of the meeting have twelve months to make ready. How should they proceed? By planning to present what will interest the people, and to omit or pass lightly over everything else. Such a program calls for much about local persons and events, with few statistics and no long talks.

The pastor may suggest that a certain group or society assume responsibility, under the official board. In almost every church some of the men, or perhaps men and women, need an outlet for pent-up energies. These friends have ability and want to use it in ways worth while. Hence the minister can suggest an assignment to the men's brotherhood, the young married people's class, or the deaconesses. These friends should begin to prepare by ascertaining the facts about annual meetings in former years. They can also confer with representatives of other congregations. Gradually the planners should secure suggestions and literature about gatherings in churches where people attend the annual meeting with eagerness and come away with enthusiasm.

The plans for the meeting a year hence may call for a congregational dinner. If so, the committee in charge may delegate this part of the arrangements to some other group. The planners wish to interest and enlist as many persons as possible. As for the actual meeting, after the dinner, the pastor usually presides. However, he gladly conforms with church law and local custom.

In conference with him the committee may decide to make large use of stereopticon pictures. Why a stereopticon rather than a motion-picture machine? Because the former does not require expensive equipment, and is less likely to go wrong in the hands of an amateur. Then too a stereopticon enables the operator to keep the same picture or display in view as long as he desires. For instance, he may wish to have the people sing, without haste, the first stanza of a hymn, before the stereopticon brings to view the second stanza.

The appeal of stereopticon pictures comes mainly through novelty of subject matter. Through the preceding year the makers of the program can gather and classify pictures that will interest the people. Instead of having the secretary of the church school read a long, dry report, replete with figures, the committee can secure a picture of the school picnic, and then have a single slide with all the school statistics that matter. Some of the reports may include simple graphs, instead of complicated displays. As for other statistics, they can be mimeographed or printed, all bound together, with an attractive cover, and then distributed to the people as they depart for home. These reports will encourage the people to attend the meeting a year hence.

The committee needs to use skill and care in selecting materials for the program, and in arranging the order. Since the gathering need not take place in the sanctuary, the people may applaud. They will enjoy the absence of tedious reports; [1] and the feeling of suspense about what will come next. For instance, the organist has resigned and will soon retire after twenty-five years of service. Or the chairman of the finance committee has led in oversubscribing the largest budget in the history of the congregation. In either case the people will applaud an appropriate picture of this good and faithful servant. In short, a group

[1] Soon after Dwight D. Eisenhower became president of Columbia University a directive went out from the office that no report, ordinarily, should exceed a single typewritten page.

of business men or women can prepare for the stockholders a program full of human interest and spiritual uplift.

After the reports may come the election of church officers. In various branches of the Church such customs differ widely. At present we have in view a large congregation where all the people do not know each other. Hence they have to rely on a nominating committee, which represents the important church organizations. In a very large body the committee may function throughout the year, so as to fill vacancies as they arise. Ordinarily such a committee acts for five or six weeks before the yearly meeting.

In some bodies the pastor serves on this committee, ex officio. If not, he may prefer to keep hands off, and let the lay members select the nominees. In order to do this, the committee may put in the bulletin a request for suggestions about persons suitable for various posts. The responses ought to come in writing. In a certain parish such suggestions recently led to the election of persons whom neither the pastor nor the other officers would have considered. Even if people do not respond with suggestions, they like to be asked. They do not wish to be ignored about anything that involves the welfare of the church they love.

If the nominating committee feels free to do so, it should present the name of only one person for each vacancy. In more than one congregation of late the committee has submitted the names of rival candidates. Consequently defeated parties have felt a sense of chagrin. Some have left the church, with their families. Then, too, many a committee meets with difficulty in finding enough persons able and willing to serve as leaders of the flock. In a church with more than one ruling board, the committee may find it hard to secure able men to serve in some posts and easy to get capable men for other offices.

Various procedures may find a place in a representative democracy. As for the pastor, he ought to know about the committee's conclusions, so that he can preside with assurance. In one case a new minister while presiding asked the chairman of the committee to state the business or profession of each nominee. When the chairman reached a certain name, he hesitated. Finally he brought out the fact that the man in view served as a financial promoter. Fortunately that candidate did not receive a majority of the votes. He could not have served for the next three years, as he spent most of that time in the state penitentiary. After that experience in the annual meeting the nominating committee each year took its duties seriously, and prayerfully. Never again did it recommend for church office a man with a shady reputation on Main Street. Nevertheless, it would have been more in order for the pastor to have known the facts before the meeting and to have had the name withdrawn privately.

Throughout the preceding twelve months the pastor can help to prepare for the annual meeting by stressing the dignity and importance of church office. When the committee has decided which persons to nominate, the chairman may ask the minister to interview some of these friends and persuade them to accept. If the pastor knows any reason why a certain man on the list ought not to become a church officer, the minister and the chairman can talk about the matter confidentially. Whatever they decide, the pastor should not gain the reputation locally of packing the board with his pets, and of keeping other people out of office.

The pastor should never have to question any selection by a nominating commitee. On the other hand, he ought to enjoy conferring with a brother who hesitates about accepting high office. When at length the minister presides over the election, he ought to feel that the battles of the next year have largely been won. In the midst of all these forward views he must not let the people forget the services of the outgoing officers. So he may suggest beforehand that the committee throw on the screen pictures of leaders about to retire from active duty.

This account may seem longer than the meeting itself. If the committee has not planned for too much, and if the pastor knows how to preside, the assembly need continue little more than one hour. Toward the end, each year, should come a climactic feature, as a surprise. It may consist of a long-distance message from the pastor emeritus, at his winter home far away. Or the foreign missionary representative and his wife, whom the church supports in Delhi, may have sent a phonograph record, with words of greeting. Again, the committee may show pictures of former members who have become ministers of the Gospel or missionaries abroad. Another year the program may feature the names—perhaps the pictures—of young people away at college. Why not show the group of stockholders the choicest of their dividends?

The climactic feature may have to do with plans for larger things in days to come. The people may have felt the need of a new organ. A month or two before the gathering one of the families may have requested the privilege of donating the organ as a memorial. Instead of making the announcement at once, the minister asks permission to wait until the annual meeting. Before that time the committee can arrange for a lay officer to announce the gift in the name of the family. Then the screen may show a picture of the organ loft or chancel as it will appear after the proposed improvement.

Elsewhere the congregation may need a new structure for Christian education. If the building committee has the plans complete, a representative may arrange for pictures of what the architect proposes, and then explain what the committee has in view. The character of this climactic feature should guide in the choice of the closing hymn. If it follows the announcement of a memorial gift, sing "Praise God from whom all blessings flow." At another time, "Lead on, O King Eternal," or "O Zion, haste, thy mission high fulfilling." Then will follow a brief prayer that the Lord may crown with His favor the work of the year to follow. Last of all will come the benediction of peace, based on Phil. 4:7.

On the way homeward the people should thank God for the privilege of belonging to a church with a forward-looking program, and of helping a pastor with a forward-looking vision. With a happy smile more than one husband will say to his wife: "Our minister always does things just right." Then she will reply, "Yes, and he gives us people the credit!"

Suggested Readings

Lane, Janet, and Tolleris, B. K., *Planning Your Exhibit*. New York: National Publicity Council, 1948. 28 pp., large.

Tolleris, Beatrice K., *Annual Reports: How to Plan and Write Them*. New York: National Publicity Council, 1946. 40 pp., large.

CHAPTER XXVIII

The Secret of Pastoral Leadership

NOW let us take a bird's-eye view. We have been thinking about the pastor as executive and as organizer. We have looked at more than a few of his problems and difficulties. At last we ought to lift the whole matter to a higher level and view it in light from God. Amid all these ideals and methods can we discern anything that will bind them together and make them a power in the work of the Kingdom?

For the answer we should go to the Book, and to our Lord. Before we do so, however, let us glance at certain Protestant ministers who have excelled as parish leaders,[1] and ask what they have had in common. Every student of church history could compile a longer list. For obvious reasons this one includes the name of no one now at work. Among pastors abroad think of John F. Oberlin and Thomas Chalmers, Richard Baxter and George Herbert, John Keble and Alexander Whyte, John Watson (Ian Maclaren) and Charles H. Spurgeon. In the homeland, Theodore L. Cuyler and Phillips Brooks, Charles E. Jefferson and Maltbie D. Babcock, Washington Gladden and Peter Ainslee, William A. Quayle and George W. Truett. Think also of an untold host whose names are written in heaven, and of their inconspicuous ministry here on earth.

What have these servants of God possessed in common? They have shown all sorts of personality, worked in all sorts of fields, and excelled in all sorts of ways. If they could speak now, they might warn us against trying to oversimplify the picture. They have left us a world of inspiration, but no quick and easy way of solving pastoral problems and transforming them into opportunities. Even so, all

[1] See Charles F. Kemp, *Physicians of the Soul* (New York: The Macmillan Co., 1947), chaps. IV, VII.

these men have had more than a little in common. By example if not by precept they have shown us:

1. *The need of faith.* Not only have they agreed with Bushnell about "Every Man's Life a Plan of God." [2] They have looked on pastoral leadership as an opportunity to carry out His will. Each of them has relied on Him for wisdom and restraint, both in determining what to do, and in devising practical methods. Such a church leader becomes a practical idealist. He looks up for guidance and yet keeps both feet squarely on the ground. If he were a mariner, he would learn from Paul during a storm at sea. [3] The mariner looks up to see the stars. He also takes account of wind and tide, with still more concern about passengers and crew.

Faith leads to courage. Like Abraham of old, every man who leaves one field and enters another must go out by faith, not knowing whither (Heb. 11:8); but God knows. Instead of equipping himself with a set of ready-made solutions for pastoral problems, with patent nostrums for people's ills, a man learns to rely on wisdom from above, both for diagnosis and for cure. Consequently the days often bring him a sense of adventure. For an object lesson of such courage, born of faith, study again the biblical records about Nehemiah's leadership in rebuilding the walls of Jerusalem. [4] Let every local leader regard himself as erecting walls that surround the City of God.

Like that builder of old every pastor today needs courage to say No: "I am doing a great work, so that I cannot come down; why should the work cease, whilst I leave it, and come down to you?" (Neh. 6:3.) In making his plans the minister has determined to do a "great work" for God, chiefly in the study, out among the people, and up in the pulpit. At least for the first few years, he may have time and strength for little else. Such a decision may seem narrow, but the narrowing of a channel brings depth and power. For many reasons, therefore, a minister should resolve to excel in his special field, the home church.

[2] See my *Protestant Pulpit*, sermon 8.
[3] For an example of leadership turn to Acts 27.
[4] See Neh. 2–6.

> The man who seeks one thing in life, and but one,
> May hope to achieve it before life be done;
> But he who does all things, wherever he goes
> Only reaps from the hopes which around him he sows
>   A harvest of barren regrets.[5]

2. *The call for strategy.* As we have already seen more than once, pastoral leadership calls for ability of a high order. The work taxes a man's creative ability. Strange as the fact may appear, a small church often proves more difficult to lead than one of moderate size. The small body may show a lack of talent in music, or in some other department. Gradually the coach ought to discover and train leaders in the various parts of the work. Meanwhile he must begin with the people where they are, and as they are, with all their limitations.

In a large body, on the other hand, the head coach faces a superabundance of unused talents. In a city church, as we have noted, the pastor may encourage some of his friends to use their talents in social work. All the while he should keep making plans for the church, as though everything good depended on its prosperity. Strategy calls for abundance of exercise by the laymen to keep the members of the body well and strong. However, the leader must never devise "work" merely to keep people busy. He should plan to guide them in worship, feed them from the Book, and send them forth to do the will of God.

A church leader may feel that no one else has to confront such a maze of problems and difficulties. He may fly away to another field, or else accept the status quo, which someone describes as "the mess we're in." Gradually the man who employs all his God-given powers can find a way out of almost every local difficulty. Better still, he can solve many problems by preventing them. According to rumor, strategy enabled a young traffic engineer in New Jersey to devise the clover-leaf method of avoiding collisions where highways intersect. Hour after hour he studied the roads that crossed each other at the most perilous intersection in the state. At last in despair he sat down by the road. There he saw a four-leaf clover. Idly he began to make

---

[5] E. R. Bulwer-Lytton, *Lucile*, Part I, Canto 2.

a pencil sketch of God's little masterpiece. All at once the engineer saw the way out of his difficulty. If the societies in the parish ever seem to become involved in a series of traffic jams, with all sorts of impending collisions, the man in charge may turn aside and study the nearest clover-leaf project. Then he can pray for like wisdom in dealing with the traffic jam back in the church. "Whoever of you is defective in wisdom, let him ask God who gives to all men without question or reproach, and the gift will be his." (Jas. 1:5, Moffatt.)

3. *The use of tactics*. With the general program in view, the leader stands ready to begin the year's work. He will need skill and tact, ability to persevere, and willingness to shift methods as conditions change. Otherwise he could not do teamwork with all sorts of human beings, one by one and in groups of various sizes. He could not encourage and inspire all the organizations, each with a different set of needs and plans. For a series of object lessons in ministerial tactics go again to the biography of George W. Truett.[7] From the beginning of his work at Dallas he inculcated the spirit of Christian stewardship. Through the years he led the First Baptist Church to financial contributions of a size they would never have dreamed of attaining. All the while he led them to grow in grace.

4. *The love of people*. For a still higher point of view we may turn to the Apostle Paul, second to none as a church leader. In his epistles to the Corinthians he deals with all sorts of local problems and difficulties. He shows that the solution lies in the spirit of Christian love. In the first twelve chapters of First Corinthians Paul deals with the needs of a worldly church in a wicked city. Then he lifts the whole matter up into the sunlight of Christ's love. This way of looking at life appears in Henry Drummond's well-known essay about Christian love as "The Greatest Thing in the World." The line of thought that appears below follows the thirteenth chapter itself. Every minister should commit these words to memory and apply them daily to his work as pastoral leader. In the pulpit, of course, he would deal with the passage as it concerns the lay hearer.

The first three verses show the greatness of Christian love in con-

---

[7] Powhatan W. James, *George W. Truett* (rev. ed., New York: The Macmillan Co., 1945).

trast with other things the Apostle counted good. At one time or another he had possessed them all, but as a leader in the Church he had learned to rely on Christian love far more than on pulpit eloquence, sound learning, mighty faith, sacrificial giving, or even willingness to die for the Saviour.

The central part of the chapter sings about Christian love as greater still in itself. *Das Ding an sich!* What then does it mean? The answer appears in sixteen details. As a whole they tell us: Christian love means being like the Lord Jesus. These words from Paul afford a picture of our Lord in the days of His flesh. They also set forth the spirit of the pastor as a Christian gentleman. Reverently let us paraphrase the words:

> The ideal minister suffers long, and is kind. He envies not, vaunts not himself, is not puffed up. He does not behave himself unseemly, does not seek his own, is not easily provoked. He takes no account of evil, and rejoices not in iniquity, but rejoices in the truth. He bears all things, believes all things, hopes all things, endures all things. The love of a Christlike minister never fails.

The closing verses of this prose poem sing about Christian love as greatest of all because it lasts. It abides. As long as a pastor lives he will love people. After he has gone home to God they will keep on loving him for his own sake, and revering him because of his work as their leader and friend. Love lasts. It stands the test of time. Partly for this reason no minister can judge the value of his leadership from year to year. Only after he has left a field can he begin to feel sure about his effectiveness. Even then he does not know, and he never will until he appears before the Great White Throne. If he has labored in the spirit of Christian faith and love, he can meet all the tests of time and eternity.

5. *The love of Christ.* The truth about church leadership appears elsewhere in still loftier forms. In Second Corinthians, the first seven chapters, the Apostle opens up his heart and shows the secret of his power as a leader second to none in the history of Christendom. In the words that follow he sets up an ideal for both pastor and people. The love of Christ here means His love for us, supremely on the

Cross. When the love of Christ controls, it leads and holds back; it inspires and transforms. "The love of Christ controls us, because we are convinced that one has died for all; therefore all have died. And he died for all, that those who live might live no longer for themselves but for him who for their sake both died and was raised." (II Cor. 5:14, 15, R.S.V.)

Controlled by the love of the Redeemer, "a wise man with love in his heart" became perhaps the foremost church leader of yesterday, at least in Britain. The biographer of the late William Temple shows the secret of his ability to ride through impending storms and out into the sunlight of peace among men. He knew how to get along with people and how to lead them onward, because he loved them in the Lord.

His courtesy and his patience both had their roots in his devotion, in that inner communion with the Lord through which it became second nature for him to see in the least of men "one of these, my brethren," and to care intensely for truth and justice. Occasionally the veil was lifted and the hidden source revealed.

I remember . . . a difficult and stormy meeting. . . . Right up to the end feelings ran high and found expression in debate. When at last under Temple's guidance we had arrived at decisions in which all acquiesced, he led us into the chapel of the school where we were meeting, for our closing devotions.

As he opened his Bible and began to read from Isaiah forty and St. John fifteen, the whole atmosphere changed. There was no mistaking the fact that in heart and soul we were being lifted up into that realm where he habitually dwelt. We knew then whence came the courtesy, the patience, the love of justice, and the calm strength with which he had led us into order out of the chaos of our controversies.[9]

"If any one is in Christ, he is a new creation; the old has passed away, behold, the new has come." (II Cor. 5:17, R.S.V.) From their minister people should learn to live and work under the controlling power of Christ's love. As soon as His love takes control of their hearts it begins to transform their lives. Then they become loyal and enthusiastic workers for Christ and the church.

[9] Iremonger, op. cit., pp. 417-18.

An example will show how this relates to leadership. In a large church the beginners' department of the Bible school needed a superintendent. The friends in charge wished to secure Miss X, a member of the congregation and an expert kindergarten leader. They asked the minister to convey the invitation. When the pastor explained the matter, Miss X thanked him but begged to be excused. She worked all week with little boys and girls, and on the Lord's Day she needed a complete change of thought and feeling. The minister saw her point of view and expressed regret that she felt unable to serve. On the way home the Spirit bade him go back and approach the matter from another angle, distinctly Christian. So he asked her to accept the additional work as a cross. He explained that the cross of a Christian meant something hard, heavy, perhaps unwelcome, which a person accepted because of love for the Redeemer. "If anyone wishes to come after me, let him deny himself, take up his cross day after day, and so follow me." (Luke 9:23, Moffatt.)

Miss X never had thought about church work in that light. After she had prayed about the matter, privately, she accepted the post. Soon her department became so nearly ideal that other churches sent young workers to learn the secret of dealing with little boys and girls. To their amazement they found that Miss X relied largely on Christian love and charm. As for the minister, he learned to use much the same approach in persuading many another to take up the cross. In recent years he has become a bishop. Now he advises young clergymen to keep the whole matter of leadership on a plane distinctly Christian. When the love of Christ controls both pastor and people, they work together in making the church a colony of heaven.

Herein lies the secret of relieving tension between "routine and ideals." When the love of Christ controls his heart and life, a minister learns to live and work without worry or hurry or fear. When the love of Christ provides the atmosphere in which laymen live and move and have their being, they find in His service freedom and joy. When pastor and people live and work together under His control, as gentle as gravity, and as mighty as God, they transform problems into opportunities. All of this may not come to pass overnight, or easily. Nevertheless the ideal can help to change a man's ministry from drudgery to delight.

For a living object lesson of a happy man's leading a happy people, turn again to Philips Brooks. In as far as a lover of biography can judge, he himself did little parish work, except in calling and in counseling. He encouraged and inspired a host of men and women to make Trinity Church a beehive of activity on behalf of the parish, the community, and the Kingdom at large. Much of his secret appears symbolically in the statue that stands beside Trinity Church and looks out toward the city. If the same spirit moved every local leader, the people about each church would learn the meaning and glory of Christian love as a transforming power.

Above the massive figure of Brooks towers the living Christ, with His arm outstretched to bless the man of God. Behind him stands the church he loved, the church for which he lived. Before him lies the open Bible, from which he preached the truth that made men free and strong. Out beyond for miles extends the city he loved, for which he would gladly have died. What a picture of the ideal pastoral leader! A lover of the living Christ, of the living Church, of the living Book, and of the living throng! Who can wonder that Brooks lived and wrought among men as a happy pastor and preacher? The love of Christ controlled him. That love went far to control and transform hosts of men and women whom he led close to the heart of God.

All of this and more the Apostle must have meant when he wrote about the secret of effectiveness in the Gospel ministry: "God was in Christ, reconciling the world unto himself, not imputing their trespasses unto them; and hath committed unto us the word of reconciliation. Now then we are ambassadors for Christ, as though God did beseech you by us: we pray you in Christ's stead, be ye reconciled to God." (II Cor. 5:19, 20.)

> Were the whole realm of nature mine,
>   That were a present far too small;
> Love so amazing, so divine,
>   Demands my soul, my life, my all.

Suggested Readings

Calkins, Raymond, *The Romance of the Ministry*. Boston: The Pilgrim Press, 1944.

Farmer, Herbert H., *The Servant of the Word*. New York: Charles Scribner's Sons, 1942.

Green, Peter, *The Town Parson, His Life and Work*. New York: Longmans, Green & Co., 1919.

Iremonger, F. A., *William Temple*. New York: Oxford Univ. Press, 1948.

Jefferson, Charles E., *The Building of the Church*. New York: The Macmillan Co., 1910.

Jowett, John H., *The Preacher: His Life and Work*. New York: George Doran Co., 1912.

Robertson, Archibald T., *The Glory of the Ministry*. New York: Fleming H. Revell Co., 1911.

Scherer, Paul E., *For We Have This Treasure*. New York: Harper & Bros., 1944.

Stewart, James S., *Heralds of God*. New York: Charles Scribner's Sons, 1946.

Index of Persons

Index of Subjects